PREACHING
ON CONTROVERSIAL ISSUES

PREACHING on Controversial Issues

A Free Pulpit in a Free Society

by Harold A. Bosley, Ph.D.

HARPER & BROTHERS   *Publishers*   New York

Library of Congress catalogue card number: 53-5001

To

Harry Emerson Fosdick

Charles Whitney Gilkey

Bishop Francis J. McConnell

Bishop G. Bromley Oxnam

Ernest Fremont Tittle

*Proven Champions of a
Free and Responsible Pulpit*

Contents

7

Preface

A BELOVED and distinguished professor of English at the University of Chicago once confessed that he was tempted to go into the Christian ministry but was deterred by the fact that he would be required to study homiletics. Homiletics, he said, "is the art of leading men hither and yon by means of inflammatory discourse." There must be some truth in this gentle indictment else the good professor would not have framed it nor have been deflected from the ministry by it. But it scarcely furnishes a significant clue to the purpose of preparing and preaching a sermon in the pulpit, or what might be called the pulpit ministry of the church.

Ideally, the sermon brings the great affirmations of faith and the great issues of life, like electrodes in an arc light, closely enough together to enable the fire of kindling knowledge, hope, and strength to leap into being. Every preacher strives for this all his life and finds the full reward for living in having had the privilege of attempting it.

Any given sermon is the personal, spoken discourse of a pastor to his people. He is talking to them about mutual problems, both personal and social, ancient and contemporary. Many if not most of the social problems thus discussed are highly controversial in nature. The sermons that comprise this book come from that particular sector of one preacher's experience. All but two of them were preached at the First Methodist Church of Evanston, Illinois, during the years 1950-1952, and some were published in the First Church Pulpit of that church. I am particularly anxious to have those who read them understand this fact. It explains the wide use of the personal pronouns—I, we, you, our, and us. It explains, further, the specific reasons behind the preaching of some of the sermons at the particular time when they were given. Because such facts are or ought to be characteristics of sermons, I have made no effort to remove them for purposes of publication. Start dressing a sermon up in that fashion and you have an essay on your hands before you know it. The essay is one literary form, the sermon another. While they have much in common, they are distinguishable and their differences ought to be respected.

9

The two sermons that were not preached in our church were presented to congregations of churchmen gathered for special purposes. "Preaching on Controversial Issues" was given to the Methodist Ministers' Meeting of Greater Chicago and must be regarded as "shop talk." I have included it because it contains the general reasoning behind the sermons in the book and is, therefore, intimately related to them. "The Christian Faith and Economic Problems" was preached at the worship service which opened the National Council on the Church and Industry, called by the Federal Council of Churches and convened in Detroit, Michigan, on February 16-19, 1950.

The sermons in this volume should be considered an integral part of a preaching program of nearly one hundred sermons over a two-year period. I mention this in the hope that it will keep them in their proper perspective in the total pulpit responsibilities assumed in our church. The issues with which they deal are now and undoubtedly will remain living issues for our generation. Some of my friends have been kind enough to urge their inclusion in a book specially devoted to them, saying that it might be of use to ministers and laymen alike. At any rate, that is the reason for the book.

Six of the sermons (II-VII) make use of what I have called the indirect or general approach to problems while the rest use the direct or specific approach. The differences between the two approaches are considered further in the opening chapter.

Acknowledgments are in order to the Woman's Society of Christian Service of the Methodist Church for permission to include Chapters II-V which they kindly published as a study book in 1950. I have already indicated the fact that some of the sermons have been published in the First Church Pulpit of our church— a publication sponsored and supported by the Men's Club of the Church. I also wish to thank the publishers who have granted permission to include poetry selections.

One reason for singling out the five men to whom this volume is dedicated is obvious to all informed people: They are proven champions of a free pulpit in our time. Another reason for their appearance here is a personal one: It has been my great good fortune to know them as teachers, friends and inspiring leaders in the Church today. They will never know how much it has meant to so many of us to have them standing firmly and openly for the right as God gave them to see the right through one of the roughest half-centuries in human history. I have the uncomfortable suspicion, though, that all they want of us by way of gratitude is that we should "carry on!"

The words "free pulpit" come easy but the fact they connote does not. That is bought with a price, and it is one that must be paid by each generation of churchmen. No greater blessing has come to me in my ministry than to have had the privilege of occupying two pulpits that are free in spirit and in truth: Mount Vernon Place Church, Baltimore, Maryland, and First Methodist Church, Evanston, Illinois. Both congregations have had to fight for the freedom of their pulpit, not once but repeatedly, and both are committed to the ancient proposition, "Ye shall know the truth, and the truth shall make you free." I may be living in a fool's paradise, but I think they symbolize the deepest trend in the Methodist Church in particular and in Protestant churches generally. If they do, the free pulpit will be a force for freedom in human life and affairs over the years ahead that must be reckoned with by every tyrant and tyrannical impulse and institution in our day.

HAROLD A. BOSLEY

First Methodist Church
December 1, 1952

PREACHING
ON CONTROVERSIAL ISSUES

I

Preaching on Controversial Issues

SCRIPTURE LESSON: Luke 19:28–40

I

NOT one but two texts suggest themselves for this theme—one from the Sacred Writ, the other a thoughtful comment made by a contemporary friend.

When Jesus and his disciples staged their triumphal entry into Jerusalem on Palm Sunday his disciples were ecstatic with enthusiastic expectations about to be fulfilled. They raised the traditional Messianic cry and bade everyone to join in it. This outcry seems to have disturbed some of the solid citizens of Jerusalem who curtly told Jesus to "rebuke your disciples. He answered, 'I tell you, if these were silent, the very stones would cry out.' " (R.S.V.). Which, as I understand it, is a vivid way of saying that the disciples of Jesus Christ have something to say, and that it is going to get said somehow by someone or, even, something. Nor can we dismiss this as a rhetorical statement. Better than anything else it accounts for the sense of urgency and relevance that has characterized Christian preaching and preachers from the beginning of our tradition.

The secular text to which I refer came from the midst of the long and far from completed struggle for academic freedom. In reply to the plea that teachers in tax-supported schools should avoid controversial issues, one critic observed, "All vital issues are controversial issues." This being true—and not more than a moment's reflection is necessary to substantiate it—the sobering corollary comes to mind: The only way to avoid controversial issues is to avoid vital issues. This the Christian preacher can scarcely afford to do. Yet there is so much discussion if not out-

15

right dissension in the Church today on this matter that we can well afford to look into it with some care.

The question of whether the preacher should deal with controversial issues was settled long ago in the Hebrew-Christian tradition, and, like so many important problems, it was settled by implication or indirection. Once the prophets of ancient Israel felt called of God to rebuke Israel for the ethical and moral sins of her common life, the die was cast. When the Rabbis who fashioned the Talmud spent all of their time interpreting the meaning of the Law in terms of ordinary daily problems, the pattern was deepened. When in the life and teachings of the Master there was a catholic concern for every human being in need, the stamp was placed on the Christian movement. The care with which the early Fathers sought to relate the Church to human life and problems is little more than an inevitable expression of this ancient trend in our religious heritage. The schoolmen of the Middle Ages might spend a lot of time trying to figure out how many angels could dance on the point of a needle, but this did not exhaust their concern. They also tried to determine the laws of usury, the limitation of the ravages of feudal strife through the truce of God, the proper approach to the institutions of marriage, universities, the state, and, later, the rising commercialism and industrialism that were among the heralds of the modern world.

Once decide in the affirmative the question as to whether the Church should concern herself with all problems that harass the thought and life of her people, and you have given answer to the question of whether the preacher should deal with controversial issues in the pulpit. As spokesman for the Church, as interpreter of the thought of the Church to his people, as guide for them as they feel their way toward the proper religious approach to the problems of living—in any and all of these roles he must deal with controversial issues. He would be clearly remiss in his duties as a churchman if he did not. Nor is he at liberty to pick and choose among the issues with which he is to deal, selecting only those that are congenial to him and permitted by his people. He is more than the conscience of his own people speaking up and back to them about their problems; he is the voice of the concern and the conscience of the Christian Church which must attempt to keep the entire range of human life under the judgment of the love and the power of God.

II

The history of our own country furnishes not one but many instructive examples of the way in which the clergy of our many churches have spoken up on highly controversial matters. The first ministers to come to this country set the pattern or, rather, fashioned here in our tradition the ancient pattern of the Church.

A quick perusal of Mary Baldwin's study of *The New England Clergy and the American Revolution*[1] or Ola Elizabeth Winslow's last book, *Meetinghouse Hill: 1630-1783*[2] will furnish ample evidence of the breadth and depth of the concern of our first preachers as they studied the problems that were troubling their people. You sense the justice of the conclusion that the clergy of the colonies were as responsible as the statesmen for kindling and fanning the flames of revolution that swept on through a tragic course to freedom.

Miss Winslow comments on the way in which the preachers concerned themselves with the moral considerations that underlay the concrete controversies over the Stamp Act and various other specific matters, and those considerations were freedom, liberty, equality, responsibility, and justice. One worthy divine, Jason Haven, preaching the Election sermon in Massachusetts said:

People indeed generally apprehend some of their most important civil rights and privileges to be in great danger.—How far these apprehensions are just, is not my province to determine. The Ministers of religion will unite their endeavors, to investigate and declare the moral cause of our troubles.[3]

It is not hard to see why Miss Winslow gives the title "Pulpit Drums" to the chapter in her book which chronicles facts like these:

Under stress of perilous events town and parish were again one as in the earliest days. The meetinghouse once more became the center of community life to a degree more nearly complete than any of the voting generation [in the 1770's] would well remember. Once again it was the town arsenal, with "Powder and Balls" under lock and key in the "Garrett" or, more conveniently still, just under the pulpit. The Rev. John Adams of Durham, New Hampshire, preached Sunday after

[1] Duke University Press, Durham, N. C., 1928.
[2] Macmillan, New York, 1952.
[3] *Ibid.*, p. 269.

Sunday with the town's supply of powder directly under his feet. So did other warm patriots among the clergy, and doubtless found their eloquence and the effects of it greatly improved thereby. The meeting-house was also the recruiting center, the place of rendezvous for troops, the point of departure when it came time to go. Later, as messengers brought back news from the front, it became the broadcasting station whenever the bell or beat of the drum called the inhabitants together for announcement.[4]

Lest we leap to the conclusion that these preachers were but following the emotional fashions of that hectic period we need to read further in Miss Winslow's account:

The "thunder and lightning" which John Adams attributed to the clergy to these war years was vehemence of conviction, doubtless also vehemence of manner, rather than radical thinking. These men were not radical thinkers, nor were they original thinkers. Moreover, they were saying nothing that they and their predecessors had not said for well over two generations on similar public occasions as well as more frequently in their own pulpits. Patiently, studiously, through the years they had built up, layer by layer, a concept of government, its obliga-tions and privileges, until fundamentals were past question. In so doing they had also made government and its ways important in their people's thought. The 1770's would have been no time for all this. Men were in no mood to be instructed. They could be reminded of what they already knew and their emotions could be aroused in its support, but they could not be put to school. The power of the familiar in a time of crisis has seldom been more amply demonstrated than in the patriotism "which burst forth like a flame," with the pulpit phrases worn smooth by several lifetimes of preaching as its watchwords.[5]

While these men lived and spoke at the time when the pulpit of the Christian Church was more widely heard and heeded than at any subsequent period in our history it would be a mistake to infer that there was complete agreement among the clergy who spoke up with such effectiveness on the great issues of that troubled period in our nation's life. The record, unfortunately, reads otherwise. Ministers loyal to the King and ancestral ways were insulted and, frequently, asked to leave their church and, usually, the town. The fissure in their fellowship was so deep that the Protestant Episcopal Church, to cite the one hardest hit by it, had to sever her legal ties with the Mother Church in England when independence had been won.

[4] *Ibid.*, pp. 273-74.
[5] *Ibid.*, p. 278.

But deeper than even these serious differences of opinion on what ought to be done about the problems at hand were two areas of complete agreement among the clergy: They agreed both in the absoluteness of their concern for the moral principles involved and in their uncompromising conviction that it was their sacred duty to speak out on them. Even as they disagreed violently on the meaning of the facts involved in the issues, they agreed that facts of far-reaching importance were involved and deserved their public attention and consideration.

If we look into the matter, we shall find that this tragic agreement-disagreement pattern underlies the creation and perpetuation of the divisions which have cropped up with appalling profusion in the church life of our country. We are indebted to Dr. William Warren Sweet's several great studies of the history of various denominations for full documentation of this point. The pre-Civil War period was easily the most trying one for all major religious bodies then in existence on a wide scale in this country. All were riven by deep splits on the issues involved in the brewing storm; only a few were able to avoid outright schisms in their polity. Preachers, north and south alike, approached the knotty problems of slavery, freedom, states' rights, etc. in a spirit of profound dedication as well as division. It is easy enough for us today to laugh (or weep) over their *non sequiturs* and special pleadings born of blind, emotional partisanship, but we would do well to endeavor, by an act of healthy imagination, to set ourselves down in their day. It may be doubted whether we would have done much better than they—and not nearly so well as some of them did. Struggling to get their hands on decisive facts that would clarify the issues before them, they plunged into Scripture, history, biology, and social and political thought, generally. That they emerged with some bizarre interpretations in all these areas should surprise no one who has lived through the last two world wars and hears all about him today the roar of the third one. The most rabid defender of slavery sounds exactly like the rabid defenders of war in our time. One such among our contemporaries made the headlines during the summer of 1952 by assuring a meeting of chaplains that there was no essential difference between the pulpit and the parade ground in the present crisis—both being component parts of an adequate defense of our country. Statements like these are more than fervent expressions of great patriotism—they are regrettably poor interpretations of the function of great religion in the life of a people beset by crisis.

Yet it is easy to miss the obvious point that, short of guaranteeing infallibility to preachers, this is precisely what we should expect when the sense of concern and commitment of the preacher focuses upon the tangled issues of our day. No one knows better than he how difficult they are; no one need tell him how inadequate he is to deal with them. But deal with them he must and will, and as wisely as he knows how—but without the claim, much less the guarantee of infallibility. Silence may be golden, as the proverb has it, for most men most of the time but not so for the preacher confronted by the unfolded issues of the life of his time. Nor will he hesitate long about speaking his mind as carefully and as forcefully as he can lest he prove to be in error in either or both insight and judgment. The one thing he cannot do is keep silence in their presence. If he belongs to the great tradition of preaching, he will know that it is better to be wrong than be silent in the face of the problems that are tormenting the thought and lives of his people. It is easy to explain mistakes for all honest men will understand and sympathize; it is impossible to explain silence, for none will listen.

Needless to say, I have little sympathy for the so-called "swing away from the social gospel" which some say is a characteristic of the last twenty years. If there is such a trend—and there is real evidence of it in certain quarters—then, in fair interpretation, it is a swing away from a forthright facing in religious terms of the vital concerns of our life and time and, strictly speaking, must be regarded as an unwitting and unintentional demonstration of the irrelevance of religion. A religious faith that will not concern itself with the vital issues in the life of a person or a people is a mean and doomed thing. It is more a delusion than an opiate and deserves the scorn which ethically sensitive people are not slow to heap upon it.

Every important person in the "social gospel movement" from Walter Rauschenbusch to Shailer Mathews and Arthur Holt knew full well the necessity of driving the roots of Christian social action deep in Christian faith. In fact, their greatest writings are concerned with this point. Something of this profound concern and commitment radiates the great social gospel documents written by churchmen. The two most influential are the *Rerum Novarium* by Pope Leo XIII and Rauschenbusch's masterpiece, *Christianity and the Social Crisis*. Neither of these outstandingly influential documents was blessed with infallibility of judgment but both exhibit what I should like to call *the absoluteness of concern* which is one of the distinguishing marks of the Christian love which seeks expression through the witness of the pulpit. Both Catholic and Protestant churches have nurtured and brought to maturity this concern in many concrete ways. Out of it has grown the strong effort of both to understand and minister to the problems of labor and agriculture, for example. In these movements and others like them individual churchmen let their aroused and informed Christian conscience come to bear on concrete vital problems and spoke their minds with real persuasiveness. No amount of criticism and opposition (encountered in tidal waves) could soften their indictment of evil, much less silence it.

III

Once the preacher has accepted this sort of responsibility as his duty he faces many problems as a craftsman in the pulpit. None of these requires more immediate attention both at the beginning and throughout the expression of the attempt to bring the resources of the pulpit to bear on vital problems than the temptation to forget, neglect, or play down the broad-gauge teaching ministry of the pulpit. The preacher must never forget that he is the teacher of the rich and multiform heritage of our long religious tradition. He will want to plan his preaching *by the year* and have, as one of his guides, a wise book on the variety of major emphases which must find expression in the pulpit: Henry Sloane Coffin's *What to Preach*. Only thus will he be sure of doing justice to the broad responsibilities that rest upon the pulpit. Actually, of course, the preacher's concern for and consideration of vital social problems will be all the more readily understood and received by his people if it is clearly a part of the larger context of the Christian gospel.

Granted vigilance on this point, he will want to plan his preaching in such fashion that he deals with all of the major problems of his day, that he deals with them not once but as long as they are real, and that he reverts to them, directly or indirectly, as frequently as can be done without appearing to be strumming a single string on his homiletical instrument. He should be careful to use both the direct and the indirect approaches. In the sermons which comprise the rest of this book, both approaches, as I understand them, have been attempted.

The first six represent the indirect approach; the rest the direct one. Both, it seems to me, are indispensable ways of creating a broad beam of Christian concern and bringing it to sharp focus on specific issues.

The indirect approach is used more frequently by most preachers, I should assume, and with good cause. As a rule, it begins with some great religious theme—like faith or humility—and develops its meaning in terms of Scripture and Christian history. Then with this as a firm foundation, the preacher is able to move with freedom and decision among the vital problems of his own day illustrating the meaning, the power, and the need of such virtues or beliefs now. This approach wears well, and it ought to be the main one used by any preacher today as it has been through the centuries.

But the direct approach is essential to realistic preaching. When some one issue—like the appointment of an ambassador to the Vatican—suddenly convulses his people he must give it his immediate, careful and straightforward attention. If it is a recurring one—like Universal Military Training or the ethics of drinking—he must keep his people facing it in a clear concise way. If it is a major issue, it deserves major treatment—that is the whole justification of the direct approach. The reaction of the congregation is certain to be definite—and contradictory! Some will think that sort of discussion "out of place" in the pulpit; others will think it appropriate and wish openly for more like it. The temptation to shrink from the former criticism and to be guided by the latter will be very great. But the preacher will do well to be on his guard against both temptations. The direct approach is heady wine, to say the least, and, if used with restraint, it may be good food, but it simply is not the fare for a well-balanced stable spiritual diet. As a rule, the exigency of time under which the preacher must labor these days (not many preachers or people long for a return of the two-hour sermons of the Puritan divines!) requires a skimping of the Scriptural and historical rootage of the Christian values which he seeks to exalt in the controversy. Wise planning of his year's preaching will enable him to build up this deficit in other sermons cast around the one which must assume them. Thus the great values of our religious heritage will receive attention both as to their rootage and their sharp relevance in our life. Which is a way of saying that the indirect and direct approaches complement each other in the over-all preaching program.

Regardless of whether the direct or the indirect approach is to be used, certain requirements lay heavily upon the man who takes them into the pulpit ministry of the church.

1. He must get the facts—not just some but as many as he can get. His research must be as careful and as conscientious as that of a lawyer preparing an important brief or a surgeon preparing to deal with a delicate and dangerous ailment. Catchwords, slogans, and rhetorical devices are or ought to be suspect as the facts are being assembled. The search for the apt phrase, the illuminating illustration is important in the finished product, but it will come later. The place where the sermon begins is in the area of public fact, and the preacher will do well to be sure of himself here before he does anything else. It is a hard, slow, grubby business, but it must be done, and done with care, or the pulpit will soon lose both the interest and the respect of the congregation.

2. He must get a clear picture of the conflicting interpretations of fact that are at work in the public discussion of the issue. While it is the counsel of perfection, he should be guided by William James' insistence that you are not able to cope with a conflicting point of view until you understand it so thoroughly that you can give it a stronger statement than one who believes it. The preacher may be sure that critics of any point of view he might espouse will be in his congregation. It might help him in working out the sermon to personalize the point of view he is contesting by seeing it as belonging to members of his church who will be listening to him. If he knows them well enough to be able to talk the matter over with them ahead of time, both he and they will profit by the experience. The resulting sermon will gain both in insight and compassion, and it need lose none of its definiteness.

3. He must reflect, whenever possible, the judgments of the general church as expressed in documents, and resolutions drawn up by representative religious groups. Even when the suddenness of the issue's coming does not permit the slow-moving conference machinery of a democratic church to be convened for the framing of an expression of the church's mind, he will want to be aware of and sensitive to probable judgments that may be rendered when such a conference does occur. It is a surprising experience to work one's way through the books and papers written in preparation for the various meetings of the World Council of Churches. Here, in brief, is a serious and dependable approach

to every major problem before men today. The resolutions adopted by the World Council itself are splendid statements of alert concern on all human problems and they are valuable summaries of the conscience of the church on such issues. Whenever possible the preacher will want and try to link his pulpit utterances with such efforts. He will not be bound by them as by law, but he will know what they are and be guided by them when it seems right and proper.

The preacher will find it expedient to make full use of certain days that are coming to be set aside for special emphasis: Labor Sunday; Thanksgiving Day; World Order Sunday; Reformation Sunday; Temperance Sunday; Memorial Sunday; Independence Sunday. Each occasion lends itself to renewed treatment of continuing problems. The simple fact that five of them occur in the fall season makes it inadvisable to observe all of them each year, thus making a judicious scattering of emphasis possible. Not all of these special days are now parts of the formal church calendar of any church, but, increasingly, they are being recognized as valuable opportunities to discuss vital problems that are certain to be emerging in various areas. Their treatment in the pulpit will be reinforced by the recognition they will be receiving in the press, on the radio, and among various interested groups.

4. He must assemble and present the considerations that seem to him to be of greatest importance with as much clarity and power as he can muster. He is preaching from conviction and he should preach for a decision. If he cannot do this, he simply is not ready to preach on the matter at hand. Both the pulpit and the problem will be better off if he leaves it strictly alone until he has found his own way to a decision in the matter. He must never forget that his people expect guidance from him in it. This awareness will keep him from indulging in the luxury of endless dalliance in the presence of an issue that is rushing to decision before his very eyes. He need not pretend to be Solomon who knows exactly the right answer (a pose too frequently associated with preaching on vital issuess), but he does need to be one who obviously has honestly grappled with the salient facts and has reached some definite conclusions which he now presents to his people in fulfillment of his stewardship of the pulpit.

5. He must preach in such fashion that everyone present feels included in the process of thought and conclusions. Even those who disagree with him should feel that neither were their reasons ignored nor their sincerity questioned. The preacher should so

present his material and conduct himself in the actual act of preaching that there will be a meeting of minds even where there is a difference of opinion. That this calls for tact, a sense of humor, as well as impassioned conviction and utterance is a fact that any preacher will admit is far easier said than done. There is or ought to be a sparkle of wit and quiet humor in well-balanced presentations of all vital issues. Intolerance, bigotry, and cruelty are out of place everywhere in life, and especially so in the pulpit. The preacher can be a crusader without being a fanatic. He can preach from and for conviction without being blinded by what he believes to be true. He must keep ever in mind the obvious fact that his deepest insight, his firmest conviction, his truest utterance are, at best, "broken lights" of Him who is the Light of the World. Let this awareness accompany him both in his study and in the pulpit and his stewardship of truth will be heard and trusted.

6. Finally, he must bear his own witness to the truth as he sees it. The pulpit requires that of the man who occupies it. It is not simply a lecture podium, nor is it a forum—though it will make full use of the fruits of both. It is the place set apart for one who feels called of God to preach the Gospel to the best of his ability. That this calls for humility of the highest order is well known—though it is as frequently honored in the breach as in the observance. It calls for courage, too; springing from the conviction that God is trying to speak His word through the preacher. In this courage he will find the strength he needs for facing the subtle as well as obvious intimidations of those who would silence the pulpit on all such issues. For those who would muzzle the preacher and mute the pulpit are always with us. They must be met and met openly. Once give in to them on your right to speak up on any issue and they will silence you on all issues—unless you propose to confine your utterance to the comfortable words they desire to hear. He who does this betrays the pulpit.

IV

Let the preacher, then, regard himself as the occupant and trustee of one of the most significant institutions in our heritage —a free pulpit. To know this, to accept its discipline is one of the most exacting and exhilarating responsibilities open to anyone. Let the preacher know, too, that he is not alone in his regard for the meaning and value of the free pulpit. He shares it with the vast majority of laymen who have found their way into the churches that exalt the preaching tradition. Such laymen come from choice and stay by decision. Not many want as their preacher one who is either afraid or unable to think for himself, to call them to task, to bring their day and generation before the judgment throne of the will of God as revealed in Jesus Christ. They want a free pulpit even when its freedom hurts them.

One is not in the preaching ministry long before he discovers that the secret of a free pulpit is a shared secret. In part, it is known to the one who must occupy it and try to speak as God would have him speak. In part, it belongs to the laymen who expect him to do just that. When he steps into the pulpit to preach it is not "his pulpit." Looking out over the congregation of those who share in the life of the Church, he knows it is "our pulpit" even as he knows that it is his duty to preach to them about the unfolded issues of the day, and do so with all of the understanding, urgency, and persuasiveness he can muster. They are joint stewards of the pulpit—he of the "spoken Word," they of the "heard Word"—and both are answerable to God for their stewardship—"lest the very stones should cry out."

II

A Faith for Revolutionary Times

1. The Discipline of Great Religion

SCRIPTURE LESSON: Matthew 7:13–23

I

AMONG the reasons why so many of us today misunderstand great religion, this one stands out: religion takes life seriously while we would like to take it lightly. We, like one of O. Henry's heroines, want to wear life like a rose on the bosom, but religion insists that both we and the rose are caught in the inexorable grip of time, of mortality—and are perishing.

> The Moving Finger writes; and, having writ,
> Moves on: nor all thy Piety nor Wit
>   Shall lure it back to cancel half a Line,
> Nor all thy Tears wash out a Word of it.[1]

We, like the star in a recent movie, cry, "I want to live, live, live, and be happy—then ring down the curtain." Yet religion reminds us that that curtain is going to be rung down whether we have been happy or not. When we are tempted to revel in our own good fortunes—food, shelter, loved ones, peace, and opportunity for useful work—religion drives hard at our dulled imaginations and challenges our complacency by reminding us of the multitudes to whom these blessings are unknown or alien or utterly insecure.

I do not mean to give the impression that religion is necessarily a grim and gloomy business, a dark and forbidding room in which

[1] From *The Rubáiyát* of Omar Khayyám, stanza 51.

27

the sunlight of happiness and hope never come. But I do mean that religion is terribly in earnest, and this is because life is terribly in earnest. Life is always on the move; it is doing something to us and through us all the time, and only death can stop it. Religion is man's most serious and sustained effort to find out what life is up to, to discover the deepest meaning of life, and so to relate our lives to it that something of that meaning will become the purpose of our daily living. Religion is not simply a philosophy of life; it is a way of life, a consciously and deliberately chosen way of life.

Small wonder, then, that the word "discipline" jumps at us out of every great religion. For he who would know peace must pay for it; he who would know joy must earn it; he who would know God must seek Him with singleness of mind, spirit, strength, and heart; he who would be a disciple of the Christ must take up his cross daily and follow him.

Throughout its long history religion has demanded many different things of its devotees in the name of discipline. As you would expect, these demands reflect, and are geared to, the cultural and spiritual level of the age in which they were made. Religion comes over the horizon of history demanding blood sacrifices, usually of choice animals but frequently of first-born sons. At a later date, the discipline demanded by religion is quite different: "What doth the Lord require of thee, but to do justly, and to love mercy, and to walk humbly with thy God?" But only a hopelessly dulled imagination would think the latter demands less difficult a fulfillment than the former.

Still another contrast in the disciplinary demands of religion will help us understand both their constant intention and their changing nature. In the days of her power the Church insisted upon absolute obedience in matters of faith and doctrine. She reduced, or tried to reduce, her people to the kind of mental slavery that causes one to say, "I will believe anything the Church affirms, no matter how it shocks my reason"; some churches still make this demand, and many people are willing to undergo the indignity of intellectual enslavement. But the churches and peoples who reject this blind obedience either forsake vital religion, or they assume the most exacting discipline —the discipline of the free, responsible mind and life. It is the sheer rigor of this discipline that makes so many of our quaking contemporaries willing to submit to the abject kind of obedience that is indistinguishable from spiritual slavery.

But this much is clear: *Christianity has always been a disci-*

plined way of thought, feeling and living. When the Christian movement was getting under way, it was a fellowship in spiritual discipline. And it had to be that! The first Christians had to match and to surpass the strength of alien cultures, customs and laws, if they were to persuade every knee to bow at the name of Jesus Christ. When a man came into that early fellowship, he came in wholly: possessions, relationships, duties, appetites— all that a man was or had was subjected to the discipline of the Christ and the Christian fellowship.

When the monastic movement that sprang up in the Dark Ages in medieval Europe started out to rescue the soul of the Church and to save the world, they advocated the most rigorous kinds of discipline: celibacy, fasting, seclusion, bodily and spiritual exercises—or, as they were fond of putting it, exercises aimed "to mortify the flesh and to save the soul."

It is a well-known fact that Wesley and Asbury were not much in favor of married preachers. Asbury was especially insistent on this point, and, if he had had his way, would have "located" every married man! Run over the writings of the pivotal leaders in the Christian tradition—men like Paul, Augustine, Luther, Calvin, and the rest—and you discover a steady preoccupation with the kind of discipline that will train a person to the point of being "a good soldier of Jesus Christ."

One thing is sure: religion, great religion, has never been content to take the world as it is, and to let life drift along aimlessly under the guidance of desire impulse, and will. It has demanded, and continues to demand on peril of losing its soul, the most rigorous kind of discipline of those who would plumb to the depths of life's meaning and purpose.

II

Yet religion is far from being unique in making severe demands of its devotees. Wherever you examine creative living you discover the fact and the demand of rigid discipline. Every scientist knows that science is an inexorable discipline. Every budding student of science soon finds it out. And the rest of us suspect the truth of it when we step into a laboratory with all of its paraphernalia for research. Not many of us would think of barging into a chemistry laboratory saying, "I am going to play around here a bit with some of this stuff. Oh, I don't know much about it, to be sure, but I'm a free man and I can do what I please here and elsewhere." Any smart person, upon hearing that proclamation, would get out of the laboratory at once, and we would soon follow either head over heels or feet first. The only safe man in the laboratory—or anywhere else in the field of science—is one who has subjected himself to the basic discipline of science—not only to master it but to be mastered by it.

The difference between most of us and the scientist in this matter is the difference between the ways in which Galileo and his friends used that revolutionary instrument—the telescope— which he had just invented. He used it to study stars and planets, and to discover data for world-shaking scientific theories. They used it to gaze and gape at stars and planets, and little more. The difference between Galileo and his friends can be put several ways, but these will do: he had accepted the discipline of re- search—they had not; he sought truth—they sought enjoyment; his contribution to human knowledge was incalculable—theirs was negligible.

When Einstein's theory of relativity was first announced many years ago, a famous American physicist, Albert Michelson, said he hoped it would not prove true because, if it did, most of the work in physical theory would have to be done over again. "But," he added, "if it is true, we will do the whole business over again!" How well this great scientist had mastered the discipline of his work!

Art, too, demands discipline of its devotees. I grant you, some of the creations that pass as art today make one wonder. I recently saw some canvases that remind me of nothing so much as of what happens when our three-year-old opens a box of water colors and applies himself to the color book—as well as to the wallpaper beside him. Some of modern art is hard to follow and to appreciate, but whatever it is, it did not just happen—it was slaved over by someone who had accepted the discipline of art. This, surely, is true of all great art. Study "The Mona Lisa" again. This time look at her hands and note the lines of repose and serenity which characterize them. Did that just happen? Leonardo's notebook is the answer. Page after page is devoted to sketches of human hands in every sort of relationship and line. Sometimes in anger and rage; sometimes in apparent sleep; sometimes limp in death. Slowly but surely the artist was sorting through the various ways of getting the hands of Mona Lisa to say what he wanted them to say, and as you see them they say it, they bespeak a spirit in quiet peace and joy.

To a person contemplating a career in art we can safely say, "You can buy, or receive as a gift, things you will need in order to be an artist. The materials through which you work, the leisure to work, a proper setting for concentration on your work—these you can be reasonably sure of getting. But there are two things you cannot buy, nor can anyone give them to you: the consuming desire to express yourself in art forms, and the disciplining of mind, spirit, life and skill actually to do it. The first of these you must have to begin with; the second you must be willing to learn through a long lifetime. Then you will have the right to say, 'I, too, am an artist.'"

Yet, ironically enough, many of the very people who readily admit the necessity of discipline in science and art object to it in religion. Knowing full well that the discoveries of science and the creations of art lie on the far side of the most exacting kind of disciplined effort, they feel that the meaning, the power, and the peace of great religion should be theirs for the mere asking. And, tragically enough, if they do not get it for the asking, they assume either that it is not there or that it is not worth the kind of discipline which seems to be required for its achievement. When they look at historic religion they cannot help seeing that the central symbols of faith are *sacrifice*, the *altar*, and the *cross*. Yet symbols like these did not just happen to emerge in our religious heritage. Far from it! They are eloquent indications of the kind of disciplined living that religion has required from the beginning, and must continue to require if it is to be a power in human life and affairs. Consider the aim of religion: the placing of the whole of one's life on the altar of the will of God as we see it in Jesus Christ. This, we may be sure, cannot be done either casually or easily. The ones who have been most successful in doing it give us their witness that it takes the hardest kind of disciplining of body, mind and spirit. They know that they must lose their life if they would find it anew; they know that only a disciplined faith can be a revolutionary faith; only a disciplined life can be a creative life.

III

Among the many ways in which the discipline of religion asserts itself, certain ones stand out in every life and movement that has discovered the power, the peace, the meaning of vital religion.

First, and truly foremost, the discipline of religion is a *discipline of worship*. Nor is this to be wondered at. The basic purpose in religion is the discovery of the will of God; the central fact in worship is God himself, the Lord of the Universe as well as of personal life, the One in whose will eternity and time, alike find their meaning, the Judge before whose bar the ages pass in solemn procession—nations and persons, kings and subjects, masters and slaves, the One in whose will there is "neither variableness nor shadow of turning," yet in whose tender mercies and infinite concern the very hairs of our head are numbered and not a sparrow falls to the ground unnoticed.

Services of worship intend, or should intend, to usher men into the actual presence of the living God. That is the ultimate thrust of the songs we sing, the prayers we offer, the sermons we preach or hear. Whatever is done in a service of worship should be done to the glory of God, to the end that His name is exalted and His will sought and served by ordinary people like us. We do not, or should not, come to church to be seen of men but to find God. We do not, or should not, come to church to please men but to find God. And a church which loses sight of this objective has not only lost its sense of direction; it has lost its reason for being. Let the church that seeks its good name primarily in the praises of men beware! As surely as God lives, it will hear the judgment, "This night thy soul shall be required of thee."

Worship is not a simple getting-together of friends and neighbors to renew acquaintance and have a pleasant time. Worship is the serious and sustained effort of social beings to approach their Creator with penitence and gratitude in their hearts, with confession and adoration on their lips, with humility and dedication of their lives.

And what is the result of worship? Two answers emerge almost simultaneously from the lives and experiences of persons who seem to know. To worship is to go with the publican through an experience in which the cant and hypocrisy, the pride and conceit, the littleness and meanness of life fall away—and, seeing ourselves for the flagrant failures, the blatant sinners that we are, we can only pray, "God, be merciful to me a sinner." To worship, to persist in worship, is to feel the strong hand of God Himself lift us to our feet and to hear Him say, "Stand upon thy feet, son of man, for I would speak with thee."

Think about it for a moment, and no sensible person will expect to be able to do that sort of thing in a casual mood and manner. He would know—even if he never tried it—that you do not happen on this kind of experience. You prepare for it: you

seek it with your whole life; you subject yourself to the discipline
of it. There is no other way to discover its power, peace, and
meaning.

Great religion is more than a discipline in worship; it is a
discipline in honest thinking. We must be able, as Paul puts it,
to give a reason for the hope that is within us. This many of us
are unable to do, and, what is worse, we are reluctant to learn
how to do it. So we look for some short cut and usually wind
up mouthing the great creedal affirmations and convictions of
our fathers. Or we take refuge in the great liturgical services
which they hammered out on the anvil of experience. Or we seek
sanctuary in some church that will promise to do our thinking
for us, especially at the critical points in our relationship with
one another and with God. Now I have no objection to the convictions and institutions of our fathers—far from it—but we cannot inherit their meaning, the facts which made them vital factors
in the life of our fathers. That we must earn, and there are no
easy short cuts to it. We must be willing and able to find a firm
foundation for our faith in terms of our own experience, our
own problems, our own day. In doing this we shall need all the
help our fathers can give us—and more too! We shall need what
John Masefield has called the "illumined mind" and the "illumined heart," the ability to become sincere, and to feel deeply
and to think clearly about the will of God, who is as much at
work today as ever in the lives of men. For the God of yesterday
is the God of today and of tomorrow as well. He has not only
spoken to men of old; He speaks to men today—and it is the
most serious business in life to try to hear what He is saying. To
crouch like cowards behind the hard-won convictions and institutions of our fathers is to be utterly unworthy of them. To regard
them as the great efforts of our fathers to state honestly what they
felt to be true, to use them as invaluable guides to a deeper appreciation of the ways of God, to be willing to use them with both
respect and freedom as we seek to find our own way in His will—
this is to use them both wisely and worthily.

He who would know the power, the peace, the meaning of
great religion, must assume the discipline of the kind of thinking
that will enable him to be one to whom and through whom the
God of the Universe is able to speak. And when due allowance
has been made—as it must be made—for the all too human shortcomings and blindness that will weaken his witness, it will still be
possible for men to say of him, "He lived near to God."

A third discipline of great religion is *the discipline of fellowship*. The streak of unregenerate individualism in each of us, as well as the incorrigible individualists among us, cries out in protest against this kind of discipline. We agree with Alfred North Whitehead's partial definition of religion as "what a man does with his solitariness." We object to his completion of it to the effect that religion is what we do with our togetherness. Let it be said once more that great religion does not try to stifle our God-given individuality and personality—our uniqueness, if you please—when it preaches and tries to create the great community, the Kingdom of God. From the very beginning, religion has been a corporate venture as well as a personal experience. And this is as necessary and as true today as ever. That is why religion is a discipline in fellowship—the kind of fellowship every church, in its high moments, seeks to be and, under God, may occasionally actually become. For the Church must be a fellowship of persons who learn to share life with one another, who trust and appreciate one another. It must be a fellowship in which fearlessness is the script, and popularity the aside. It was of this kind of fellowship T. S. Eliot wrote in "The Rock":

> Why should men love the Church? Why should they love her laws?
> She tells them of Life and Death, and of all that they would forget.
> She is tender where they would be hard, and hard where they
>   like to be soft.
> She tells them of Evil and Sin, and other unpleasant facts.[2]

You will look a long time for a more revealing explanation of why so many of our contemporaries so studiously avoid the Church. For in the fellowship she engenders, the whole of one's life and times is brought under the judgment of God. We are weighed in the eternal balances, and all men are found wanting. The truth of Paul is felt at all points in the fellowship, "For all have sinned, and come short of the glory of God." If a person wants to keep himself in the proper perspective for creative living, he will need the steady assistance of a vital fellowship, he will need to see himself as others see him, he will need his fellow men, not alone at a hundred times in his life, but, more especially, in the continuing experience of belonging to humanity, of being an integral part of the common life of mankind.

I do not mean to give the impression, in even so brief a description of the religious fellowship, that the Church is faultless and

[2] From Chorus VI of "The Rock" in *Collected Poems*. Copyright, 1936, by Harcourt, Brace and Company, Inc. Used by permission of the publishers.

above criticism. I have been a churchman too long to entertain, even fleetingly, that illusion. I get as impatient as the next one about the glaring shortcomings of the Church; yet, I confess to an even greater impatience with those critics who stand outside the Church and tell her how to go about her business. There is a time and a place and a person for the criticism of the Church. The time is when the Church fails to be the messenger of the will of God as we see it in Jesus Christ; the place is on the spot of her transgression; the person is someone—anyone—who stands within the Church and has earned the right to criticize her. The Church has generated her own sharpest critics—this is the witness of the ages. The indictments leveled in love against the Church by those who are proud to be, and to be known as, her children have been unsparing; so much so that they make outside critics look like rank amateurs! The Church stands in constant need of criticism as well as of prayer—if her fellowship is to be vital. Consequently, it is no little or light thing to step within the fellowship of the Church. It is a discipline—a discipline in shared responsible living that requires of a mature person the best that he has.

IV

When we have accepted the multiple disciplines of great religion, we shall be as nearly ready as it is humanly possible for us to be to accept Jesus' austere invitation: "Enter by the narrow gate; for the gate is wide and the way is easy, that leads to destruction, and those who enter by it are many. For the gate is narrow and the way is hard, that leads to life, and those who find it are few" (R.S.V.).

Then and only then will our faith be down to "fighting weight." Then we will be able to bear the Christian witness in the face of the injustice and inequity of our common life. Accept the discipline of religion, and then some of the towering tasks of our time will not seem so impossible of achievement: the conquest of war, of nationalism, of racism, and of denominationalism. No man wants to tackle problems like these unless his faith so links him to the living God that, as he labors at them, he knows he labors not alone but that God works in and through him; that when he falters, God will speak a strong word of encouragement in his ear; that when he is driven to despair, God will make his life luminous with hope; that when he falls, God will set him on his feet and on the pathway again. Truly, the future belongs to men like that.

III

A Faith for Revolutionary Times

2. The Faith That Strengthens

SCRIPTURE LESSON: Hebrews 11:32–12:4

I

WE SPEND too much time praising the faith of our fathers and too little time seeking to understand it. And as far as our meeting the problems of our day with a faith that matches the one they threw against theirs—the less said about that the better. Who can honestly doubt that one of the great tragedies of our day lies in precisely this area?

We sense the fact that the faith of our fathers is once more caught up in a time of severe testing. For, as we have been told again and again, the basic battle in our time is not between armies; it is between ideas, or systems of ideas, or rival systems of belief and faith. Standing, as we do, in the midst of this conflict, we sense the fact that the faith of our fathers is infinitely deeper and broader than its modern antagonists, and we have the deep impulse to rush to its support. But we know, and how well we know, that our every effort to defend it is crippled by our lack of understanding it. We find ourselves in our candid moments doubting whether we are able to defend it intelligently, let alone embrace it effectively. The winged faith of our fathers flops around on broken pinions when we try to borrow it for our life and times. To alter the figure, when faith led our fathers to the frontiers, they followed it fearlessly, but we flee from its leading.

One thing to our credit is this: we are aware of our needs. Let a crisis envelop us, and we reach out for a vital faith. When the

36

last war started its sweep over the world, and men's hopes grew dim and their courage alternated with their fears, book after book on faith was written and eagerly devoured by faith-hungry people. Men who in earlier days thought they could either get along without faith, or could manufacture all they needed out of whole cloth, suddenly found that in order to have anything solid at all, they had to come to terms with the tradition of great faith that is an essential part of our religious heritage. Hence the upsurge of interest in religion both then and now.

While it is difficult to expect too much of the faith of our fathers, it is easy to expect the wrong thing of it. We who look to it for pat answers to our problems are certain to be disillusioned. In fact, the triumphant religious faith like that of Jesus and Paul, so far from furnishing us with ready-made solutions to our problems, in reality sharpens up both the problems themselves and our responsibility for them. There is no question but that their faith was victorious, was strong enough and radiant enough to prevail over the darkest kind of difficulties they faced. But there is abundant reason to question:

1. Whether we can achieve a faith like theirs in a day like ours.
2. What a faith like that would contribute to persons like ourselves.
3. Whether we are willing to pay the price of achieving, nurturing, and perpetuating that kind of faith.

II

Look for a moment at what I have just called the solid tradition of great faith which lies at the core of Western culture, and you will see not only that it did strengthen those who embraced it, but also why it served them in this manner.

For Jesus, the fountainhead of our tradition, faith was both deeply personal and social in nature. It rested on the broad base of a belief in God as love. For him, there is both an ultimacy and an intimacy in the will of God, in the activity of his love in life. Jesus drew his conception of the will of God both from the prophets of Israel and from his own personal experiences. With the prophets, he discerned the activity of God everywhere in life and history. No one ever got away with the effort to influence him to refer to religion as "a purely personal matter." That travesty on, that final indignity to, the world-shaking and the world-shaping power of great religion was reserved for later generations of Christians, including our own.

The faith of Jesus knew no such compartmentalization of life. And it is a good thing it did not! For it had to carry him to triumph over questioning friends, doubting disciples, carping critics, and ruthless foes. Small wonder he assured his disciples that their faith could move mountains, could cast out demons, could empower them to face their enemies, could escort them to the ends of the earth, could lead them gently, as the good shepherd leads the sheep that are with young, even through the portals of death itself, and into "my Father's house [where there] are many mansions."

This faith, incarnate in his life, both preached and lived by him, became the gospel—the good news—that *God loves man.* And that, from his day to ours, is the faith that overcomes the world.

This faith bred true to itself as it passed from Jesus to Paul. Like Jesus', Paul's faith rests on the broad base of the richest of all religious traditions in the ancient world—Judaism. Paul's own personal experience of the activity of God in his own life gives his faith a ring of authenticity which echoes throughout his letters. Like Jesus', Paul's faith was tested in the fires of daily living. It enabled him to triumph over his own doubts and sinfulness, over the inertia which always tries and sometimes succeeds in stifling the inherited forms of religion, over the factionalism among his followers, and over the many personal trials and sufferings he was called upon to endure. Argue with some of his statements of faith if you must—no one will deny you that right and responsibility—but you cannot argue with a life like his. Nor can you deny that the secret of it lies in his faith in God as revealed in Jesus Christ, and in his own experiences through a long lifetime. Standing at the known end of his journey on earth, he could bear this witness: "I have fought a good fight, I have finished my course, I have kept the faith."

Study for a moment, as a historian, the results of Paul's life of faith, and this is approximately what you will find: a faith that made him ready to go to the ends of the earth; a cosmopolitan fellowship, instead of a small group of Jews, bound together in a faith strong enough to survive the decline and fall of the Roman Empire and the centuries of confusion that followed; a faith mobile enough to adapt itself to crisis after crisis in human affairs without once losing its grip on the love of God as revealed in the life and teachings of Jesus Christ.

III

Yet a vital faith like that to which we have been referring cannot be burrowed out of history books—even books of sacred history. However much we may be stimulated and inspired by the faith of Jesus and Paul, however much we are inclined to rejoice in the solid tradition of great faith which they injected in our culture, the simple and searching fact remains that such a faith begins by confronting us with our own lack, our own need of it, or something like it, if we are to be equal to "the living of these days."

Is it possible for us—all of us—to share the belief in God as love, in the ultimacy and the intimacy of the activity of the will of God both as seen in Jesus Christ and as experienced in a profound sense of Christian fellowship?

A faith like this is largely a question mark for most of us. Yet each of us, alone, can transform it into an exclamation point, can change the permanent possibility of a faith-filled life into the vibrant actuality of faithful living. Even so, is a faith like this one we have been talking about sufficient for our problems today?

Can belief in the love of God triumph over the rising tide of hatred, ill will, fear, and suspicion—fostered by racism, classism, and nationalism the world over? Can belief in the unity, the oneness, of God actually prevail over the sectarian differences in the Christian tradition, let alone all the other divisions known to man? Can belief in the ultimacy of the love of God prevail over our blind, hysterical preparations once more to elevate as the saving symbol of mankind the Power of the Sword rather than the Power of the Cross?

Put the problem positively rather than negatively: can this solid tradition of great faith so come alive in us and our day as to pave the way to a deep harmony among men who now hate and fear one another? Can it pave the way toward a hopeful picture of co-operation among men who now mistrust one another? Can it lead us out of the wilderness of fear and frustration into the promised land of a confident comradeship with God himself?

Many of us feel about this as did a skeptical professor about an earnest freshman's effort to persuade him of the glories of the Kingdom of God: "Good—if true!"

The Christian faith faces these bewildering questions I have been citing with an earned confidence that it is not only good but true. It approaches any and every man with the assurance that a great faith is necessary to creative living, that it makes all the difference in the world, and that it is open to all—not for the asking but for the earning.

IV

Here, briefly, are the contributions which you can expect a great faith to make to your life as you face not only your personal problems but also the social problems of our time.

A great faith brings the confidence of fundamental beliefs. You must and you will believe in someone, in something. As a rule, the things we believe in lie on the surface of our lives—as a result, they are the first casualties of adversity and confusion. It is a dangerous thing to try to live without clear-cut basic beliefs. Whittaker Chambers, Alger Hiss, and other children of an age which, thinking it had outgrown the discipline of historic faith, adopted the use of Russian communism. Manners, conventions, and traditions usually monopolize our living, our thinking, and our believing. Like Jane Austen, we operate within our own set of accepted conventions or customs, and never once raise the problem of their ultimate validity. And when tremendous social changes sweep them aside, or cast them in doubt, we are bewildered, helpless, angry. Great religion knows that our beliefs must drive a taproot to the heart of the universe if they are to have steady and sufficient nourishment. Religion is more interested in morals than in manners, in convictions than conventions, in living relationships than traditions. Great religion believes that the Sabbath was made for man and not man for the Sabbath.

Consequently, the Christian religion urges upon all who would know its inexhaustible power the importance of clear, honest, creative beliefs about God, Christ, and man—to cite but three. These are the taproots of "peace of mind" and "peace of soul" which all men need and for which modern man searches so avidly. The Christian faith invites us to take these beliefs seriously and to see in them the real foundation for our confidence that God is a real fact and factor in the world. For we, like our stalwart forefathers, stand in the need of the conviction that God is love, and in need of a faith in the ultimacy and the intimacy of the will of God for all men.

If this conviction becomes real for you, it will be your clue to history—not in the sense that it will explain everything to your satisfaction, but in the deeper sense that you will be able to bear with calm confidence and with a sense of creative responsibility the exigencies of any given moment or event. For great faith meets the future that way, firmly confident that threading the uncertainties of the present and future, as a firm road threads through the swamps of the South or the muskeg bogs of the North, is the will of God over which men may travel. This belief, this confidence, is ours for the searching, the testing, and the living. It is no good on paper; it is invaluable when incarnate in human thought and life.

A great faith brings the warmth of a great hope. When hope dies, humanity, strictly speaking, dies. Without hope, man would slip back to the level of animalism. This retrogression is one of the most ominous signs of these times. Shortly after the war, a revealing book about the spiritual condition of the British churches was written by British churchmen. In their judgment, the greatest danger they faced was summed up in the single word: *despair*. They found their own people—the churchmen of Britain—facing the future without the kind of radiant hope and joy that is the hallmark of Christian faith. The writers of the book agree that there was nothing more important for the church to do than to accept the challenge of despair, and redeem it by Christian hope.

The same despair which our British brethren discovered in their ranks is now found everywhere in the world. It is doubtful whether man's confidence in himself and his future has ever been at a lower ebb than now. I would not ape Pollyanna, nor any other apostle of a superficial gospel of sweetness and light, in what I am about to say. I stand firmly in the solid tradition of great faith—a faith that saw Jerusalem leveled, yet continued to talk about the New Jerusalem; a faith that witnessed the collapse of the Roman Empire, yet talked of a greater empire, the kingdom of God—I stand in that tradition when I say that the chill of despair which now numbs our sense of responsibility can be driven out by the Christian hope that the God of the universe is struggling to realize His will in human events, through lives like ours. Wherever you touch the Christian faith you hear that stirring message: "Hope thou in God." So far from meaning that you will go through life with a set grin on your face, *hope* means simply that you have fellowship with One who from the beginning has been trying to bring order out of chaos, peace out of conflict, love out of hatred. In this fellowship—a working fellowship, mind you—there is real spiritual peace.

A great faith brings the strength to hang on in the face of discouragement, disaster, and loss.

There are times—such as the present—when we need what

might be called *the survival value of faith*. This is the faith on which to hang if we are to weather the beating storms of the present. The matter in question is not of our being able to build the Kingdom of God in our time; it is keeping the hope of God's Kingdom, and the sense of responsibility to it, alive in the human heart.

When I answered the call to the ministry in the 1920's, our church was resounding with the cry of the Centenary movement: "The world for Christ in one generation." And we thought it could actually be done! We thought that within the compass of a thirty-year period—by 1950—we could present Christ so effectively to men that at his name every knee would bow. Now we ask for enough co-operation to preserve peace, enough good will to avert another war, enough progress toward a better world to make up for the appalling amount of ground we have lost of late in our effort to reach the goal of security for all men. We need faith—great faith—simply to hang on when, all about us, men are letting go, when we are tempted to believe that all is lost, and that we ourselves might just as well let go.

Faith helps us hang on to life itself when we stand at the side of a grave as wide as the world and see it receive a loved one. The temptation to quit from the inside out will present itself to everyone in such moments—yet the answer comes through faith in One who knows the meaning of life and death and in whose love, life and death find their full answer. We may not be able to phrase that answer even to our own satisfaction; yet to know that it is there is to feel solid ground under the feet of our spirit, and we are ready for life—ready to live again.

It is dogged strength like this that we need; and we can have it through faith and only through faith. I repeat: it is ours for the searching, the testing, the living.

A great faith gives us the courage to start anew after defeat and disaster. In addition to sheer *survival value*, faith has what might be called a *revival value*. Slowly but surely the courage to believe in and work for the Kingdom of God will come again with power in human thought and life, and we will begin to dream dreams and see visions of the world as God intends it to be. We will be sobered but not dismayed by the problems we face, asking with Paul, "If God be for us, who can be against us?" We will know what Gandhi meant when he answered a British threat of death in case he did not comply with the law, "If you deprive me of this life, I'll come back in another and yet another life and carry on until my people are free!" Or the confidence with which Gladstone faced a hostile Commons in debate on a reform bill, "You can force us to dip our colors today if you choose—but the future belongs to us!" The God in whom we believe is one who makes all things new, is one who never tires, whose rebuffs by us and through us only encourage Him to persist in His purpose for us— this is the witness of Christian faith. If we listen carefully, we will hear it being proclaimed in every quarter of the world today!

Listen to China and you will hear it there! When the Red wave recently gained momentum in China, Christians in America were justifiably anxious about the future of Christians and Christianity in what is commonly called Red China. From the midst of the confused scene itself came a letter from a well-known Christian leader, T. C. Chao, who said that there was cause for rejoicing in China because of the new chance to correct heavy abuses that had existed for generations. And only recently the Christian leaders of China published a strong statement of faith in the life, work, and witness of the Christian fellowship in China.

No one of us has planned this kind of world to live in, much less to pass on to our children. But, for whatever reason, it is our world and both accept and redeem it we must—this is the clear responsibility of our faith.

V

In days like these when the Christian faith is locked in mortal combat with what Paul so aptly called "the powers and principalities of this world," the ancient cry goes up, "God, send us men!" Men of great faith! Faith in God; faith in Christ; faith in one another; faith in themselves. Let us not waste time—precious time—envying men like Paul, Luther, Wesley, and Father Damien their great faith in God and Christ. I say to you: There is not a man in that company but who envies us our opportunity to bear faithful and daily witness to the love of God in the life of man. That is why their faith prevailed in their time. That is why, and how, ours can prevail today.

You must have heard the story of the eager young man who visited the aged James Russell Lowell at the turn of the century. Thrilled again at his stories of the struggle against slavery, the young man exclaimed, "How I wish I could have stood at your side then!" The aged warrior for righteousness stepped to the window, pulled aside the curtain to reveal the smoking stacks of a great industrial plant with wretched hovels housing its workers, and he asked, *"What more do you want?"*

IV

A Faith for
Revolutionary Times

3. The Sin That Kills

SCRIPTURE LESSON: Ephesians 2:1–10

I

ONE of the most significant differences between us and our spiritual forefathers is this: *they took sin seriously; we do not.* They prayed over it; we jest about it. They regarded it as the open and crowded road to hell; we regard it as an unfortunate religious term for a pathological condition. They thought the power of God the only force strong enough to cope with it; we counsel disturbed persons to watch their diet, their exercise, their rest, and to try not to think about the matters that upset and disturb them. I know of no better contrast between their attitude and ours than T. S. Eliot's parody on Oliver Goldsmith's quatrain. Oliver Goldsmith writing in the eighteenth century asks:

> When lovely woman stoops to folly,
>   And finds too late that men betray,
> What charm can soothe her melancholy?
>   What art can wash her guilt away?[1]

T. S. Eliot faces the same question in the spirit of the twentieth century and recasts Goldsmith's lines to read:

> When lovely woman stoops to folly and
> Paces about her room again, alone,

[1] "Song," stanza 1, in *The Vicar of Wakefield.*

44

> She smooths her hair with automatic hand,
> And puts a record on the gramophone.[2]

In simple fact, one of the most alarming characteristics of our day, a profound and disturbing portent of the state of our spiritual health, is this inclination to brush by the idea of sin, to treat it lightly, to act on the assumption that it can safely be put in the same general category with witches and magic. We have all chuckled over the famous story of Calvin Coolidge's laconic report to his wife on the preacher's sermon. She asked what it was about. Coolidge replied, "Sin." She persisted, as wives will, "Well, what did he say?" "He was agin it!" was the reply.

It is the serious, studied, often reconsidered but always reaffirmed, judgment of religion that all thoughtful men will be "agin" it once they understand sin in the light of true religion, once they consider carefully what it means in human life and history. Put the matter negatively, and this is how it reads: only the atheist can afford to dismiss the idea of sin as unimportant or irrelevant. The rest of us, professing belief in God as the moral order of life and history, will, in the words of Anselm, the medieval theologian, "consider the gravity of sin."

Let us inquire with some care into its meaning for our forefathers, then ask what it means concretely to us today.

II

Sin, to our forefathers, meant disloyalty to God. Break a man-made law, and you are guilty of a crime. Break a divinely ordained precept, and you are guilty of sin. Sin, if you please, is a crime against God—a conscious and open violation of his holy will. But, you ask, how do you know what the will of God is? This must be known—at least in part—before a man can actually be guilty of breaking it. Our forefathers were nothing if not specific in their answer to that query!

To the ancient Hebrew, sin meant disobedience to the will of God as expressed in the revealed law, the Torah, the divine law as given by God to Moses on Mount Sinai. By means of this law, God made a covenant—a binding agreement—with Israel. He would be her god if she would be His people. She agreed. He told her, through Moses, what He wanted her to do. He promised to do certain things for her if she would accept

[2] From "The Waste Land" in *Collected Poems, 1909–1935*. Copyright, 1936, by Harcourt, Brace and Company, Inc. Used by permission of the publishers.

and obey the covenant. Israel, through Moses, agreed to the conditions in the covenant and accepted the moral responsibility of living in obedience to it.

The burden of the prophetic denunciation of Israel through the eighth and seventh centuries B.C. was based on the conviction that Israel had broken the covenant, that she had been disloyal to God. She had no claim on His mercy and reward because she had not been governed by His expressed will. In unforgettable phrases, the prophets etched their indictment upon the consciousness of Israel: she had "sniffed up every breeze" of desire, passion, and greed; she had "played the harlot"; she "hath dealt treacherously against the Lord." Even as her obedience was a mockery, her repentance is pure hypocrisy: "They [the Israelites] return, but not to the most High: they are like a deceitful bow. . . ."

The prophet could see only one result: "Israel is swallowed up. . . . Ye have plowed wickedness, ye have reaped iniquity; ye have eaten the fruit of lies. . . ." Though the prophet could bewail the fate of his people, he could not protest against it. For it was richly deserved. Let famine, earthquake, fire, pestilence, war, and destruction come upon Israel from God—Israel had earned them all by her sins.

Looking back over the tumultuous years that led to disaster and exile, Ezekiel, writing in the heart of the experience of the Exile, could only conclude, "The soul that sinneth, it shall die." For him, sin can and does kill in very specific and tragic ways. He had seen it kill the rich life his fathers had begun to build in Palestine. He had seen the fine sense of being "the chosen people" die by developing into the conceit that God would back them in anything and everything, that somehow, no matter what they did, He would support them. He had seen the deep religious conviction that supreme loyalty to God would give Israel all the strength she needed give way to a mad scramble for security and power through prosperity, treaties, and alliances. In Israel's effort to become a great nation, the royal word and court had taken precedence over the word of God and the temple. And, standing amid the wreckage of his people's life and hopes, Ezekiel concluded that sin does not pay, that the soul that sinneth shall die. He would not understand our taking sin lightly—of this we may be sure!

To Jesus, sin was the bitter, tragic fact which underlies much, if not most, of the evil of life. He believed that God had made it possible for men to live together in such fashion that love would bless their common life. He centered his life and teachings on the things that separate man from man, and man from God. To him, loyalty to God means loyalty to God's will that men shall dwell together in peace and brotherhood. Sin is conscious disloyalty to God's will for life. When men separate themselves from one another through hypocrisy, when Jews draw apart from Gentiles, when saints fear the company of sinners—men are disloyal to God. Sin, as Jesus saw it, is essentially a spiritual condition. He warned his disciples, "And do not fear those who kill the body but cannot kill the soul; rather fear him who can destroy both soul and body in hell" (R.S.V.). He seems never to have doubted the simple fact that sin can kill.

Later thinkers in our religious tradition accepted Jesus' teaching in this matter. For Paul, sin was disloyalty to God revealed in Jesus Christ. Augustine regarded it as "the great destroyer." The medieval Church organized its sacramental life around the effort to cope with the "seven deadly sins" that, unredeemed, would damn a man's soul to eternal hell. Luther and Calvin never thought of treating sin lightly. If anything, they took it with even greater seriousness than did the medieval Church. Calvin came close to being so obsessed by the reality, the power, the universality of sin, that to him there seemed no way for most people to escape its fatal consequences, no matter how hard they might try. Dr. Paul Scherer once wrote, "Calvin couldn't stop sin, but he could take all the fun out of it!" Read Calvin's *Institutes* sometime and you will give Dr. Scherer a medal for masterly understatement!

No historical survey of the weighty nature of the idea of sin can neglect to mention, at least, the dark and difficult notion of original sin. Though it is flirting with heresy to say so, I cannot help feeling that this is one of the least useful ideas ever to be developed in our religious tradition. It has an ambiguous ancestry in the realm of ideas, and its progeny in human affairs have been cause for constant concern. As good an informal statement of its meaning as I have found is in *McGuffey's Reader*:

> In Adam's fall
> We sinned all.

This is pure fatalism—and the Church, from Augustine's day to our own, has had to evolve dubious theories of miraculous cleansing from the taint of original sin. The wise words of a New

England preacher put the truth of the idea of original sin in a
much more useful way. Paraphrasing McGuffey, he said,

> In Adam's sin
> We all jined in!

So far from lessening the seriousness of the meaning of sin in
human life, this second attitude increases it by making us morally
responsible for the mastery of sin. This, Richard Baxter, the
great British preacher, saw with clarity as he penned these impassioned words, "Use sin as it will use you; spare it not, for it
will not spare you; it is your murderer, and a murderer of the
world; use it, therefore, as a murderer should be used. Kill it
before it kills you. You love not death; love not the cause of
death." This, I would say, is taking sin seriously! But not too
seriously if you agree that sin is a fact, an evil fact, a fact that not
only can destroy all that we hold dear, but also can actually turn
us away from God.

III

When we consider what sin, what disloyalty to God, really
means translated in terms of ordinary people and daily living,
we will be driven to the conclusion that our spiritual forefathers
most assuredly did not overemphasize it. And for the simple
reason that, *dealing as it does with the issues of life and death, it
cannot be overemphasized.*

Disloyalty to God means disloyalty to that which is truly best
in the universe. Put it in personal terms, and it means disloyalty
to our own good, our own best interests, our truest self. Neither
a house divided against itself nor a self divided within itself can
long stand. Sin kills that which is best within us by separating
us from that which is best for us. Sin drives a wedge between us
and the great values that ought to dominate our thinking and
our living: truth, beauty, goodness, love. Instead of walking
humbly in the light cast by their glory, we turn away from them
and, extending the candle of our conceit against the enveloping
darkness, we grope ahead confident that somehow or other we
will find our way because we are the masters of our fate.

Sin strikes at us with various weapons. *Rationalization* is one
such—and probably the most vicious. We try to console ourselves and persuade others that we are all right after all. The
best definition of rationalization I have discovered is this: rationalization is giving a good reason in place of the real reason. It is

the effort to make the worse appear the better cause. It is a form of essential dishonesty and, as quickly as any other attitude, will either kill one's self-respect, or the ability to be critical of oneself. But, either way, it kills something in us that is essential to the life we might live, the person we might be.

The criminal rationalizes crime. Al Capone regarded himself as a public benefactor, it seems. "I give people what they want," he said.

The gambler rationalizes gambling. A taxi driver in New York City once asked me which horse I was betting on in a certain race. I replied that I wasn't a betting man. He studied me carefully in the rear-vision mirror for a moment, then said with that air of judicial omniscience that seems to settle on those who man the taxis of New York City, "Why not? All life is a gamble, anyway. Yer can't even walk across the street widout takin' a chance." (And the way he was driving, that was most certainly true!) Former Mayor William O'Dwyer of New York City agreed with this taxi driver, and said, in effect, "Let's legalize gambling and then tax it." So the taxi driver, and millions of others, daily add their two-dollar bets to a multibillion-dollar criminal racket—but, note this, they rationalize it, they seek to make it appear to be normal and natural, and quite, quite the thing to do.

I know of no form of moral laxity that does not cloak itself in rationalizations of one kind or another. Is it simply low moral standards? Is it premarital sexual relations? Is it adultery? Is it some form of sexual perversion? All these have their apologists; all don their rationalizations that give the appearance of plausibility, if not actual innocence, when it appears that severe judgment might fall on them. The commonest rationalization presented by these sins is that their prevalence is due to the moral letdown following the war. There is a measure of truth in this, of course—there is always a measure of truth in every good rationalization—but it is not enough to avert the judgment that these practices are sinful and that those who engage in them are sinners and that the consequences of sins like these were truly described a long time ago: "The wages of sin is death." For something dies, is killed within one—anyone—who seeks to order his life so as to include sin.

The tendency to rationalize the sins of society is written large all over the world today. The effort of the Soviet government to rationalize the slaughter of the small farmers in the 1920's was and continues to be a sickening performance. The effort to rationalize the concentration camps, the slave labor of war prisoners, and the grim and ghastly technique of control and suppression in police states—the effort to justify these as being essential to the establishment and maintenance of a "people's government" is too thin a rationalization to deceive many people outside Russia itself. Would to God Russia were the only sinner in this regard!

Not long ago I saw a newsreel, one portion of which was devoted to the amount of unemployment in the United States today. Mr. Leon Keyserling, a presidential adviser, was doing the talking. He pointed out that we did have an unemployment problem—some three million breadwinners were out of work—but, he concluded, "That is not a large number for a country like ours which has nearly seventy million breadwinners!" Not only was I not reassured by that rationalization, I could scarcely credit my ears! Only three million—not a large number! Break that three million down into persons and homes—then meet these persons and walk through their homes! Have you ever done this? I did, in 1930 to 1933 in South Chicago, in Grant Park, on Halsted Street, under the Chicago River bridge. I saw fear, insecurity, worry, frustration, malnutrition, and their kin slowly strip life of its poise, its sense of worth, its actual strength until it was beaten into a sodden bundle of despair.

That is *evil*: an open, conscious sin against God. Whatever causes it is sinful because it distorts and degrades the true self in man. Whoever consciously and openly either causes it or accepts it as necessary is a *sinner*—is one who seeks to block the will of God for human life and society.

I have attended too many annual, jurisdictional, and general conferences of our own church to think for one moment that churches are untainted by the effort to rationalize the sins that exist both within congregations and in interchurch relationships, as well as within the social order in which they exist. And we are neither better nor worse in this regard than every other church in the Christian tradition. You cannot study the deliberations of the National Council or the World Council without sensing the same temptation to rationalize rather than to repent of our sins.

I have heard almost every sin known to men, with the certain exceptions of drunkenness, prostitution, adultery, and dope-peddling, rationalized in some way or other by fellow churchmen. I have heard such evils as war, obliteration bombing, the use of the atomic bomb on Hiroshima, seriously rationalized as being unavoidably necessary and therefore in some sense Christian. I have heard racial discrimination debated and defended as properly belonging not only to a social order which aspires to be Christian but, God help us, to a Church that seeks to present Jesus Christ in life as well as by lip to all men.

If that were the whole story, who could help turning away from the Church with the feeling, "There is no health in it!" For sins like these actually kill something vital in our faith and life and witness. To cherish them or to rationalize them is to introduce into our common life dissension, distrust, and, finally, an open break with our historic mission to preach the fatherhood of God and the brotherhood of man. But it is far from the whole story! Written in the deliberations of the General Conference of 1952 is as strong an indictment of racial discrimination as a sin as you can find anywhere. And it is implemented by a determined effort to move against that sin in our common church life.

One of the proudest moments I have had as a churchman came, all unexpectedly, at the 1949 meeting of the Woman's Society of Christian Service of the Southeastern Jurisdiction, held in Louisville, Kentucky. I had slipped into the business session that preceded the lecture hour just in time to hear a resolution dealing with the problems of race in the church presented for consideration. As I listened, I fully expected the heavens to fall! For racial discrimination was condemned root and branch; our church was called upon to revamp our institutional policies and life until there is real comity and community among races; and we were told that the time to begin is *now!*

Listening to that report were four hundred Southern women, and when it was finished, I thought, "Now the fur is really going to fly." For one fevered moment, I considered asking for the floor and, in the interests of peace, reminding them that Paul had forbidden women to speak up in church. But I waited—*for the tumult that never came.* Without a dissenting vote, they endorsed the report and passed it on to the next General Conference for action. Mind you—these women are not going to be spectators in these reforms, and they know it. They are going to have to bear the brunt of them—and they know that, too. But they had the courage of their Christian convictions that it is their duty—their Christian duty—to raise the standard of the Kingdom of God in our common life.

Robert Browning suggested as the symbol of unused wisdom, the "unlit lamp"; and as the symbol of unused strength, the

"ungirt loin." Both were and are prevalent—they tempt everyone and will score many victories over anyone. Both are deadly
because they strike at the soul of man. The sins I have been
describing may have resulted in either the unlit lamp or the
ungirt loin, or both, but whatever their cause, their consequence
is sure—unless the person or people engaging in them can find
their way in God's will.

IV

That is a big "unless," I know, but enough people like Mary
Magdalene, Peter, Paul, and a host of others have done it to
encourage us to believe that it can be done by anyone, anytime.
The man who said, "Every sinner has a future, and every saint
has a past," gave a true word to guide us at this point.

Great religion confronts the sins of man, and man the sinner,
with the word: "Repent ye for the kingdom of heaven is at hand."
Confession, not *rationalization,* is the proper approach to sin.
"Sin can be cleansed! Life can be redeemed! You can find the
right road and walk therein!" Like Nicodemus of old, we ask,
"How can these things be?" And the answer comes steady and
sure, "We are surrounded by the love of God who seeks the
abundant life for all his children. When anyone is lost, God
persists in the effort to find him and bring him to the fold again.
He asks only that man become conscious of his plight, and, like
the Prodigal, say, 'I will arise and go to my father!' At that
moment and in that act of repentance, the healing love of God
takes hold of man and begins to make him whole again."

I would not give the impression that repentance comes easily.
The Prodigal had to go through plenty before he came to his
senses—and so do we all. Healing begins with a conscious awareness and repentance of our sins. Healing began for Paul when
he could say, "For all have sinned and come short of the glory
of God." Healing began for the returned exiles when Ezra led
them in the prayer of communal repentance, "Lord we have
sinned." Healing was far along the way when the Prodigal could
say, "Father, I have sinned against heaven, and in thy sight, and
am no more worthy to be called thy son."

Following hard after the initial act of penitence comes the
necessity of repentance. "Aye, there's the rub!"

As a Church we must repent of many sins before we can speak
of the love of God without having our life give it the lie. We
must tire of the husks of our separateness and seek the Father's

home of communion one with another. We must cease feeding on the poisonous diet of racialism and nationalism and seek the nourishing food of the God who wills the good of all His creatures. We must put first things first. We must be willing to lose our life in order to find it. We must preach the Kingdom of God without fear or favor and in complete faith in God. We dare not be deflected from our duty by the cautioning cries of prudence. If need be, we must remember that we are called upon to be "fools for Christ's sake." This is no call simply to ignore, much less forsake, the world: It is the only known way to be an instrument in its redemption. As a nation we must repent of the sins of spiritual blindness and self-righteousness which bid us seek our own welfare first and foremost, and, if necessary, at the expense of other peoples. There rests upon those of us who call ourselves Christian an especial responsibility at this point. We must both call this people to repentance and lead them in the act of true penitence that will serve to bind this broken world together. It is our Christian duty to strive for the kind of national life and policy that will make our common life a blessing to all men. It is our Christian duty to strive for the kind of common life that will exalt the welfare of men above every other good known to man.

Recognizing sin, then repenting of it and conquering it—both in our personal and communal life—is our Christian duty, our Christian calling. I wish it were an easier duty, a lighter calling. But it is both what it is and has always been—*The King's Highway of the Cross*. The Way of the Cross is the way of the cross— but it leads home—and there is no other way.

V

A Faith for Revolutionary Times

4. The Life That Endures

SCRIPTURE LESSON: Romans 12:1–21

I

TRADITIONALLY, Christians have never been satisfied with either the mere fact of life or life as it is. We are always looking at it with some adjective in mind: the *good* life, the *Christian* life, the *abundant* life, the life of *faith*, *eternal* life. This, I suppose, does not necessarily mean that we are ungrateful for the gift of life itself—at least, it need not mean that. Most of us, when we stop to think about it, are all but overwhelmed by the fact of life. But gratitude is not enough. Life is a most exacting and responsible gift. It must be lived somehow from day to day on the high road or on the low road. It must be shared with our fathers before us and with our children who will come after us. At the end of our earthly journey, death stands waiting to relieve us of certain privileges and responsibilities here, and, we believe, to introduce us to others that we now "see through a glass darkly but then face to face."

Tennyson was profoundly correct when he exclaimed, "As though to breathe were life!" It is not given to us simply to live out an animal-like existence; we must live in the light of some meaning, guided by some star, according to our understanding of some divine intention or plan—put it how you will.

One of the great privileges of working on or near a college campus is to be associated with large numbers of persons whose lives are beginning to move through the latter stages of adoles-

54

cence into full maturity. Although they usually manage to have
a very good time in college, their minds are restlessly probing
for the deeper meanings of what life is all about. They are trying
to formulate "a philosophy of life"; they discuss it incessantly,
in forums, classrooms, sandwich shops, in every sort of group.
And, like their elders before them, they occasionally come up
with some staggering answers! I recall one young man arguing
for an entire evening that since life was basically physical, health
was the absolute good that men should seek. That, in essence, is
and was to be his philosophy of life. Yet most thoughtful people
manage to come up with something more comprehensive than
he did.

What these young people do when they seek a philosophy of
life is what every person must do; and, I hasten to add, what
great minds and spirits have always tried to do. We can no more
live without some philosophy of life than without food and
drink. That is why men have always wrestled with the twin
problems of the meaning of life and the fact of death. Their
efforts are important because they are unavoidable. The decisions
we make from day to day are determined, in part, by our thoughts
on these basic problems. That is why the Christian faith needs
to be translated into a Christian philosophy of life. The Christian interpretation of life, the Christian standard of values by
which to make choices, frame policies, and direct personal and
social affairs—this is basic to putting the Christian faith in
action. Let it be emphasized, the Christian faith must be planted
in the sphere of action as a seed must be planted in soil, or it will
never mature, flourish, and live. The uniqueness of the Christian
philosophy of life can be appreciated better, I think, if we set it
against the background of other interpretations.

A physiologist once defined life as "the recurrent satisfaction
and dissatisfaction of a protein molecule." This, of course, is a
true description of one of the processes that are fundamental to
life. But whether it is the bottom on which all else must rest is
surely open to question. Yet it would be difficult to find a more
concise, trenchant philosophy of life for those who are inclined
to charge off life as an instance of animalism.

James Branch Cabell, the novelist, gives us this interpretation
of the meaning of life: "Life is a comedy perfectly re-enacted."
This interpretation differs from Ecclesiastes at only one point—
on whether life is a comedy or a long adventure in boredom.
The writer of Ecclesiastes gives as his opinion: "The thing that

hath been, it is that which shall be; and that which is done is that which shall be done: and there is no new thing under the sun." Cabell, apparently, thinks life is much too superficial to deserve the designation "tragedy," so he calls it a "comedy"—an incredible mixture of laughter and tears, irritations and perplexities, and one long or short, as the case may be, succession of trivialities.

You are familiar with Bertrand Russell's memorable phrasing of the philosophy of pessimism: "The life of Man is a long march through the night, surrounded by invisible foes, tortured by weariness and pain, towards a goal that few can hope to reach, and where none may tarry long."[1] Nor is Russell alone in this view of the human enterprise. Jean-Paul Sartre insists that we do not appreciate our situation as human beings until we accept the fact that "we are isolated [from everyone else]. We are conscious of our isolation. We make foolish and pathetic efforts to escape it. . . . Man can do nothing unless he first understands he must count on no one but himself, that he is alone, abandoned on earth in the midst of his infinite responsibilities, without help, with no other aims than the ones he sets for himself, with no other destiny than the one he forges for himself on this earth. . . . Life is absurd, love is impossible. . . . There is no way of knowing the true meaning of what we are doing; perhaps our actions have no meaning."[2]

There are times, of course, when this sort of philosophy has so many counts on its side that it makes, or seems to make, sense. When the eager idealism that nerves a young person to try to set the world aright fades into the calculated caution that keeps an older person from attempting anything; when the universal hunger of man for peace, security, and brotherhood is offered the "serpent" of another world war; when churches, after struggling to greatness through sacrificial loyalty to great causes, seek the serenity of conformity; when small colleges consecrated to their task of Christian education become great universities and forget or neglect this spiritual intention; when nations grown great through devotion to freedom become fearful of freedom, in the day of their power, and curtail it—when you see or share in experiences like these, you feel the full force of the philosophy of pessimism.

[1] *Mysticism and Logic* (Norton, New York, 1929), p. 56.
[2] From "French and American Pessimism," *Harper's Magazine*, September, 1945.

II

The Christian faith has a long-standing acquaintance with these contrasting, if not conflicting, philosophies of life. It was born amid the welter of philosophies that vied for attention in the Greco-Roman world of the first century. Materialism, idealism, pessimism, escapism—all such philosophies had eloquent spokesmen, then as now. The Hyde Parks and Washington Parks of the cities of that day must have been busy indeed with the many ideas then in circulation. I mention this in order to correct the impression some have that the Christian faith is a sort of other-worldly affair. As a matter of hard historical fact, the Christian faith is very much at home in this world—and has been so from the beginning. It won its way in the market place before it built places of retreat and retirement, such as nunneries and monasteries. What happened in the early centuries has happened repeatedly in Christian history. Read Kenneth Scott Latourette's seven-volume *History of the Expansion of Christianity* sometime, and you will encounter a veritable deluge of facts to support that statement. Yet we do not greatly advance the solution of our own problem by simply noting that Christianity has become a powerful historical fact. What we need to know is how this was accomplished. What was the philosophy of life that swept on to victory at various crucial periods in the last two thousand years? The answer to this question will suggest the essential elements in a life that endures. Fortunately, certain facts stand out.

For the Christian, *a life that endures is a life of faith in God as revealed in Jesus Christ.* Belief in God as seen in the life and work of Jesus Christ, confidence in the accuracy and adequacy of that belief, a willingness to be guided by it in the planning and the living of life—these are fundamental. There can be no Christian philosophy of life, no Christian community, no Christian family without them. They are the star by which the Christian thinker charts the course of his thought and life.

Gamaliel Bradford was making confession for many of us as well as himself when he wrote: "I have long been convinced that the greatest need of American civilization today is the need of God. . . .

"Personally I am in no position to make any effort in the matter, because, while I feel that the whole universe crumbles without God, I am myself utterly unable to find him. I am only deploring what I am sure is an imperative need, without

being able to suggest any means of meeting it. I trust someone, with a more positive faith, will be able to do better."[3]

I wish it were possible to assure persons like Mr. Bradford
that there is an easy path to a confident belief in God, but that
is not possible. God can be found—that can be stated with
complete confidence—but only by a never-ending search amid
all the difficult and tragic problems of life and history. As long
as we live, the search for a more adequate idea of God looms
as one of the major obligations of life itself. I would emphasize
the phrase "more adequate idea" because it highlights the real
crux of our problem. We do not need to create the idea of God;
we inherited it. But much of the content and meaning which
the idea of God holds for us derives from the experiences of our
ancestors. Our fathers gave us an idea of God geared to their
experiences of Him. Their interpretations of these experiences
may be in need of revision, and this we must feel free to make.
But over and beyond this, we must assume the responsibility of
relating the idea of God to our ever-changing pattern of knowledge about the world and experience of it. Why we should
have any hesitation about the propriety of doing this is hard to
understand. Every generation has had to do it, and it has
proved to be harder for some than others. With a world in
turmoil, as ours is today, with old landmarks disappearing in
every area of life, with mankind facing as ominous a future
as was ever envisioned by apocalyptical writers, it goes without
saying that we must be prepared to rethink, restate, and reaffirm
our faith, our belief in the reality of God. But this must not be
done in a rotelike manner, or it will be "love's labor lost."

It is gratifying to record the fact that an awareness of this
urgency seems to be abroad in the Christian fellowship today on
a wholly unprecedented scale. Our own church has had phe-
nomenal success in distributing the booklets dealing with the
fundamentals of our faith. This is all to the good, provided the
process goes steadily on until each one of us is able to give a
reason for the hope that is within him.

Remember, Gamaliel Bradford insisted that "the whole universe crumbles without God," and begin at the beginning. Belief
in God—not alone in the generalized sense as a principle of order
and purpose in history, but more especially as seen in the life and
teachings of Jesus Christ—constitutes the foundation of our
Christian faith. When wholehearted, it gives a meaning to life

[3] *The Letters of Gamaliel Bradford* (Houghton, Boston, 1934).

that can be found no other way. Yet it must be reached in a thoroughly honest manner and held with humility as well as conviction. Our belief in God must never be shielded from the facts of sin, evil, and death. Actually, it must try to find some kind of meaning for them in the divine economy of the universe. The Christian belief in God has grown to a rich and strong maturity because it could meet and master the many challenges put to it through two millenniums. It is, therefore, no broken reed on which to lean; rather it is a firm foundation on which to build a life that will endure.

III

The life that endures is one of faith in man. And this in spite of what man is and what men do to one another. Our Lord knew what was in man and yet loved him enough to die for him. We live in a world where there is brute passion and uncurbed hatred of man for man. The fruits of this passion and hatred are becoming more and more apparent. One tyrant no sooner passes away than another—yes, many others—arise to take his place. Concentration camps, slave labor, stock piles of atom bombs—are not these the true symbols of man and all his works? Why talk about Utopias when we seem utterly unable to fashion even a peace for our own time? How is it possible to have faith in man when men are what they are and do what they do?

In answer, let it be said that even as some men cause us to doubt mankind, there are others who rebuild our faith in mankind. Each one of us will know many such people, and as I relate certain incidents that have helped me believe in man, you will be thinking of those in your own experience that have helped you to the same end.

Many years ago an incident occurred that has helped me repeatedly in later life. The First World War was near, and hysteria was mounting. Atrocity stories were going the rounds, and the measure of patriotism was the ability to accept them without question. One day I accompanied my father to town, and there we fell in with the street-corner forum that was discussing world affairs. One of the men, a banker, knowing my father's reputation as a stubborn thinker, said that a trainload of maimed Belgian children was in Iowa. He asked my father what he thought of that. Father replied, "I don't believe it." The banker said, "You ought to be taken out of town on a rail."

At that point I was ready for action, and waited eagerly for father to fell him with a mighty blow—as well he might. Instead, he said to me, "Come on, Harold. It's time to go home." I could hardly believe my ears. I was angry and humiliated half to death. As we crossed the street, I asked, "Why didn't you hit him? Why didn't you knock him flat?" Father replied, "There are lots of things you don't settle by knocking people around." Right then, that was hard to believe, but the truth of it has been growing on me steadily ever since.

Incidents like this in the lives of people like us provide insights into the essential validity of a firm faith in man. When the Christian faith asks us to have faith in man, it does not gloss over the fact that Peter denied Jesus; it records the final movement in Peter's life in which he was truly "the rock." It does not lighten the infamy of Saul's persecution of the Christians; it records as of greater importance his conversion and his leadership of the early Church. In fact, the amazing growth and expansion of the Christian movement must be written in terms of ordinary people like these who were made extraordinary by their faith in God as revealed in Jesus Christ. Study it for a moment, and you will exclaim, "What hath God wrought!"

Truly, the heroic souls, known and unknown alike, are living examples of an insight attributed to Emerson: "Most people worry themselves into nameless graves while here and there a few choice souls forget themselves into immortality." What happened in the early centuries has recurred again and again over the centuries. It is going on today, and will continue until, in the fullness of time, God's will is done on earth as it is in heaven. Men and women from common walks of life, from ordinary homes—so far as wealth, fame, and power are concerned—will continue to step forward, to become uncommon, extraordinary crusaders for the Kingdom of God. Let the hand of God fall on the shoulder of any man in whose heart there is the will to follow, and that man is literally born anew through the power and in the purpose of God. Study this panorama of what has been done by God through people neither better nor wiser than we are, and you will find it both possible and necessary to say, "I believe in man, under God." There is reason to have hope and confidence in the future of the human enterprise. There is reason to believe that the Christian faith can bring into existence a community that deserves to endure.

IV

The third essential of a life that endures is complete commit-ment to the will of God.[4] In His will we find our purpose, our peace, our power. It is our business, our vocation as Christians, to build the Kingdom of God in the affairs of men, and to be satisfied with nothing less. It is our calling to lift the banner of a great purpose, God's purpose, as the only fitting challenge to men who would march to the Promised Land of a better world. We cannot study the records of the Christian faith with-out finding our categorical imperative in the idea of the King-dom of God, and in the conviction that it is relevant both to human life and to history, but incumbent on confessing Christians as the final purpose and goal. The Kingdom of God is the end and the only end plainly prefigured in the Christian gospel of the love of God. Several facts about the nature of the Kingdom of God stand out with such prominence that they deserve to be etched upon the minds of all who name the name of Jesus Christ and say they would be citizens of the Kingdom of God as un-folded by him.

1. It is God's Kingdom, not man's. No one—neither a Caesar nor a modern dictator, nor even public opinion—can, by his will, either create or dominate the Kingdom of God. In that Kingdom only one will will prevail—God's will.

2. The Kingdom of God is the Christian vision of the true condition of life. It is a vision rather than a blueprint of the divine purpose at work in human life. It is a mystical, ethical sketch of what God has in mind as to the meaning and fulfill-ment of life. Jesus seems to have had this in mind when he likened the Kingdom of God to a seed that can and will grow to full stature when given the chance and the care. When he said, "The Kingdom of God is within you," his thought was mov-ing in that direction. If it were not possible to demonstrate the reality of God, then there would be no conception of divine pur-pose. But, given that basic idea for good and sufficient reason, then the acceptance of the Kingdom of God as a vision of the fulfillment of God's purpose for life is neither incredible nor unimportant. It is as reasonable as the idea of God and quite inseparable from it.

When we say we are ready and willing to find the true mean-

---

[4] Much of the material in this section is contained in an earlier book, *A Firm Faith for Today*, chap. X (Harper, New York, 1950).

ing of our life in the will of God, we are saying several significant
things. We are saying: (1) that God is real, (2) that He is at work
in the world, (3) that His will provides man his only way to
growth and permanence, (4) that the discovery of this will is, or
ought to be, the major concern of our lives, (5) that in the life
and teachings of Jesus Christ we have our clearest revelation of
the nature and meaning of God's will for life, (6) that we ought
in all humility to seek to build our life and society along the
lines so clearly laid down by him.

We are saying that we propose to lose our lives for Christ's
sake. We are saying that we both believe that the world can be
saved in and through him, and that we are prepared to do our
part in bringing this about. But let us be sure that we make
ourselves clear on what we are trying to do. We are trying to
save the world, the whole world; not just a part, our part, of
it—not one part at the expense of another—but *the whole
world*. We are trying to *save*, to rebuild, to reform from foundation to superstructure, the world, until, as William Temple
said, "the sovereignty of love" characterizes the whole structure.
That this will call for the most serious kind of recasting of our
common life ought to be both axiomatic and accepted without
alarm.

Risky business? Of course it is. How do we think the cross came
to us—from playing it safe? What makes us think that we can
talk about the Kingdom of God without tragic sacrifice? Who,
in his right mind, thinks we can challenge sins, now so open and
so old they have become respectable, without cost or price? The
Christ whom we seek to serve is no easy master. H. G. Wells
once wrote these words of solemn warning to all who would
follow him:

He was too great for his disciples. And in view of what he plainly
said, is it any wonder that all who were rich and prosperous felt a
horror of strange things, a swimming of their world at his teaching?
Perhaps the priests and the rulers and the rich men understood him
better than his followers. He was dragging out all the little private
reservations they had made from social service into the light of a universal religious life. He was like some terrible moral huntsman digging
mankind out of the snug burrows in which they had lived hitherto. In
the white blaze of this kingdom of his there was to be no property, no
privilege, no pride and precedence; no motive indeed and no reward
but love. Is it any wonder that men were dazzled and blinded and cried
out against him? Even his disciples cried out when he would not spare

them the light. Is it any wonder that the priests realized that between this man and themselves there was no choice but that he or priestcraft should perish? Is it any wonder that the Roman soldiers, confronted and amazed by something soaring over their comprehension and threatening all their disciplines, should take refuge in wild laughter, and crown him with thorns and robe him in purple and make a mock Caesar of him? For to take him seriously was to enter upon a strange and alarming life, to abandon habits, to control instincts and impulses, to essay an incredible happiness. . . .

Is it any wonder that to this day this Galilean is too much for our small hearts?[5]

And yet—the miracle of human hope, courage, and strength in Christ continues to be enacted. Although he may be too much for our small hearts, if we try to find our way in his will, we can do it. If we are faithful to the end, our lives will bear such fruit as passes belief, and our children will see "our good works" and "glorify our Father which is in Heaven."

[5] H. G. Wells, from *The Outline of History* (Macmillan, New York, 1920).

VI

Science and Religion[1]

SCRIPTURE LESSON: Proverbs 8:1–4; 22–36

I

THE Old Testament's love of wisdom and the New Testament's devotion to truth were so deeply implanted in our religious tradition that almost from the beginning it was inevitable that our religious faith was going either to co-operate or collide with every other activity or institution that was interested in knowledge and truth. This fact, better than anything else, explains the uneven and hectic relationship between science and religion. When I asked myself whether I would be threshing over old straw if I were to look into this matter, two facts immediately assured me that that would not be the case.

In the first place, I suppose more young people have been and continue to be alienated from the Church during their college years by the conflicts between science and religion than by any other single cause. Over and over again in student conferences I have found this given by intelligent, alert collegians as the reason for not being interested in or for the waning of their interest in religion and the Church. They argue that science is moving ahead; religion is retreating. Science is the hope of the world; religion is hypnotized by her concern with another world. Science is interested in real problems; religion is concerned about problems many of which seem to be wholly unreal. Hence—they conclude—why bother about religion?

Thus reason many of the young men and women who throng our halls of ivy today as well as in earlier days. And this same attitude carries over in their life after they leave college. That, I am convinced, is why so many people are, to use a vivid and reasonably exact phrase, "lost to the Church" as a result of their

[1] This sermon was preached January 13, 1952.

college training. Churches deplore this fact, as well they may.
They usually wind up by blaming the colleges and especially
those "godless professors." Colleges deplore the fact, somewhat
more mildly as a rule, and they blame the churches for poor
preparation of young people religiously for the new problems
and shifting scenes of interest that they will confront in college.
There is just enough truth in both accusations to make this a
very real problem.

The second fact which encourages me to look into this relationship between science and religion must be obvious to everyone
today. Preparing as we seem to be to commit suicide with the
most advanced scientific techniques, we are either loudly blaming
science for our plight, or bellowing frantically for religion to
hasten to our rescue. Some of our leaders have called for the now
famous moratorium on the physical sciences until the social sciences and ethical concerns catch up with them and get them
under control. All of this puts both science and religion in a false
light. They are and ought to be integral parts of every thing that
really matters. You do not de-emphasize one in order to re-
emphasize the other. They co-operate or collide with each other,
and this is the promise as well as the peril of the day in which
we live.

II

Recurrent collisions between them have rocked Western civilization for nearly four hundred years now. And this is one of the
most dangerous as well as deplorable facts of our heritage. When
we think of them we think of them in collision with each other as
indeed they have been upon many occasions. We are witnessing
in our time—at least I hope we are witnessing—a sustained
effort to encourage and promote an era of understanding and
good will between these two great concerns. " 'Tis a consumma-
tion devoutly to be wished" because everyone has suffered from
their collisions and everyone will be benefited by renewed co-
operation. We cannot get along without either one of them,
though upon occasion both have been sure they could get along
without each other. Both are essential to the preservation of such
civilization as we have, and there is no hope of reaching beyond
what little we do have without the help of both concerns. Science is fundamental to modern civilization. But no more so than
historic religion whence came many if not most of the guiding

ideas and ideals of our culture. Both are so deeply intertwined with our civilization as to be inseparable from it.

The recognition of this profound interdependence between science and religion has been a long time coming. We may be guilty of wishful thinking if we think it's here now. It is still possible to meet some professors as well as some preachers who need to be taken to one side and have this fact explained rather quietly to them. As recently as sixty years ago Andrew D. White, president of Cornell University, wrote *A History of the Warfare between Science and Theology,* and he felt that the war was far from over as he wrote. At an even more recent date—1920— Professor C. E. M. Joad, one of the most popular philosophers in England, felt safe in writing, "So far as present indications go, it seems not unlikely that science will deliver the final blow to organized Christianity within a hundred years." It is only fair to note that Professor Joad has radically revised this judgment within the last ten years, becoming an ardent apologist for both individual and organized religion. But there are many among us who still wonder whether his original judgment may not be the true one. As a ministerial student in college, I well recall the quiver of alarm that passed over me when I read the pontifical judgment of a learned man that religion was now outmoded, half way between yesterday and tomorrow, having been stripped of all her usefulness by science on the one hand and philosophy on the other. I was not only alarmed, I was mad. And, I must confess, I read with great glee a counterblast written by an outraged thinker against *Science, the False Messiah.* And I was all for the subordination of science to religion and the removal of a few scientists here and there!

Judgments and attitudes like these could have been avoided— would have been rendered impossible—if a little closer attention had been paid to one interesting fact about the great controversies between science and religion: *They emerged from each battle more solidly united, and more deeply in need of each other, than they had ever been before.* A quick look at some of these conflicts will help us appreciate the permanent importance of this point.

III

I grant you it was a rough day for traditional religious ideas when Copernicus, Galileo and their colleagues brought forth proof of the claim that the sun rather than the earth was the center of the universe. For with this conclusion the neat little bandbox universe with the earth as the main theater of operation and with man as the principal actor strutting upon that stage was swallowed up in the awful immensities of space and time and motion of the vast universe then unrolled. Everyone, whether scientist or religionist, got more than a little giddy when he thought about where he was. While science might justly celebrate the magnitude of the discovery, the individual scientist was no better equipped to face it than was the individual religionist. Both were in danger of losing their sense of personal worth, dignity, and destiny in the vast reaches of what, to science, appeared to be a mechanistic universe, quite devoid, they feared, of soul or spirit.

The final outcome is well known to us, even though the road to it lay over a hundred years and had to be built every step of the way. Religion accepted—as indeed she was forced to accept—the new conception of the universe, but she flatly refused to entertain the implication that spirit or soul were alien to the universe. And when the echoes of the battle began to die down, man found that he still lived much as he had lived before even though in a vastly different setting. Science discovered that it needed two of the great words of religion in order to go on living in this world that it had discovered: *mystery and purpose.* For great scientists suspected, from the outset, that what we did not know was infinitely more important than what we did know about this world in which we live. Science needed the help of religion and needed it badly. The only escape from the nightmare of a universe of endless and pointless wheeling planets lay in religion's historic confidence in the reality of the mysterious and continuing purpose of God in creation. The individual scientist was far from through when he discovered and described this new universe: he had to live in it, he had to work in it, and he had to justify the importance of the work he was doing. This is why he turned again—and turned quickly—to historic religion without, for one moment, sacrificing his science. Of both scientist and religionist, in that day and of one as truly as of the other, it may be said:

> As wider skies broke on his view
> God greatened in his growing mind
> Each year he dreamed his God anew
> And left his older God behind.

Now what has been celebrated frequently by amateurs with adolescent enthusiasm as the victory of science over religion ought to be described in all seriousness as the emergence of a truer conception of the nature of the universe and the consequent struggle to interpret all life in terms of it. It was a victory for truth, and, as such, a victory in which both religion and science shared. Science and religion emerged from this period of discovery and adjustment wedded in an even closer union than had been the case before.

I can still feel—and I think most of you can—the heat of the second period of tension between science and religion: the one touched off by Charles Darwin in 1859 and brought to the extreme limits of absurdity in the Stokes trial in Tennessee when a teacher of biology was declared a criminal because he taught the validity of the idea of evolution.

When Darwin advanced his thesis, everyone—scientists and religionists alike—believed that man was the result of a special act of creation and unrelated to any other form of life. But Darwin blew this notion sky high by relating man to a long line of animal ancestors. Actually, man's life was not changed so much as one iota by this announcement. But his pride was considerably damaged. Instead of being the one for whom the whole creation waited breathlessly in that primal day when he stepped forth from ancestral clay the darling of Deity and the master of all else, man had to come down to and face the fact that he was the latest arrival in a long progression of life forms, and that he had arrived so recently as to be hardly here at all!

It was hard for everyone to assimilate this new notion. Obviously, it played havoc with all traditional scientific and religious ideas, and, as I read the records, scientists as well as religionists were exercised about it. In fact it is hard to say which one had the more difficult job adjusting its inheritance to the discovery. Both went to work rethinking the whence, why and wherefore of life—questions that until then had not been seriously challenged for nineteen hundred years. I shall not deny for one moment that religion faced a colossal task. Its traditional notion of salvation assumed that the entire universe was created as a gigantic stage on which was to be enacted the drama of man's creation and salvation. But now—man and all his works seemed, at least for the moment, to be an insignificant aspect of an obscure corner of the cosmos. Dr. Harlow Shapley, famous astronomer at Harvard, once cut us down to size with this judgment: "The earth is a grain of sand with a whiff of atmosphere and a smear of biology plodding its way around the sun with monotonous regularity."

Now there's just enough truth in this to keep us humble, but no one knows better than Professor Shapley that it is a little less than the whole story. The larger outline of the meaning of life on this earth is beginning to emerge for both science and religion. Man belongs here. He is no alien intruder, no stranger here within a foreign land, whose "home is far away beyond a golden strand." This earth is his home: he is a part of it; it is a part of him—*and God is the creator of all*. Man is not only a created being; he was created a *human* being. And whether that process took four thousand or four billion years, whether it involved a few or an inconceivable number of preliminary life forms— these are matters of detail. The main point stands firm: We are here, equipped with a sense of duty and destiny, and guided by a sense of responsibility to the God who is the Creator of the entire Universe. That is enough to keep both science and religion forever humble and everlastingly grateful for such help as each other can give in the adventure and the discipline of living.

We are still surrounded by that third period of tension between science and religion; one growing out of certain forms of psychology, particularly behaviorism and depth psychology, or what we usually know as Freudianism. For a while it looked as though John Watson and his fellow behaviorists were going to sweep all before them and reduce us to a bundle of conditioned reflexes. We were blandly informed that who we are depends upon where we've been; our babies were called "animated vegetables" or, at best, "candidates for personality," and we were told that if we could control their environment perfectly we could determine their character exactly. There were some pretty ugly scenes between religion and this brand of psychology before it was unceremoniously dumped overboard by Freudianism.

In its early days, and for Freud to the end of his days, Freudianism regarded religion as an illusion. The new psychology toiled unceasingly at the problems of ideas, fears, loves, hates, and desires, and it probed steadily in the unconscious and subconscious life of man. It cut us up into such nasty little psychological pieces that we were almost afraid to shave of a morning. In its heyday, it made a tremendous stir! It labeled a son's affection for his mother an "Oedipus complex" and a daughter's affection for her father a "father fixation." An entirely new jargon came into fashion: wishful thinking, complexes, inhibitions, fixations, frustrations. We became curious about, even suspicious of, every altruistic impulse, dream, ideal, or emotion we might have. Everything had to be pursued into the depths of one's emotional nature before it could be understood. And when you finally caught up with it, if you ever did, it wouldn't bear inspection. It soon came to this—that you almost had to be psychoanalyzed in order to be respectable. Not that the good psychiatrists themselves ever said this! I once asked the head of a famous psychiatric clinic whether he had ever been psychoanalyzed. He said, "No." When I expressed surprise and asked why, he said, "I want to let well enough alone."

Now after that early period of collision on almost every score, an era of co-operation is growing up between religion and the new psychology. Jung, Adler, and Fromm, to name but three, are typical of the move to bring the two concerns more closely together. Religious workers gladly follow the lead of our own friend and member, Dr. Carroll Wise, in saying, "It is primarily to Freud and his fellow workers that credit must be given for the discovery and development of techniques for dealing with the psychological factor in illness. . . ."

There is every reason to believe that in this and every future period of tension between science and religion, we will discover a deeper need for and solidarity with one another. It will not always be easy and it will not be had for the simple asking. But serious and disciplined minds and spirits will work for it and will find it. This is no fatuous hope; it is a reasoned conclusion that drives its roots in a long period of human history.

IV

I have had the feeling many times that if scientists and religionists knew their Bible a little better they might have avoided much if not most of the trouble they have had with each other. It is as true for one as the other: "Ye shall know the truth, and the truth shall make you free." And the book of Proverbs was serving an ultimatum on both science and religion when it caused Wisdom to say: "Blessed is the man that heareth me, watching daily at my gates. . . . For whoso findeth me findeth life, . . . But he that sinneth against me wrongeth his own soul: all they that hate me love death."

Most of the trouble science and religion have had with each other has grown out of their failure to realize that they must stand together. Literally, there is no way in which they can avoid coming to terms with each other. And there is no way any one of us can take one and ignore the other. They talk about the same universe. They seek not two kinds of truth but one kind of truth about this universe. They talk about the same man and they seek the truth about him. They have made and they will continue to make enough mistakes to keep them humble and in a teachable frame of mind. Arrogance and dogmatism are as out of place in one as in the other. It is not enough to seek a truce with each other; we must find a new sense of comradeship in the great tasks of helping mankind face this hour. The gravest need of this hour is not bigger bombs; it's better men. Better men in every walk of life—men with purer motives, a higher morality, and a more sincere concern for the welfare of all men everywhere. This does not call for more religion and less science; it calls for more religion and more science and for a greater degree of co-operation between the two.

Professor Niels Bohr, a Nobel prize winner, recently told a conference of atomic physicists that "not only scientists but men in every walk of life must be responsible for devoting the new truths and revelations of the universe to peaceful rather than war-making ends. . . ." Dr. Harrison Brown, who recently addressed the World Affairs Forum in Great Hall, was not asking an idle question when he titled his book, *Must Destruction be our Fate?* That question must be put to everyone, and it must be answered by everyone to get the right answer. Scientist and religionist alike must divest himself, for the moment, of the peculiar concerns of his own calling to ask where he fits into that answer. Churches and schools have no more important problem than asking where they fit into that answer. We in our homes must take it as a primary concern or we are not preparing ourselves or our children for the problems of this day.

The answer to that question, I am convinced, will run something like this. In the idealism of great religion and through the instrumentalities of great science, standing together, we can find our way toward life. Separate them, and all is lost. For, in separation, religion becomes irrelevant—at least unrelated to—many of the most powerful forces in the world, while science becomes the blind engineer at the throttle of the most powerful civilization man has ever known. Keep them together—in thought, teaching, and life, in home, school, laboratory, and church—and we have our one chance to find life, the life of justice, brotherhood, and peace. To get them together, to keep them together is not only the measure of our maturity; it is also a true indication of our awareness of the seriousness of the hour in which we live and of our determination to meet it with every resource at our disposal. To do less is to "love death."

VII

An Obituary of Modern Civilization

SCRIPTURE LESSON: Amos 1

I

EVERY good newspaper has its file of materials that are going to be used in writing the obituaries of prominent people when the time comes. Obviously it is the mark of wisdom to keep this file of materials up to date. This could be a morbid business, but, sometimes, when properly handled, it has its lighter moments. I well recall the time Shailer Mathews, Dean of the Divinity School of the University of Chicago, came to class a few minutes late. There was a twinkle in his eye as he explained his tardiness: "A reporter from one of the papers was calling to find out whether I have written or done anything lately that deserves space in my obituary!" This serves to remind us that obituaries, while published after death, are actually written in life.

Civilizations, like men, have their separate envelopes in the obituary file of history. And, on separate cards in that envelope, are listed the assets and liabilities of the men, institutions, and movements that constitute that civilization. These cards contain the materials from which the obituary of that civilization will be written. Amos, for example, in the opening chapter of his prophecy, pulled out the envelopes of half a dozen nations, including his own, and with terrifying brevity and lucidity told his startled listeners what he saw. Any number of historians have gone to the file, pulled out the envelope marked "Greece" and have written their interpretation of the life and death of that unique culture. Gibbon extracted the envelope marked "Rome" and wrote *The Decline and Fall of the Roman Empire*. In our time men like Spengler, Toynbee, and Sorokin have written the

73

obituaries of various civilizations and, with this as background, each has attempted one of our own.

Their interest in this does not seem as premature now as it did as recently as ten years ago. A dour professor at Harvard, Ernest A. Hooton, writes us off in a single sentence: "Modern man moves toward extinction." After the atomic bomb burst, Norman Cousins decided that "Modern Man is Obsolete." Several other careful students have brought in the judgment that what might be called modern civilization isn't dying, it's already dead. The consensus of opinion, however, seems to be that while modern civilization isn't dead—yet!—it is acutely ill and is surely lying at death's door.

Against this somber background, it is in order to have a look at some of the cards in the envelope marked "Modern Civilization" in the obituary file of history, and this is a good time to do it. If we had the time to go through the entire file, card by card, studying the achievements of our civilizations, we would be brought to our feet time after time with exclamations of joy and pride. And we must resist the temptation to center our attention exclusively on these cards as though they told the whole story. If they did, we would not now be in so grievous a plight. Something has gone wrong, terribly, tragically wrong, and we had better keep thumbing through those cards until we get hold of the ones that help us understand what is the matter.

I do not like what I see on these cards any better than you do. We will react to some of them as an agent in *Oliver Wiswell* did to the battle of Bunker Hill. He was one of the Tory citizens cooped up in Boston by aroused patriots. These unhappy people were gathered at upstairs windows and on housetops watching the British Army form at the foot of the hill and move slowly toward the crest. This particular Tory shuddered as he saw the soldiers mowed down as if by a giant scythe. He saw them flee down the hills, reform ranks and start up again toward the waiting riflemen. He hastily abandoned his place at the window crying, "I can't watch it!"—but he was back in a minute muttering, "Can't look and can't not!" That's the way I feel about some of these cards: "Can't look and can't not!"

But difficult as it is, we must do it, so I propose to pull out four of the cards in our file that will at least suggest the nature of the struggle between life and death in modern civilization. One deals with major trends in the national and international scene, another with trends in our economic life, a third with trends in education, and the last with trends in the Church itself. We shall find that these cards are not so much cold resumés of impersonal facts as they are living alternatives among which each person must choose. For these cards are not wholly filled out as yet. We are writing on them day by day, decision by decision. And the determination of life or death for our civilization lies as truly with what we write in our generation as with what any preceding generation has written.

II

Consider for a moment the card which chronicles trends in national and international policy. We've been filling in the facts which appear on it for a long time—and the entries over the last two hundred years have been both rapid and ominous. In that period of time we have witnessed giant concentrations of power, wealth, and culture grow up centered in various geographic localities. Not only have they been powerful; without exception they have tried to become all-powerful. We have seen these centers of tremendous power fall upon one another in a series of utterly vicious wars that resulted in the destruction of at least the imperial aspirations of all. Simply to call the roll of these casualties is as sobering an experience as one could want: Italy, Spain, Portugal, Holland. As a result of events since the turn of the century, the list must be extended to include Germany, Japan, France, and England. Each one of these in the heyday of its power produced leaders and apologists who were certain that they were the darlings of destiny. The pronouncements and analyses of those leaders must have sounded fine then—but they do make strange reading now!

Looking back on that historical scene several things should be axiomatic: (1) The materials out of which we build power and security are international rather than national in scope; (2) No nation is powerful enough nor can any become powerful enough to go it alone with safety; (3) To keep on going this way means the ruin of modern civilization. I say these truths should be axiomatic but, if we are to judge by what is going on now, they are not.

For once more power—political, economic, military, technological power—is being gathered around two great nations—Russia and the United States. Each one is "sold" on its own way of life and believes that, given a chance, all mankind would embrace it. Each has come through the last quarter century with mounting power and self-assurance. Each one proclaims the innocence of its own intentions and is suspicious about the other's plans. They have maneuvered themselves by word and deed into a state of mind where neither believes the other when words of peace are spoken, but dire threats are taken at twice their face value. Each is in quest of allies yet wonders just how much dependence can be placed upon them. Each wants to influence, if not determine the foreign policy of all allies. Each is willing to arm allies that seem to be trustworthy. And, if the worst should come, each is willing to stand alone against the other. Sensing the imminence of a cataclysmic showdown in the near future, each is arming with utmost dispatch. If this were a new situation, we would not be so completely overwhelmed by despair and futility. But it is old—as old as the era of nationalism in our history. The ghosts of Spain, Italy, Germany, and all the rest appear, Banquo-like, at our celebration of power and shake their heads in solemn warning. But not many see them and those who do are more frightened than guided by this warning.

Several efforts have been made to halt this homicidal, if not suicidal, mania of modern civilization by some form of co-operation under law. We have tried Peace Tribunals, Peace Pacts, the League of Nations, the World Court, and now the United Nations. And then the advocates of a strong, centralized world government come among us, seeking a hearing. The men who have believed that there is some other way, some way of peace and justice, who have persisted in this belief through disappointment after disappointment, have written one of the most glorious chapters in the history of man's struggle for a better world. Oh, I know, they are regarded as "fools" by many but, if they are "fools," they are "fools for Christ's sake"—and in Christian parlance that is the highest form of praise.

I will not pretend to know nor does it do much good to guess about how we are going to fill out this card in our file. But there can be no ducking the grim fact that we are filling it out by our policies and deeds day by day. These are our answer to the question: Do we work ahead toward a more perfect union of the nations of the earth, or do we beat a retreat to the patterns of power of yesterday? I do not know what answer we will finally make, but I do know that if we make the wrong one, the historian of tomorrow, trying to account for the death of our civilization, will say, "This is where they went wrong." The future of modern civilization, if it is to have a future, rests with those who not only believe in the possibility of a more perfect union but who also are willing to work toward it.

III

The notation on the second card in our file is "Economic Trends." One look at it reveals the fact that the modern world is the scene of a desperate race between achievements and disasters. Any effort to celebrate the former without confessing the latter is a most dangerous form of hypocrisy. It is true that the standard of living in some sections of the world is higher than it has ever been before. And, thanks to the technical genius of our age, it is also true that a higher standard of living is now possible for all men. These facts stand in such sharp contrast to earlier eras of famine, semistarvation, and stark need that, instinctively, we want to thank God for them. But who can honestly let the matter rest there? Our own higher standard of living is at the mercy of an increasingly militarized economy. There are too many hungry, homeless, fear-ridden peoples all over the world for us to get much comfort out of the knowledge of how well off they might be.

When we ask what has gone wrong with modern civilization on this score, many answers are given. Dr. Northrop's study, *The Meeting of East and West,* published as the war drew to a close, opens with these disturbing words that are as much a forecast as a summary: "Ours is a paradoxical world. The achievements which are its glory threaten to destroy it. The nations with the highest standard of living, the greatest capacity to take care of their people economically, the broadest education, and the most enlightened morality and religion exhibit the least capacity to avoid mutual destruction in war. *It would seem that the more civilized we become the more incapable of maintaining civilization we are.*"[1] The most convincing, as well as the best-known answer, was suggested by Arnold Toynbee over a decade ago. Underlying the social and economic confusion of our civilization is the basic conflict between democracy and modern industrialism, he says.

Modern industrialism, centering its vast genius in the production of goods, has completely transformed the life of peoples wherever it has gone. When the history books call it "the industrial revolution" they are dead right. Its demand for the tre-

[1] F. S. C. Northrop, *The Meeting of East and West* (Macmillan, New York, 1946), p. 1. Italics mine.

mendous concentration of men and materials has produced large cities that, inevitably, have become the fulcrums of economic, cultural, and political influence. When the yeomanry of England were swept off their farms and out of their unbelievably peaceful and lovely rural villages to the mining, manufacturing, and trading centers, a new era had begun in British history. Industrialism grew to gianthood overnight. It promised much, and it wrought an authentic miracle in the production of almost every kind of goods man might need, and let it be confessed, a great many he seems not to need. It centered power in the hands of a few men, giving them the responsibility—the penalties and the rewards—of leadership. Not only were workers dependent upon them; kings, presidents, and political bosses walked softly in their presence. The domestic and foreign policies of nations bloomed in their smile and withered at their frown. They were a strong breed—these men whose insight, daring, courage, and driving hard work brought industrialism from infancy to maturity.

But industrialism failed to make good its promise of security, prosperity, and peace for mankind. Its concern for its machines and its markets and its dividends was noticeably stronger than its concern for the personal welfare and the personalities of the workers. Its belief that competition was the law of its life, growth, and continued usefulness did something more than stimulate individual effort and enterprise; it encouraged conflict, it praised hard-driving ruthlessness and, in extreme cases, it put a premium on actual brutality.

Grave social and moral deficiencies like these could not go unchallenged, and the challenger was already in the field. For democracy, schooled in the Christian teachings that man is a child of God and that we are to build the Kingdom of God, had set itself to champion the rights of man wherever these were curtailed or impeded by institutions and conventions. It had scored early but difficult victories over the medieval Church in certain sections of Europe, over feudalism, and over the idea of the divine right of kings. It believed, and believes, that man is the bearer of intrinsic worth, that institutions are made for man, not man for institutions, that he is entitled to have a voice in the determination of any decision or policy which affects him and his welfare, that he must learn to live with his fellows on a plane of equality and common concern, that the final word in human relations is co-operation rather than conflict, peace rather than war. The issue was joined between the convictions of democracy and the deficiencies of industrialism more than a century ago, and the outcome is still in doubt.

Can we rediscover man now lost in the pentagons of modern society? Can we individualize, personalize, and save the souls of the increasingly anonymous and faceless units in the mob of mass-men? Can we save our men of power from the illusion that power means righteousness? Can we build a social and economic order in which all people feel that they belong, in which co-operation is the rule of procedure, in which they share both work and profits, both responsibility and reward?

Day by day we are writing our answer to questions like these on this second card in our obituary file. I wish I knew exactly what we wanted to write. If we get the wrong answer down, some Gibbon of the future, writing of the Decline and Fall of Western Culture, will say, "This is where that society went wrong." He may even quote one of our own poets:

> O we could build these towering buildings
> With their thousand gleaming lights
> But we could not find the formula
> Of simple human rights.

IV

A third card in our file—and one on which we are writing an immense amount of material these days—bears the notation: "Educational Trends."

Schools are one of the greatest formative forces ever developed by a society. The emphasis on education, public education, is one of the characteristics of our time. Formerly schools were small and for the few. Now they are large and for everyone. The deepest problem in education today does not lie in the size and scope of schools, however; it lies in their *purpose*. Schools once regarded themselves as the creative leaders of a society. They thought it their function to take young men and women and train them to stand on the frontier of every problem known to man. They tried to train them to become fearless, useful thinkers with both the skill and the freedom to bring in new answers when older ones seemed inadequate. The little College of William and Mary did that for Jefferson. The College of New Jersey, forerunner of Princeton, helped Madison on his way. Harvard College had no reason to be other than proud of John Adams. I would be a little less than human if I did not hear Madison's years of training and reading in theology and philosophy echoing through the nine amendments he proposed to the Constitution which, when amplified and adopted, became the Bill of Rights.

Despite and deeper than all the fun that our immediate ancestry poked at "book learning" was the sincere conviction that the fellow who had it had an added measure of responsibility for finding answers to pressing problems. It was as though our fathers said to the schools, "Give us men trained to lead at those points where the issue is life or death." And schoolmen were proud as well as humbled by that responsibility.

Now a new mood is discernible both in schools themselves and in society. Schools are no longer the creative leaders of society; they are to be the creatures of society. Increasingly our great educational institutions particularly in critical periods are chanting, "Tell us what you want and we will give it to you. Tell us what's right and what's wrong, what's true and what's false, what's good and what's evil—and we'll abide by what you say." Would to God this were a caricature of our situation! With few exceptions, any man coming into a position of responsible leadership in colleges and universities, whether tax-supported or privately endowed, feels compelled both by conscience and by constituency to frame so broad an indictment of social radicalism as not only to damn communism but also to put an effective damper on creative social criticism. The utter seriousness of this situation breaks upon us when we realize that the only social order that can safely neglect or stifle criticism is one which either thinks it is perfect or knows how to become perfect and is willing to do so. Every other form of society will make way, will welcome, the kind of criticism that keeps it conscious of defects and experimenting with new ways of correcting them.

Our schools must not so much be permitted as be expected to study with freedom the great issues of the day. And how sadly we need their help here just now! General Omar Bradley has warned us that "we live in an age of nuclear giants and ethical infants." This, surely, is one of the gravest problems we face. This being true, you would suppose that the schools would rush at the problem of correcting our ethical infancy rather than accelerating our nuclear gianthood. But no—nuclear research is the order of the day. According to one estimate, the government has expended six billion dollars for nuclear research to date— and much of this through university budgets. It is not recorded that any such new money has been advanced toward correcting our ethical immaturity. While we continue to hope the ethical infants will somehow become mature before it is too late, we bend every effort to increase the power which we put in their hands.

And we ought to encourage our schools to investigate the controversial issues of our day. This business of drawing up a special oath of loyalty for teachers and demanding the signature of men and women who are as truly citizens of this country as anyone else is more than an affront to their integrity and a transgression of their freedom: it is a sure way of depriving ourselves of potential Adamses and Jeffersons and Madisons at a time when they are needed as badly as they were at the end of the eighteenth century in these United States. To one who argues that this kind of freedom will be abused in a dangerous way by our schools and must, therefore, be curtailed by law, one reply, and one only, needs be made: We, as a society, can more safely tolerate the occasional abuse of this freedom at the hands of the very few who will abuse it than the suicidal policy of reducing our centers of leadership training to a goose-stepping regiment of *"Sieg Heilers"* of the status quo.

As I let this card on "Educational Trends" fall back into the file, I wish I could assure you that we are going to fill it out the right way, that we are going to urge and insist that our schools once more become creative leaders of society—but I honestly do not know what we are going to write from here on out. I only hope the historian of the future is not forced to say, "At this point, and in this fashion, their fear for freedom became a fear of freedom, and in their frantic determination to preserve the forms of freedom they stifled the love of it in the hearts of their youth."

V

There is one more card in our file that, in fairness, we ought to study, though I am most reluctant to do so. Like the Boston Tory, "I can't look and can't not!" It is the card marked "Church." Small wonder we who are confirmed churchmen are loath to go further. Organized religion has a lot to answer for before the conscience of man as well as the judgment bar of Almighty God. For three hundred years the Inquisition shackled the mind and conscience of Europe with fear and hatred. The Inquisitors in their effort to crush heresy stopped at nothing. Confiscation of goods, torture, death: all were used to the glory

of God—or so the inquisitors thought! Then, as if that were not
enough, the so-called modern era in Western history opens with
the wars of religion raging all over Europe for a hundred years,
impoverishing the land and filling up the as yet unemptied vials
of bitterness everywhere. Even when we haven't been fighting
one another with physical weapons, we have found it difficult to
be on speaking terms with one another.

We have been so busy combating one another that, to borrow
a phrase from John Dewey, we have let "burly sinners rule the
world." Instead of finding common ground on which to stand as
we tried to build a spiritual foundation for the world community,
we have chosen to try to further our claims at cost to one another,
to seek privileges which we had no intention of sharing with one
another. Instead of doing everything in our power to help build
peace on earth and good will among men, we have been the
prolific mother of much discord. Instead of subjecting one another to endless criticism, we might be bringing the Christian
ethic to bear upon the great issues of our day. Who knows what
a difference that might have made in the long run?

We have spent so much precious time and energy over small
matters that there are moments when it seems to me a fitting
epitaph for the Church would run something like this: *She had
great convictions about little problems and little convictions
about great problems.* Yet that is far from the whole truth. We
have spoken out with clarity and conviction on such issues as
drinking and corruption in public office. This is all to the good—
but it is not enough. Other evils are equally real and as desperately serious, and need attention: racial discrimination, war, the
exploitation of many sections of the human family—this too
should have been done—done by the Church in the name of the
God of all men.

Thank God, the light of a new day is breaking over much of
the life and work of the Church. We are learning how to work
together as we never dreamed possible as recently as fifty years
ago. Now we have a World Council of Churches and are studying
how to increase its strength. In the National Conference of
Christians and Jews we have at least a meeting place for the
three great religions in the Western world. Not enough, to be
sure, but, let us hope, a beginning of a period of increasingly
close co-operation.

And we have begun to speak our mind on the major issues in
the common life of mankind. You cannot attend conferences of

world churches without sensing a new awareness of responsibility for everything that is going on in the world today.

But we have so far to go before we build a spiritual foundation strong enough for world unity—and so little time remains! Can it be done? I do not know but with a faith bolstered by prayers, I think it can be done.

When the historian of the future drops that card back into the file he will say at least this: "After wasting many precious opportunities over nineteen hundred years, the Church finally woke up, but it was then too late to halt the processes of disintegration that had been gaining momentum in every walk of life over several hundred years."

And, in the Providence of God, he might hold it up triumphantly and say, "Thank God, though the hour was late and the issue desperately in doubt they came through and lighted and pointed the way to the new world which we now enjoy."

The end of modern civilization is not yet come. It may not come in our lifetime. It may not come at all, in the Providence of God. But if it does not come, soon or late, it will be because people like us suddenly came alive to our serious responsibility for determining the fate of our civilization. As I have said before, I am not a pessimist but I am the soberest optimist you ever saw. We are not fated by God to perish—but the issues of life and death are clearly in our hands.

VIII

Shall It Be War or Peace Today?[1]

SCRIPTURE LESSON: I Corinthians 13

I

ONE of the most creative Christian thinkers of our time is John
Baillie; he has spent his life teaching first in America and now
in Scotland. In one of his last books he gives us an eloquent
biographical note: "My earliest memories," he writes, "have a
definitely religious atmosphere. I can not recall a time when I
did not feel in some dim way that I was not my own to do with
as I pleased but was claimed by a higher power which had
authority over me. For, as far back as I can remember anything,
I was somehow aware that my parents lived under the same kind
of authority. They too behaved as though they, even they, were
not their own."

This witness of John Baillie is important because it is the
simple human description of the Christian conception of life
and duty. Once we have felt the full force of the belief that in
Jesus Christ we have our clearest revelation of the will of God,
and having seen it, embraced it as our way of life, we are not
our own. We belong to Him.

We accept as the great vocation of our life the responsibility
of trying to be living witnesses. We enter into every situation
then both bound by, yet freed through our loyalty to Him. He
is relevant to every problem that we face and the rightness of
every answer that we get derives from Him. All this, I am sure,
is why, as the Quakers say, "I have a concern this morning and
feel I must bear witness to what my Christian faith means to me."

As I face the problems of war and peace which press in upon
us all today, I do this not in the spirit of trying to tell you what
you as a Christian must think and do—that would be sheer pre-

[1] This sermon was preached January 21, 1951.

84

sumption and no one knows it better than I—but only what one aspiring Christian thinks he must do and thinks ought to be done. What has been called "The Great Debate" is now on in the Congress of the United States. It will deal, we are told, with two major problems: the foreign policy and the rearmament program of this country. That it will affect each one of us is a well understood fact. Equally well understood is the further fact that it will affect every person on the face of the earth. It will be studied with care by responsible men everywhere. The conclusions reached by it, when embodied in national policy, may well constitute another major decision in the history of mankind.

For my part, I am here trying to lift up in our common thinking certain Christian convictions that seem to be getting lost in the scramble of fear and alarm. Each of these convictions bears directly upon certain cardinal facts in the contemporary situation. Only their transcendent importance and inseparability justify the all too brief time devoted to each one. But if I can remind even some of you of the reality and relevance of great Christian conviction to concrete issues, this effort will have achieved its objective.

II

Here is the first of several facts that are getting misplaced with appalling regularity in much of our Christian thinking today and can only be properly rediscovered by seeing it in the light of our Christian duty: The question "Shall it be war or peace today?" has not yet been answered. It is still up for free discussion. Influential journals like the *United States News and World Report, Life* and *Time* are openly calling it war; but in simple and most important fact, we are not now at war with either China or Russia or anyone else. If we were at war in the full constitutional sense of that phrase, both this discussion and The Great Debate would be equally academic. But we are not now at war. We are getting ready for war and we may soon be fully at war by congressional declaration, but that is not now the case.

I am not blind to what is going on in Korea and Indo-China. The lengthening casualty lists that reach for many of our homes mean that men are fighting with almost every instrument of war and are dying as truly as if we had a congressional declaration of war. What is happening now may well prove to be the opening phase of a full war, but the time for diplomacy is not yet over. Until war is actually declared, bringing into conflict the full resources of the great powers of the world, there is a strong chance that the present conflict can be brought to an end somehow, not without tragedy, but without the irreparable catastrophe of a world war.

It may be a forlorn hope, but it is not to be neglected now because it is the only one we have. It must be seized upon and used as a brake upon the drift toward a fatalistic acceptance of the existence of war.

And, along the same line, I refuse to believe that the determination of whether it is to be war or peace rests solely with Russia. She can make it war if she desires, but so can we. Yet, ironically enough, neither of us can make it peace without the will and co-operation of the other. Russia has been notoriously unwilling to co-operate toward any peace but that of her own choosing—of this I am fully aware—but, I must say, the facts require that exactly the same judgment be passed on us. We know what we want; she knows what she wants. Both hope to achieve our end short of war but are quite willing to run—indeed are running—the risk of war if necessary. But it is not yet clear that either is willing actually to go to war without extreme and direct provocation by the other. I submit that this reluctance demands recognition and explanation by thoughtful people. So long as it lasts, it provides an interval and may provide an opportunity for a new try at peace.

As citizens, we owe it to our country, and as Christians we owe it to our father God and our brother man to work with patient and untiring strength toward peace no matter how late the hour seems or how difficult and complex the task is. Our faith theoretically prepares us to cope with pride. Now is an excellent chance for us to find out how well prepared we are! Knowing that "pride goeth before a fall," we must not let false national pride lead us from bad to worse, from the present difficult and desperate situation to one of irreparable tragedy.

Sophocles would counsel us, "He only who persists in folly is a fool." But we must go farther than that. Our faith theoretically prepares us to admit errors and repent of sins. Now is an excellent time to determine, if we can, what our mistakes have been and are and correct them forthwith no matter how much "face" we think we will lose in the process.

Hanging over us, we know, is the judgment, "The soul that sinneth it shall die," and alongside it is the assurance, "With

God all things are possible." Counsels like these are the deepest reasons why we must continue to assert our personal responsibility for seeking the answer to the question, "Shall it be war or peace today?"

III

Another fact that keeps slipping out of focus in these days is our unfitness as a people by temperament and tradition to endure a prolonged period of tension with poise and patience. We have suspected for some time now that we are going to live in a war of nerves for at least ten years, probably much longer. We have realized, too, that the fissures between and among the nations are so numerous and so wide that no power on earth can close them overnight.

Nothing, literally nothing, in our national heritage has prepared us for life under these circumstances. We have had the habit of forcing issues to a showdown in our history. When we do not like something we propose to remedy it right now. When we do not like the way things are going, we propose to step in and change them immediately.

France and Germany are historic enemies, having fought three terrible wars since 1870. Their hatred for and suspicion of each other is deep-seated to say the least. These facts we know. But, confronted today by the threat of Russia, we have tried to get them to work together. And when, for good historical reasons, they are reluctant to do so, we want to do something drastic in order to bring them to their senses and to see it our way.

The New York Times, among others, is losing patience with Nehru these days. Nehru wants to stop all wars in Asia and to get non-Asiatic soldiers off that continent. This seems highly unreasonable to the *Times,* and I can see how it would. But what we fail to understand is this: To a citizen of any part of Asia, a white soldier means imperialism and exploitation. That has been their history for the last two hundred years, and they want no more of it. "But," we shout, "we do not want so much as a square inch of Asia. All we want is to protect you from communism." We do not understand it when the Asian eyes us steadily and asks, "Protect whom from what, did you say?"

These are well-known examples of the kind of problems we shall have to live with over the rest of our generation. And how we hate that prospect! We keep feeling that there must be a way, some way of getting them answered once and for all. If no one else comes up with a quick answer, we think it is up to us to find one. Once we've found it, or think we've found it, we insist that everyone else fall in line, or else!

Russia is hard to live with—there's no doubt about that. Hard—and dangerous. We are hard to live with, too. Even our best friends in Europe and Asia will admit that—and our reckless impatience is one of the biggest reasons for their anxiety these days. It comes hard for us to realize and admit that we have neither the right to tell another nation what kind of government it can and cannot have, nor have we the power to enforce our recommendations on one if we should be so ill-advised as to try. Yet we are constantly tempted to do both, and when we are ignored or rebuffed by England or West Germany, we are irritated no end. We are not constitutionally able to appreciate the remark of a thoughtful leader in West Germany: "You Americans have brought us freedom and democracy. You must not be surprised if we use the freedom to reject the democracy."

We are in the slow and difficult process of learning, as a nation, that issues great enough to separate peoples are not easily resolved, not even if we want it done. We need to learn what a former professor of mine learned when told he would have to have his leg amputated above the knee. Said he to the physician, "Go ahead, I have long since learned to co-operate with the inevitable." We would do well to aspire to that kind of wisdom in our national life and thought.

When Jesus was preparing his disciples for one of their missionary journeys, he made it plain that they were in for a rough time of it. Prison, misunderstanding, persecution, ridicule, hatred —these lay ahead. Instead of sympathizing with them, he said simply, "In your patience possess ye your soul."

Those of us who, by Christian commitment, bring our present irritations with others and desire for speedy results under this kind of judgment will strive to achieve a new kind and quantity of patience. It isn't easy, even for those who try most sincerely, to do it. It looks too much like a counsel of quiescence, of sitting back and letting nature take her course. Actually, it is far removed from the philosophy of the quitter. It is a thoroughly alert, responsible way of living in a time of great tension.

If we seem not to be able to resolve our difficulties at once in a creative fashion, then rather than blunder around with hasty answers, we would be well-advised to learn to live with them. Instead of losing all patience with the Germans and the French because they do not fall on each other's necks at our behest, let our knowledge of historical facts and human nature plus a great faith in the healing power of God accept the simple fact that it will be a long time before they can honestly trust and co-operate with each other.

When we are tempted to pass bitter judgments on Russia's high-handed tactics all through eastern Europe, it might help us to ask what we would do to Mexico or Canada if twice within a generation nearly fatal invasions had been launched at us from their territory. Memories like these are not easily erased. They take time—and much more than time. Almost always they require security measures exaggerated by our fears if nothing else.

Once we take seriously the simple fact that what the Indians used to call "great peace" will not come easily or quickly, we shall be better prepared not alone for the slowness of its coming but for its costliness all along the way.

IV

A third fact that is getting submerged these days is the absolute necessity of believing in and working for some kind of unifying agency among the nations of the world.

One of the most alarming things in the contemporary crisis is the way so many of us are writing off the United Nations as useless. The two senators who only this week urged our country to break with the United Nations, the gloomy post-mortem of the United Nations conducted in the last issue of the *United States News and World Report* are indications of how an increasing number of us feel about that body. Even its staunchest supporters cannot claim to be pleased with its history. But I doubt whether even its bitterest critics will contend that the effort to establish a meeting place of the nations of the earth, to nurture the growth of international law, and to encourage the development of a world-consciousness was a mistake.

It has been obvious from the outset that no infant world organization would be able either to work effectively without the great powers or to survive a collision between and among them.

But until that collision comes, the United Nations continues to be the one place where the world thought and opinion can be focused on world problems. So long as it is in being, it helps remedy what Quincy Wright once called "the basic defect in the structure of the world before World War II," namely, "the lack of consciousness in the minds of individuals that they are related to the world community." Knowing that "those who cannot remember the past are condemned to repeat it," the United Nations is our concrete effort to remember rather than to repeat.

Bernard Baruch's word of warning leaps to meet those who retreat from the United Nations these days: "We must embrace international co-operation or international disintegration." Here, then, in minimum terms, is the reason for believing in and working for the continuation of the United Nations.

But those of us who consciously choose to live under the Christian judgment or in the Christian perspective have an even more compelling reason for keeping faith in and with every effort to achieve and extend co-operation among men. We believe that we are brothers one of another, that we are members of the human family and ought to conduct ourselves accordingly. We are committed to the task of trying to build a society in the world which is the true expression of our faith in the fatherhood of God and the brotherhood of man.

Practically speaking, then, we will want to sustain and strengthen the United Nations in every possible way until a better instrument for bringing about co-operation among men has been devised. We need not—must not—blind ourselves to the grave weaknesses in the United Nations. These must be removed as soon as possible. But to break with the United Nations because Russia has misused the veto, because the Security Council is presently helpless, and because the assembly will not back our proposals or, having backed them, seems to let us down in the execution of them, is to throw away something we have because it isn't all we wish it were—and then to be left with empty hands.

The United Nations is our last concrete manifestation of a will toward world community. We have done much toward its creation and support, but we have not done enough. Although we have contributed more in terms of dollars and cents toward its support than any other nation, even that vast amount of 5 billion dollars is dwarfed by the budget presently before congress—71½ billion dollars, more than half of which is for war purposes. There you have an indication—not a true measure, I am sure—of one of the reasons why organizations for peace are so ineffective. Five billion dollars for peace and 50 billion dollars for a wartime economy! Is it any wonder we get war rather than peace?

I know we cannot buy peace by signing checks, but it ought

to be plain to all of us that even if the organizing of the world for peace should come as high, financially speaking, as the organization of it for war, peace would be cheap at that price. Ninety-five per cent of the citizens of the world would vote for it, of that I am certain.

V

The final fact—and in one sense the most difficult and the most important one of all for us to get and keep in perspective—is the complete inability of military power to get and keep peace.

There is disagreement among equally sincere Christian folk on what ought to be done in these critical days, but there is no disagreement among us on the completely evil nature of war and of moral and spiritual bankruptcy of human relationships based on the coercions of military power.

We agree that war is evil. We have said so in the great corporate gatherings of Christianity for the last twenty-five years. We agree that war is the prolific mother of every other evil known to man: disease, want, cruelty, destruction, hatred of man for man, dictatorships of every kind. We agree that whatever values may come out of war are far offset by the brood of evils it invariably spawns. We agree that the eradication of war is the prime business of both the Christian faith and modern civilization. We simply refuse to accept the inference or assertion that war is natural and unavoidable. When Cordell Hull said, "War is not an act of God; it is a crime of man," the Christian conscience said, "Amen."

Through the World Council, the Federal Council, the General Conferences of our church, we have left no doubt about the Christian condemnation of war as one of the greatest, if not the greatest evil known to man. And we are in complete agreement in this simple judgment that drives to the heart of the matter: *All wars are civil wars in the sight of God.* They are one son hating and killing another son.

Slipping as we are again into the war psychosis—and it is a bona fide mental illness, a hysteria born of hatred and fear—we need to remind ourselves, and assume responsibility for reminding the world, that war is a hypocrite, a cheat, and a liar. It is the greatest destroyer known to man—and it destroys every fine and fair thing in human life. It promises great and good ends like "a world safe for democracy" in 1917—it even promised "a war to end war" then!—and it delivered five military dictatorships, in Russia, Japan, Italy, Germany, and Spain. It prates about "the preservation of our way of life" and requires for its pursuit a modification of that way of life to regimentation and control that we seem never able wholly to cast off when it is over. Even now, in the name of freedom and democracy, and for the third time in our generation, we are being asked to accept "thought control" as well as every other form of control in the interests of national security.

Does any sane person think that this can go on indefinitely without indelibly affecting the ideals and institutions of freedom and democracy in this country?

"Give us your eighteen-year-old sons—all of them; give us universal military training; give us the apparatus—financial, economic, social, legal, and spiritual—for calling the nation to arms overnight, and we will be able to defend America," plead militarists.

Does anyone honestly believe that the disciplines of freedom and democracy can be taught in an efficient army? Beginning with conscription; proceeding every step of the way by coercion and indoctrination until a portion of God's family is literally read out of the human race fit only to be destroyed like wild animals—is this either recognizably or even remotely related to what we are trying to do in this church or in Evanston High School or in Northwestern University?

Slip any one of the virtues attributed to conscription under the microscope of historical inspection and you will find it infected with bacteria fatal to the deeper meanings of democracy, freedom, and Christian ethics.

We have the right and the duty to call attention to the way in which proponents of military training are blandly taking advantage of the tense world situation to sell us a bill of goods on the blanket conscription of our eighteen-year-olds and a plan for universal military training for all—to take effect when the crisis is over. Give the military leaders of this country these measures, and they will have everything they have been seeking for thirty years, things that we have wisely and rightly refused to give them on penalty of losing our democracy.

VI

Two of our congressmen—Walter H. Judd, a Republican from Minnesota, and Brooks Hays, a Democrat from Arkansas, have just announced a joint speaking tour in the principal cities of the United States to stress bi-partisan unity in the seeking of a just Christian peace. "The great challenge of our age is to lick the problem of war," they assert. This kind of statesmanship needs to be encouraged and echoed by Christians everywhere. Think what it might mean if thirty-one million Protestant Christians and twenty-five million Catholic Christians should begin to walk up and down in our common life talking and thinking this way!

Do not think for one minute that the congressmen and all who agree with them—as I do—are inviting us to tackle a less difficult task than that of "licking Russia." We are tackling a far more difficult task than that: one that will require the finest idealism, the best brains, the most sacrificial living and giving we have ever dreamed of. We cannot hope to win without the sincere, thoughtful, conscientious support of the rank and file of men and women who not alone hate war, but love God and their brother man and believe it their duty to express that love in terms of our common life.

God alone knows how late the hour is for our civilization. It may be later than we think yet not nearly as late as we fear. But, until the hour of midnight strikes and all hope vanishes, we must work at our task of seeking peace without fear or alarm. For we believe that there is a more perfect way than hatred, than the vast conscription and destruction of life and means and good called war—and we believe that that way was described by Paul in his letter to the Corinthians concluding with the great affirmation: "And the greatest of these is love."

We do not enter these troubled times and tangled issues able to switch back and forth and tacking this way and that as we work with them. We are *not our own*. We are witness to the better way. We enter them conscious of the fact that we are called upon, of God, to bear daily and costly witness to our conviction that God is love, that love is the only ultimate power on earth, that no other human attitude or emotion is anything like as strong as love, that the policy and the people rooted in that power can no more be destroyed by the other powers than the cross could destroy Jesus Christ. It is our precious privilege and high calling to seek to find our way and the way of our day in the love of God as we see it in Jesus Christ. More than this we cannot do; less than this would be quite useless.

IX

The Christian Witness for Peace[1]

SCRIPTURE LESSON: Matthew 5:1-14

I

IT IS one of the minor ironies and major tragedies of our time that Christian churches are having more dissension over the meaning of peace, the way to peace, and the Christian responsibility for peace than over any other single matter. We find ourselves as churches coming under the satirical judgment we frequently pass on rampant militarists: They love peace so much they are willing to fight for it. Only we must amplify this somewhat to do full justice to our plight: We love peace so much that we are willing to fight among ourselves about it. That, in sober truth, is what we all too frequently have been doing and are doing right now in this all-important matter.

Looking back as I do on nearly twenty years of keen interest in this matter, I am merely reporting facts when I say that the bitterest debates, the sharpest cleavages, and the deepest feelings of our church conferences have revolved around the Church's attitude and policy on matters of peace and war. This has been true of The Methodist Church and other churches as well as of the great interchurch movements—the Federal Council of Churches, the World Council of Churches, and, if every sign be not deceptive, of the new National Council of Churches in this country.

As you would suppose, the public statements of church bodies on such matters have been confusing and, I'm afraid, of little use as "light-bringers" to a world groping in darkness. The least, and probably the worst, thing we can say about such resolutions is

[1] This sermon was preached November 25, 1951.

94

that they fail to lift a clear Christian witness for peace. The resolution recently adopted by the National Council's Department on International Justice and Goodwill (of which I am a member) is a case in point. The resolution cries out for disarmament in general but favors the rearmament of the United States and her allies in particular. This kind of reasoning, of course, is of a piece with the general practice of the Christian churches. We denounce war in general but finally approve any and every particular war for some reason or other. We deplore the steps that take us into war, but, once in it, we accept it and wage it to full victory if we can. I am not now passing a judgment upon any other church before our own or upon anyone else before myself when I say that it all adds up to this one simple and tragic fact: The Christian Church has not lifted a clear witness in these matters of war and peace. She has sounded her trumpet, all right, but the sound it emits reminds one of nothing so much as a sturdy boy's first attempt to play a horn—an awful alternation between unbelievable silence and unbearable sound.

I do not pretend to have a pat and easy answer to the question of how to fashion and bear a strong witness for peace, but I know we have no greater responsibility than trying to do just that. The difficulties we face in clarifying our witness are many but the two most important ones appear to be these: a sense of despair over the apparent futility of the entire effort; a lack of appreciation of the total meaning for life of the Christian witness for peace. I am certain that a careful examination of these two will disclose the fact that they belong together. Once we grasp the grand strategy of the Christian conception of peace we shall not be driven to despair by even so calamitous a period as the one in which we must bear our witness.

II[2]

There is a fine story about the last days of George Lansbury, one of England's tireless workers for peace. He had spent all of his mature life wrestling with the knotty problems which lead to war. He had lived through the First World War and as he died the guns of the second one were echoing through the world. To the realist, it seems as though he had thrown away his forty years of struggle. A close friend asked him how much nearer he

[2] Much of the material in this section has appeared in an earlier book, *Main Issues Confronting Christendom*, chap. I (Harper, New York, 1948).

thought peace was as a result of his effort. Lansbury replied, "Forty years nearer!"

There is an antidote for the pessimism we so easily fall into about the inevitability of war and the hopelessness of peace! There is an even better antidote in a consideration of the seventh beatitude of the Sermon on the Mount: "Blessed are the peacemakers: for they shall be called the children of God." In a day when peacemakers are called pretty nearly everything else, it will repay and chasten us to inquire into the meaning which Jesus, in his life and teachings, pours into this beatitude. We shall find it a difficult saying, difficult to comprehend, difficult to fulfill—and the deeper we dig into it, the more difficult it becomes.

Gerald Heard, in his book, *The Creed of Christ,* devotes a penetrating and suggestive chapter to this blessing. As we study his analysis we shall find ourselves surrounded by a ring of probing questions. How many of us are qualified to be "peacemakers" as Christ seems to have meant the term? No one doubts our present fitness to wage war, but will anyone lay claim to the moral fitness to initiate peace, thought, and action, as Christ understood them?

Obviously, before the Christian Church can work effectively for a lasting peace it must be composed, more generally than it now is, of ministers and laity who will make a serious and sustained effort to be Christian peacemakers. This is not a matter of knowing the right words; it is a matter of maturing, spiritually speaking, the right way—through the four general stages—in the growth of the Christian peacemaker. I propose to describe each one briefly and as we move through them, ask yourself which one you are in at the present time. Or if you find that you are not in any of them, that you have not even made a start in the direction of becoming such a peacemaker, ask yourself, "What, in God's name, am I doing anyway that I think is more important?"

In the first stage of his growth, the Christian peacemaker *finds peace with God.* He accepts God as the basic Fact and Factor in human life and history. Whatever questions he has about God will fall within the circumference of confident faith in His reality. The inquiring mind will always be raising questions about God's meaning, will, or purpose. There is no other way to push back the horizons of our limited understanding and experience. There is no better way to pay tribute to the all-encompassing glory and richness of God than by determining, with Job-like stubbornness, to ask questions and to keep right on asking them until a reasonable answer is found. Finding God, so far from resolving all doubts and questions, actually stimulates them by making them useful and creative. They have in God a worthy object, One in whose fuller truth they find their answer. For the Christian, peace with God means acceptance and commitment to the belief that God is love. What a difference that concept "love" makes! If God be love, then love is woven into the very texture of the universe and must be accepted as real in every sense of that term. If God be love, then love is the most powerful fact and force in the universe. If God be love, then peace with God means acceptance of the plain fact that only a life of love can be a life at peace with God. To find peace with God is to accept the further fact that "in His will is our peace," is to learn to say, "Not my will but Thine be done." To find God in this sense is to desire supremely to serve Him, to be willing to put first things first, to resolve to "seek first the Kingdom of God and His righteousness," knowing that all other needful things will be added.

Having found God in this profoundly personal sense, the Christian peacemaker moves imperceptibly into the second stage of growth, *one in which he finds peace with himself.* He lays a firm foundation for finding peace with himself by finding peace with God. He gives himself to God because that is the only sensible thing to do with his life. Simply to drift along without rhyme or reason, without purpose and plan is gross negligence. To say that he believes in God yet deny that God has a claim on him, to assert that the Creator has no rights to or in His creature, to oppose His manifest will—this is sheer idiocy! The Christian peacemaker is driven to the ancient and humble confession: "Our hearts are restless until they rest in Thee."

With this decision, the Christian peacemaker's self ceases to be simply the plaything of desire and impulse and seeks to become the instrument of divine purpose and will. His life ceases to stew in the juices of words, fancies, and prejudices and is set to *work*, is absorbed in the *act*, the *deed*, is put on the *way*. In truth, the dynamic, ongoing quality of life demands some such outlet in work in order to become wholesome, and creative. Life never stands still. It is always going somewhere, somehow. It may be treading the high road of noble purpose and fine ideals, becoming, thereby, progressively richer and stronger. Or it may be taking the lower road of unguided impulse and ungoverned desire, becoming, thereby, progressively poorer and weaker. In the one case, life rises to new meanings; in the other, whatever meaning it has is slowly but surely debased and degraded.

The Christian peacemaker knows that, under God, the only way to keep himself from being a knot of frustrations, to keep his sanity as well as his spirituality, is to set himself to a mighty task. And, looking within himself as well as into the world of social relations, he sees no mightier task than that of peacemaking. But it will not be easy for the Christian peacemaker to find peace with himself. At least, this is the all but unanimous testimony of Christian history. The Gospel narratives, to cite but one instance, are dotted with people who could or would not find peace with themselves. Poor Judas is the extreme example. But for a long time in the life of stalwarts like Peter and Paul it looked as if he were going to have a lot of company! They too were known to kick against the pricks of God's will for them even after they knew what that will was! They were creatures in inconsistency and torment until they learned to say what a later hymn writer said, "Take my life and let it be consecrated, Lord, to Thee!" They finally learned to say it, finding grace and strength to humble their proud wills and spirits to the voice of God, thus finding peace with themselves.

The third stage in the growth of the Christian peacemaker is *that in which he finds personal peace with others.* Manifestly there can be no such thing as complete peace with God and self when enmity toward others is raging, tornadolike, through our spirits. Jesus saw this and described what he saw in that sobering parable about who should and who should not approach God's altar with a gift. When a man is at peace with his brethren he may profitably place a gift on the altar. But if he "has aught against any man" he wastes his gift unless he puts it aside, while he makes peace with his brethren. This done, he may put the gift on God's altar.

The Christian peacemaker will *want* peace with others; he will take the initiative in peaceful attitudes and actions; he will risk rebuffs; he will be prepared to fail; he will seek and find the strength to persist indefinitely until he is successful. He will strive for peace in the full sense of a mutual, two-way relationship of good will and understanding. Yet he knows that the possibility of failure to win this objective is always at hand. There is no way he can storm the citadel of another's soul. The wounds in the spirit of another may be too deep, too grievous, for any healing unguent he can place on them. But, so far as it lies in the peacemaker's power he will have peace with even those who resist, rebuff, and seek to take advantage of him. If he cannot achieve peace in the full sense of a two-way relationship, he can do no less than make it a one-way affair. He will stand at the edge of every chasm in the human family with hand and heart outstretched in the spirit of Christian fraternity. If the one on the other side refuses to respond in similar spirit, the Christian peacemaker will not walk away angry, calling down fire and brimstone upon his head. He will stay right there bearing a continuing witness to the reality of the love of God in human relations, knowing full well that there is no other way in which the wound can be healed. So far as his attitude toward others is concerned to the extent that he can control his own tongue, his own actions, his own plans, he will "seek peace and pursue it." He knows that in this way he is making the supreme effort to overcome enmity; he knows, too, that it bears the seal of God's approval—which, for him, is enough.

In the likely event that others, in anger and greed, lay violent hands on him and seek to put him to death—even then his loyalty to peace does not succumb to the fear and anger which ignite as hatred and retaliation. Before we dismiss this as weakness, consider St. Francis' poignant parable of how the misunderstood and sadly mistreated Christian should greet each indignity. He should welcome it with the inner assurance that that is just what he deserves for having been so long blind to the glory of God, to the peace of Christ. The proud and powerful men of the day laughed at St. Francis' idea. They knew the "proper" way to deal with indignity and opposition! Yet when they by force of arms were unable to batter their crusade into Jerusalem, St. Francis, armed only with his meekness, walked through the battle lines and sought to persuade the sultan to become a Christian! Talk about courage and strength!

St. Francis' advice is not alien to the spirit of him who prayed in behalf of his persecutors. "Father, forgive them, for they know not what they do." That, I am certain, is why one New Testament scholar holds that the very best commentary on the beatitude, "Blessed are the peacemakers: for they shall be called the children of God," is the admonition made later in the chapter, "But I say to you, Love your enemies and pray for those who persecute you, so that you may be sons of your Father who is in heaven; for he makes his sun rise on the evil and on the good, and sends rain on the just and on the unjust" (R.S.V.).

This spirit, and none other, will enable the Christian peace-

maker to face any and every possible situation which may arise
as he seeks peace with others. When the Christian peacemaker
meets the challenge and threat of the powers of the world in the
spirit of love he is not meeting strength with weakness. He is
meeting a lesser power with a greater—the power of man with
the power of God in man.

*The final stage in the growth of the Christian peacemaker is
one in which he is equipped to be an instrument in peacemaking
between others.* By the time one has found peace with God, with
himself, and with others, he will have acquired certain characteristics which are essential to this highest and hardest kind of
peacemaking. He will be trusted by others because he is trustworthy. He will not be feared because of harm he can inflict since
the entire set of his life will be against doing that. His word will
be his bond; he will speak openly, honestly, and courageously;
he will have none of the double talk which discourages friends
and stimulates enemies. His motive in all his dealings with
antagonists, be they persons or nations, will be that of finding *an
enduring relationship* between them. He will not be the advocate of this person or nation against that person or nation; he
will seek to be the advocate of justice and good will for all since
these virtues alone bring peace.

The very integrity of the Christian peacemaker will be a
danger to him because selfish, hateful men among the disputants
will want to secure his name for their cause, will want him as a
front, an *appearance* of virtue behind which they can mask and
further their evil designs. Flattery, threats, and solemn warnings
will be used to cajole him into making "the worse appear the
better cause." But he will have learned how to conquer similar
tactics in his struggle for peace with himself and others. He will
not succumb even though flattery, threats, and warning come to
him in the guise of patriotism. His mission will be central in his
life and mind—he is a peacemaker; by the mercy of God, he is a
Christian peacemaker, one whose task it is to measure the contesting causes and claims by the mind of Christ, since there is no
other sure road to permanent peace.

Now, quite obviously, the Christian peacemaker will not be
permitted to intercede and institute the process of conciliation
and reconciliation until the combatants have tried all known or
available means of imposing their will on one another. But,
finally, when the descending spiral of recurring conflicts reveals
the pit of utter catastrophe into which both are falling, they may

be willing to listen to what they have hitherto been content to reject as the counsel of perfection. There is reason to believe that the prospects of an atomic war have reduced contemporary civilization to some such state of moral desperation. After the last war, Lloyd George, powerful leader of a victorious nation, said, "The next great task of humanity is not deliverance by the sword, but deliverance from the sword." Arnold Toynbee's discussion of "The Saviour with the Sword" deserves to be studied by all who believe that we can guarantee peace by an overwhelming preponderance of military power.

The sword is only wielded in the hope of being able to use it to such good purpose that it may eventually have no more work to do; but this hope is an illusion; for it is only in fairyland that swords cut Gordian knots which cannot be untied by fingers. "All they that take the sword shall perish with the sword" is the inexorable law of real life; and the swordsman's belief in a conclusive victory is an illusion. . . . The Saviour with the sword may perhaps build a house upon the sand but never the house upon a rock.

But, thank God, not many people are honestly prepared to stake the future of our civilization on force of arms. They will do so only as a last resort, for it is pitifully plain to all that wars are social earthquakes which no one wins. If the common man accepts war as inevitable, the blame will lie squarely on us who desire to be known as Christians but will not make the effort to be Christian peacemakers! There rests upon us the infinite obligation to discover and explore all possibilities for peace in the concrete conflicts which are now raging. "Blessed are the peacemakers: for they shall be called the children of God."

III

But, you object, none of us are or ever will be peacemakers in the full and complete sense of being a Christian peacemaker. It's too hard, too exacting for mortal man! It's impossible!

Not many will think that the supreme gift of being a child of God would be given us for the asking. The supreme achievement open to man requires nothing less than the supreme efforts of a lifetime. Only the man who has tried it with his whole soul has a right to say that it is impossible to be a Christian peacemaker. And, let it be noted, the ones, like George Lansbury, who earn the right to answer it, assure us that, with all its enormous difficulties, the task of Christian peacemaking is possible, and it alone is hopeful.

Actually, we have no way of knowing how good a Christian peacemaker we can become until and unless we devote the best efforts of a lifetime to it. This means finding peace with God, with ourselves, with others, before we are equipped to be an instrument in peacemaking between others. These four stages of growth are tied together like infancy, childhood, youth, and maturity. They are related to one another as the base and peak of a pyramid are related to each other. Neither by itself is or can ever be a pyramid. So it is with Christian peacemaking. Beginning with the broad foundation of peace with God, we toil upward stone by stone until finally we aspire to be a humble but willing instrument of God's will, a child of God, in the work of establishing "peace on earth, good will among men." We must be willing to say: "I propose, under God, to labor at the whole structure, limited only by my ability and opportunity." We must forswear the temptation to measure ourselves by any other standard than that of "the mind of Christ." This temptation will beset us daily, hourly, not only from without but even more desperately from within. We will want some lower, some easier, some more convenient standard. Appalled by the task before us, dismayed by our failures, our inadequacy, we will be tempted to make more convenient gods in our own image, rather than brave the miracle of creation of being remade in the image of God. But the price of idolatry continues to be death while the reward of true religion is strength and peace.

The Christian witness for peace will be felt and found in the way the individual Christian keeps putting the accent in the right place in very difficult areas.

The Christian peacemaker will strive for disarmament because he knows that the existence of great military establishments drains off the money and confidence needed by the constructive and creative programs for international co-operation. He will strive for disarmament, not simply by negative votes on arms, but by positive votes for international law, organization, and community. He will seek to remove the need for any kind of armament by dealing constructively with the social, racial, economic, and political causes of fear, insecurity, and ignorance.

The Christian peacemaker will oppose such steps as Universal Military Training for this country because he sees it to be an integral part of the war system. He will want to keep it entirely out of the life of our country, knowing that it more than anything else is the policy which can undermine our basic concepts of democracy and freedom. He will pierce to the heart the specious plea that Universal Military Training is the democratic way of self-defense. If anything must be said along these lines, Universal Military Training is the road away from democracy and the free men and institutions so fundamental to democracy.

These are two instances of concrete ways in which the Christian witness for peace can and should be lifted in terms of the issues before us today. They do not stand alone in a sense that they are the only issues to be dealt with, but they do illustrate the many day-to-day problems on which we have to pass judgment and to try to reach some kind of decisive conclusion. There can be no clear witness from the Church on matters like these until and unless individual Christians accept their role as peacemakers. When that happens the Church will speak with wisdom, authority, and power.

Although the conscientious Christian will say "No" to every effort to deepen and make permanent the hold of the war system on the minds and in the affairs of men, the Christian witness for peace is positive rather than negative in its approach to the problems of injustice, fear, and hatred. When the Quakers, for example, wanted to open up new channels of communication and understanding between the Soviet Union and the West, a delegation of Quakers from England went to Russia and took with them a series of proposals for peace. The Quakers simply ignored the fiction of the iron curtain which throws so many of us into paroxysms of fear, and they were able to do so because of their historic commitment to the cause of peace. In fact, the Quakers are a living verification of the possibility of a clear Christian witness for peace by a church. What the Quakers did, the Methodist Church could do if Methodists believed in peace as much as the Quakers do. What the Quakers did, the National and the World Council could do if peace seemed as important to these groups as it does to the Quakers. We have every reason to thank God for the existence of a determined, fearless, consecrated group like the Quakers who continue to bear their witness for peace and by so doing become a literal norm by which the rest of us can measure ourselves.

Paralleling the efforts of the Quakers, the World Peace Commission of the Methodist Church has been and continues to try to awaken us to the need for bearing a clear Christian witness for peace. The resolutions studied and adopted in the recent meetings of the Commission in our church are evidence of this concern and determination. When these resolutions are presented to the General Conference ʼof our church in San Francisco next spring, the representatives of our communion will have an opportunity to determine whether they want a clear or a clouded witness for peace. More than I like to think hinges upon the decision of the General Conference in this matter.

Let it be underscored, then, that Christian men and women cannot stand idly by while the disintegrative forces of war reach, like a sword, into our standards, our homes, and our whole society. Christian homes, as they cherish their faith, will get a new grip on the spiritual resources of fellowship and trust. They will seek to be islands of complete understanding and sympathy in a world in which men are being forced to grapple with mistrust and hatred. Christian churches must not forget their mission— the proclamation of the gospel. This is a *world* mission. Our hardest task is now at hand—preaching the gospel of love and brotherhood in a world either at war or filled with the hatreds bred of war. There is no occasion for self-pity in that. Our task is no more hopeless than that which has confronted the Church in many earlier periods. We bear in our body the scars which were their wounds. The cross will slip into the focus of our thinking as the only adequate and relevant Christian symbol for such trials of men's souls. As persons seeking to be Christians in our living, no one will need to urge us to a deeper consecration of ourselves to the Christian way of life as we see it in the life and teachings of Jesus Christ. Out of this experience of humble, sincere, and persistent dedication to him will flow hope, courage, and purpose sufficient unto even this day.

Consider, then, these manifold tasks: tireless efforts toward permanent peace; the determination to keep alive a fellowship of faith in God as we see Him in Jesus Christ. This is our work and we ought to be doing it. It constitutes the Christian witness for peace. And when Christian churches appeal to men and women like us to carry on in these undertakings, they are making their supreme effort to alter the tragic ending which is fast closing in on the drama of our day. Nor can we expect peace in our time or any other until and unless we lift a clear witness for peace as individual Christians and as Christian churches. Peacemaking begins here or nowhere.

X

Why Christian Churches Oppose Universal Military Training[1]

SCRIPTURE LESSON: Isaiah 59:1–15

I

THE united opposition of the Christian churches of this country to Universal Military Training is not new. They have become increasingly concerned and alarmed about it over the last thirty years. And well they might! For the effort to introduce this fundamental alteration in our way of life began in dead earnest immediately after the First World War, and, although defeated time after time, it has bobbed up in each new crisis with its specious guarantees of security. The churches have declared themselves in opposition to it repeatedly and with unqualified vigor— that is a matter of simple historical record. I do not know of a single major church or council of churches in this country that has not made itself both articulate and clear on this important matter. The resolution adopted by the General Confernce of the Methodist Church in 1948, on motion of Ernest Fremont Tittle, was strong, and in line with similar positions taken by the American leaders of the Roman Catholic Church in 1945, and by every other major church. We said, "Seven church-wide organizations of the Methodist Church, led by the Council of Bishops, have declared their opposition to any system of peacetime universal military training. We reaffirm this stand. We appeal to the United States to give bold leadership looking toward the universal abolition of peacetime conscription by or through the United Nations."

Yet, strangely enough, despite this unanimity among churches on so important a matter we were never nearer defeat on it than

[1] This sermon was preached April 1, 1951.

105

now. Actually, within a matter of days, the Christian churches of this country may be informed by the Congress of the United States how lightly their convictions on this matter are valued. Knowing churches as I think I do, I know we will not let the matter rest in defeat, if defeat it is. We have appealed from Caesar to God before and we will do it again, if need be.

II

In the interests of precision, may I, at the very outset, say what I am not talking about? I am discussing but one of the several provisions in the manpower legislation now pending in Congress. That one is not the draft or mode of selective service—a debatable matter, to be sure. I shall deal directly and explicitly with the proposal to make Universal Military Training a permanent part of our way of life here in the United States of America.

Before plunging into a discussion of the principle of Universal Military Training, a word about the manner and the timing of the presentation of the proposal is in order. Seldom if ever has so far-reaching a piece of legislation been presented in so confused and confusing a manner. This confusion is so great that it gives every indication of being intentional. The proponents of the measure are both trying to confuse the issue in every possible way and take full advantage of the tense international situation to secure its passage now.

Universal Military Training is not an emergency measure, yet it is presented in a bill all other items of which are emergency measures. It is not to take effect during the present international crisis, yet it is being presented along with measures designed specifically to deal with that crisis. It is permanent, not temporary, legislation, yet it is presented along with other proposals that admittedly are temporary. To one who argues that Universal Military Training belongs with such other proposals, the reply must be made that this is the first time they have ever been presented together. Heretofore, and time after time in 1920, in 1944-1945, in 1947-1948, Universal Military Training has been presented, considered, and defeated as a separate issue.

The question will not down: Why is Universal Military Training being presented at this time and in this utterly confusing manner? There is, I believe, only one answer to that: Its proponents, from the President right on down, know that this is the only way they have a chance to get it adopted. Why, otherwise, would the powerful military clique which now influences all and dominates most legislation in Washington be afraid to let this permanent measure be separated from emergency measures for consideration? We have General Marshall's word for the fact that *he is responsible for the combination.* Why else would they resist the effort to let a specific date for the review of Universal Military Training as a policy be inserted in the bill which proposes to create it? The powers in and in league with the Pentagon are taking full advantage of the present crisis to get what they've worked for for thirty years. And, I must say, they are closer to success now than ever before. Their refusal to let Universal Military Training be considered on its own merits, their deliberate cultivation of confusion about it, their determination to rush it through before the people of this country have had an opportunity for a full review of it—all this may be "good strategy" from their point of view, but it is part and parcel of the rotting moral fabric of so much of our public life these days.

Even though the hour for remedial action is late, it is not too late to remind ourselves of the reasons why we as churches have been opposing and continue to oppose Universal Military Training. So far from walking around, like the fabled philosopher who was so intent upon the stars that he fell into an open well, we have three very good reasons for this position:

1. We believe that a wholesome Christian character can best be developed in terms of normal social relationships, and are convinced, from experience, that the effort to place all young men in the decidedly abnormal atmosphere of training camps for any period of time is morally dangerous.

2. We believe in freedom and democracy as valid ideals for America, and are convinced, from experience, that the enactment of Universal Military Training here will jeopardize both.

3. We believe in the possibility of world peace, and are convinced that the enactment of Universal Military Training by the United States will endanger its achievement.

I am sure most of you feel as my father did when we would come to him with some tremendous reason or other: "Better tell me a little more about that, if you want me to believe it." I'd like to do just that—within the limits of the time at our disposal.

III

1. *We believe that the wholesome Christian life is better attained in normal social surroundings, which, most emphatically, are nonexistent in the military training camps.*

We are persuaded that the proposal to take young men eighteen years of age out of normal social surroundings is a major moral blunder. To put it bluntly, it amounts to a moral holiday for a certain period and under the protective covering and anonymity of the uniform. The ordinary social restraints of family, home, church, school, and community are entirely lacking. Long time acquaintances are replaced, temporarily, with short time ones, with a premium being put on the principle of getting what you can while you can with no questions asked.

I am not simply conjuring up bogeymen. We who lived through the last war in a city like Baltimore know all too well how the red-light district became a thriving business the moment war began to bring men near us in large numbers. We know that the venereal disease rate leaped to alarming proportions among the men in the services and the girls of comparable age in cities adjacent to training camps. We are familiar with the moral laxity which infected the entire community when there were so many persons in it for brief periods of time and utterly unchecked by the normal social relationships of their own communities. Live through that for five long years, and you know at first hand some of the moral problems which will stretch before every young man as an alluring possibility, if this proposal of Universal Military Training became permanent policy.

I am not saying that more than a fraction of men in training will misuse their period of service in this fashion, but I am saying that more of them will use it that way if they are in the service rather than under normal social conditions. This is a risk that must be run in wartime for a few brief years, but it is not a risk which we should accept lightly as a permanent problem. We are having enough trouble already holding our homes and families together, keeping our crime rate down, keeping our standards of moral values up, to take a step like this unless, literally, there is no other way.

The armed services have all too little concern about the moral welfare of their men—our sons. Promiscuity and drunkenness are viewed, not from the moral angle, but from that of military efficiency. Consequently, if a man is able to report back to duty from a week-end leave, it makes no difference to his superiors where he has been, or who his companions have been, or what he has done. Could the situation be summed up better than by citing the fact that, to the armed services, promiscuous sexual relations are no offense, but the failure to report them and to receive proper prophylactic treatment is a serious offense?

You cannot meet many of the officers in the armed services—the ones under whom our eighteen-year-old sons will be placed—without being impressed with their uneven concern about moral standards. Some are completely dependable and morally ready for leadership, but there are at least as many who, whatever their military qualifications, are, at best, moral derelicts themselves and utterly unfit to possess assigned influence over anyone else. They say, "What the men do when they are not under orders is their own affair." They wink at the escapades in the red-light districts, and say, "Well, boys will be men!" Or, they will tell you with a seriousness that borders on truculence, "It's our business to build an army, not to run a Sunday School."

I am making the deliberate charge that, on the basis of facts, the armed services leave much to be desired as morally trustworthy influences; that they should not be permitted to offer a standing temptation to moral degradation to every young man in America—yet this is the clear import of the proposal to make Universal Military Training a permanent part of our way of life. Although our homes and communities are far from perfect as moral influences, *at least they care about the moral welfare of our youth.* To place our young men in organizations which have, at best, a most uneven moral concern is an indefensible blunder and should be avoided at all costs.

IV

2. *We believe that the proposed measure will endanger freedom and democracy in America.*

This is a serious charge, I know, and one that can be made only when overwhelming evidence is at hand attesting its truth. That evidence is what has happened in the two outstanding nations that have used peacetime military conscription over many years: France and Germany.

France, under Napoleon, actually started this business of peacetime military conscription, though Machiavelli had advocated something like it in the sixteenth century. When the

Revolution had destroyed the small professional army of France, her new leaders were forced to find men in another way. Conscription seemed to be the fairest way; so it was inaugurated, and, after more than a little blundering, it was brought to a satisfactory level of achievement. Napoleon, blunt if not brutal, told his foreign minister, "I can use up 25,000 men a month." And he did—until France ruled most of Europe and numbered her dead by the hundreds of thousands.

But notice this: a study of the French government over the last one hundred years is a study of the increasing role of the French army in the life of that nation! It became the bulwark of conservation, bigotry and, in these latter days, of totalitarianism. It had its own newspapers whose editorial policies were determined by the General Staff. It did not hesitate to mix in local elections in order to secure strong support in the Chamber of Deputies. It was always the most decisive factor in the determination of the foreign policy of the country. Every liberal premier and every liberal movement in France had to fight the strongly entrenched conservatism of the French Army leaders. All of this was highlighted in the Dreyfus case which was the scandal of the liberal world prior to the First World War. This exposé of the bigotry and corruption of the army leaders and the War Department brought about an effective curbing of the army's influence—until the World War raised it to new heights again.

Pertinax, a French journalist with high standing for integrity, tells in his book *The Grave-Diggers of France* of the frank sympathy for totalitarianism which existed throughout the High Command of the French army both before, during and after France was involved in the second World War. The positions of Petain and Weygand are too well known to need more than a passing mention. They and their kind were not and had not for a hundred years been interested in the ideals of freedom and democracy. Whenever they came into power—and that was with appalling frequency—these ideals withered away.

Germany learned about peace-time military conscription from Napoleonic France. After her land had been ravaged time and time again she began to fight fire with fire. She learned how Napoleon did it, and, with her famed efficiency, brought the system of conscription to such perfection that she became a shining example of "a nation in arms overnight." All of her neighbors will testify to what this has meant to them over the last seventy-five years! Within the last twenty-five of those years, nations four thousand miles away can join in the chorus of those who have not found any good reason yet for giving thanks for the benefits of German militarism. And with good reason: The Prussian military class, the Junkers, were little more than sullen, dissident groups in one of the German states until they had every male German, sound of mind and limb, handed over to them for training, indoctrination, and control for a long period during the most formative years of his maturing life. Then they really got going—and the whole world has had to bend every effort to stop them. Under their leadership the German army became the seedbed of a mystical, fanatical love of country, culminating in a kind of cult of those who ask only to die for the Fatherland. The terribly efficient German Military Staff (which we broke up a few years ago and are now trying to reassemble!) would not have become the threat to world peace which it did had it not had increasing millions of German men to train and throw into one war after another.

How interested was the German army in the ideals of freedom and democracy? To ask the question is to answer it. They wanted order, efficiency, discipline, and obedience. They streamlined the schools, conventions, laws, and governments of that great country over a period of seventy-five years until freedom and democracy became bywords and epithets.

The late Charles A. Ellwood, a thoroughly competent sociologist, wrote an essay on Modern Germany which is not only a review of what happened there but also a preview of what can happen here if we enact Universal Military Training as a permanent policy:

One hundred and fifty years ago Germany was noted for its piety and general religious spirit. Its philosophers and theologians, along with its great literary men, made it, as was often said, "the home of the human spirit." But Germany about that time entered upon a policy of universal compulsory military education of all its young men. Every German youth was conditioned to think and feel from the military point of view. The military tactician came more and more to rule in this land that had been frequently acknowledged to be the most cultured country in all Europe. More and more, Germany became a military garrison. . . . There is no mystery, however, in the fall of this "most cultured land" down to the level of a military garrison. It was all accomplished by a century of training in which every German youth was conditioned to think, feel, and act as military tacticians taught that they should think, feel, and act; namely, to uphold always *at all costs* the military system, because only in that system "was there safety for the Fatherland."

France is the first, and Germany the second illustration of a well-founded historical rule: *to be prepared for war is to be predisposed to war.*

Add these historical facts together and you have another tremendous reason why the Christian churches are opposing the enactment of peacetime military conscription in this country. While it is true that the theory of "a nation in arms overnight" makes for strength in war, let us never forget that it also makes for several other ends, too. It means that we propose to place our entire economy on a semiwar footing, to keep it permanently geared up to the needs of and governed by the controls of a war economy. It makes for the rationing of liberty in peacetime as well as in wartime. It will make for the most powerful pressure group in America—with leaders on the spot in the Cabinet in Washington.

Recall, if you will, the enormous influence exerted by the veterans of the Civil War on the political life of America until that organization disappeared through the death of its members. Recall the way in which the American Legion became a tremendous fact in the public life of this country after the last war, actually controlling many powerful state machines, and always sought after by every political party. Now it is proposed that to the powerful but temporary influence of the men who go through a war together we add the widening influence of the vast majority of the men of the country and make of them the most potent political pressure group this country has ever seen. That is the record in France and Germany—and we would be blind beyond all healing if we thought that by some miraculous chance we could avoid the selfsame result here.

So far from being a bugaboo created by an idealistic few, these possibilities appear to be looming large in the minds of some of our more thoughtful military men. Mr. Hanson W. Baldwin, columnist on military affairs for *The New York Times,* shares them. Writing on March 22, 1951, he protests that the "permanent features" of the manpower bill "are monstrous." Why? Because they are "a potential political, social and educational danger." He argues: "Above all, Congress should not endorse in the guise of emergency a permanent measure that would commit us forever . . . to peacetime conscription, which has always been alien to our concepts of democratic and non-militarized government."

As we believe in freedom and democracy, we will fight this

proposal to the end. For, the very day it wins they will begin to wither away.

V

3. *We believe in the possibility of World Peace, and are convinced that the enactment of Universal Military Training by our country will further endanger its achievement.*

Let it be stated at once and written in letters so large that he who runs may read that the Christian churches have not, will not, and cannot accept war as a necessary and inevitable part of human history. Along with Charles A. Beard, we reject "the devil theory of war." Along with Cordell Hull, we affirm, "War is not an act of God, but a crime of man." We insist with Herbert Hoover that war is "the world's greatest scourge." We deny as inconclusive and denounce as blasphemous the glib assertion and easy belief that since there always has been war, there always will be war. We therefore propose to oppose any and every effort which proceeds upon the assumption that war is inevitable, that lasting peace is impossible. Since so much of the support for the measure under consideration proceeds upon the cynical assumption that man is, by nature, a warring animal, and that we must deal with ourselves "realistically," the churches are on principle bound to be critical of it. But our opposition is not based solely upon this ground, important as it is. Our opposition just now grows out of the fact that we are not impressed by the reasoning and marshaling of evidence which protagonists of the proposal are producing.

We hear it said that the only way to have peace is to be strong, i.e., to be prepared for war. We hear the old saw: If you want war prepare for peace, if you want peace prepare for war. *But history supports neither of these positions.* I have already mentioned the truth which history does support: *"To be prepared for war is to be predisposed to war."* So far from being my judgment, this is the judgment of careful historians like Quincy Wright, Professor of International Law at the University of Chicago, and Arnold Toynbee and F. A. Woods, two English scholars. Read their works and you encounter well-documented assertions like these: "The great powers have been the most frequent fighters; it is the stronger nations that have devoted the most time to war." Professor Wright has an unusually telling section in which he is studying the history of military equipment and preparation in the United States. He points out that each time we have begun to develop a military establishment we have either found or created an occasion to use it. As one instance of this he tells how in the 1880's naval building was begun on a large scale and what we then called "the white fleet" was developed. In 1896 Theodore Roosevelt voiced "the popular sentiment that 'this country needs a war.' " Well, we got it! The Spanish American War broke out in 1898.

Another bit of evidence for the assertion that to be prepared for war is to be predisposed to war is found in various studies that have been made in what happened to the attitudes of men toward war as a result of R.O.T.C. training in our colleges and universities. One study contrasts the attitude of men before and after they had the training. This is the conclusion: "People are favorable to war in proportion to the amount of military education and military service they have had."

The late Jan Smuts, elder statesman of the British Empire, summed it up nicely and conclusively when he said, "While the Great Powers are allowed to raise conscript armies without hindrance or limit, it would be vain to expect the lasting preservation of world peace. If the instrument is ready for use, the occasion will arrive and the men will arise to use it. I look upon conscription as the taproot of militarism; unless that is cut out all our labors will eventually be vain."

It is the position of the Christian churches that the enactment of Universal Military Training is more than a misreading of the clear meaning of history; it amounts to a breach of faith with the declared intentions of the United Nations to lift the crushing burden of armaments from the peoples of the world. It is a breach of faith with the citizens of this country who have gone into two wars moved by the belief that one of the reasons was to destroy the militarism of dangerous powers, thus removing the necessity of our having to support a huge peacetime military establishment in the interests of national security. We did not want "to live with a gun in our hands" as President Wilson once put it. What an irony it would be if we emerge from the first half of the twentieth century saddled with one of the very things we said we were fighting against in both world wars, namely, the threat to world security of a highly militarized people!

It is the position of the Christian churches that the proposed measure, if adopted, plainly serves notice to the entire world that we have just about lost all faith in the United Nations and every other pacific way of keeping peace. We say more, much more, than that we intend to protect ourselves from aggression and to fulfill our obligations under the United Nations and the North Atlantic Pact. We are keeping these commitments now by means of Selective Service, and can continue to do so. It amounts to a junking of every serious effort at disarmament that can be made by the United Nations or any other group. Actually, that is the most threatening part of the entire picture. For us, one of the most powerful nations on earth, to say that we intend to get and to stay armed to the teeth will be the only incentive needed to bring into existence the most colossal armament race this world has ever seen in peacetime, and to create occasions of new tension all over the world. We conclude, therefore, that "that way madness lies."

VI

It would be interesting—and sobering—to know how many of us here this morning have ancestors who fled Europe in order to get away from the military systems of Germany and France. Two in our own families did, so I get a bona fide disturbance in my chromosomes every time I face up to this matter of Universal Military Training.

I do not want to be forced by events to say of my country what Isaiah said of his: "The way of peace they know not, and there is no justice in their tracks; the paths they have made for themselves are crooked; whosoever treadeth thereon knoweth not peace." Rather, I honestly covet for my country the responsibilities of leading the nations of the world in the paths which are straight and point toward peace. Yet if we keep on talking about wanting peace even while we lay permanent plans to orient our total life toward war, who will believe our words?

Christian churches are committed to the dream of the day when swords will be beaten into ploughshares. We shall keep right on opposing every effort to beat the ploughshares into swords. Knowing that "they that take the sword shall perish by the sword," we urge not only our countrymen but all mankind to make every effort to get rid of the swords before they do us all to death.

As I consider the current uncertainties of Congressional action, I have been recalling as food for my spirit an incident from the life of Gladstone. When his famous Reform Bill was facing defeat at the hands of the Commons, he took the floor. Addressing his opponents, he said: "Gentlemen, you may vote down this bill, you may make us dip our colors today—but the future belongs to us." And it did! And it will! We shall not accept defeat in this matter. Proponents of Universal Military Training may write it on the law books, but they can't keep it there. As God lives and as we live to serve Him, we'll take it off!

XI

What Is Freedom of Religion?[1]

SCRIPTURE LESSON: Joshua 4:1–9

I

THE meaning of great events has a way of getting mislaid among the trivialities of daily living. And when we need it the most we have difficulty laying our hands on it.

It was so with the ancient Hebrews in that portion of their life recounted in the Scripture lesson. Surrounded as they were by a series of momentous events that had caused them to erect great memorials, they realized that the time would come when their children and their children's children would confront them with the query, "What mean ye by these stones?" In a very real sense the writers of the Old Testament books set themselves to the task of singling out the great meanings in the life of the Hebrew people that deserved to be known and perpetuated throughout the ages to come. This was their only guarantee that the meaning of great events would not be permanently lost.

We, too, mislay the meaning of our great events. Of none is this truer than this national holiday—the Fourth of July. We agree that it is an occasion for celebration, but we are more concerned with the "how" and the "where" than with the "why" of that celebration. Some of us, I fear, simply will not be bothered with that problem, either. We are blood brothers to the mountaineer in the Ozarks who went to the county fair to hear a political speech. He shouted himself hoarse in his cheers for the speaker. Someone near him asked what he thought of the speech. He answered, "I didn't come here to think; I came here to holler!" Some of the rest of us will dip hastily into the meaning of the day, then beat a quick retreat to an enjoyment of the celebration itself. You may have heard Gabriel Heatter in a radio

---

[1] This sermon was preached July 2, 1950.

broadcast some time ago. After spending a fearsome ten minutes hurling defiance at Moscow and giving advice to Washington as well as to the rest of the country, he confessed that the future was most ominous. But, he said, "make the most of such a joy as you can get." Whereupon he gave us his personal recommendation that we use Kreml Hair Tonic.

But for many, and I am persuaded most of us, the pleasant round of activities of the day—family outings, picnics, fireworks, et cetera—will not be enough. For, underlying these lesser activities, made deeper by the darkening outlook in international affairs, is a growing awareness that this particular holiday ought to serve a great and good purpose in our common life. They take to heart the warning of Somerset Maugham: "If a nation values anything more than freedom, it will lose its freedom; and the irony of it is that if it is comfort or money that it values more, it will lose that, too." That is why we want to be able to give our children a clear and convincing answer when they point to this great day and ask, "What mean ye by these stones?" We ought to be able to tell them why we believe in this holy fact of freedom, and why we dedicate this day to celebrating it.

We celebrate the day in which this fact came to birth in a new way and with new meaning in human history through the resolution, the courage, and the confident hope of the men who wrote the Declaration of Independence, and then prepared to seal it with "their lives, their fortunes, and their sacred honor." We stand to salute men like that and days like this. For with the adoption and publication of that Declaration the die was cast, we had crossed our Rubicon, or, as airplane pilots might say, we had passed the point of no return. And the men who did it are among the greatest benefactors of humanity. They deserve to be called the Founding Fathers. With good cause "the crowned heads of Europe" trembled when they heard the news. And by the same token the spirits of ordinary people everywhere took a new lease on life and hope and, from that day to this, have turned eyes of longing to this country. Emma Lazarus' famous inscription for the Statue of Liberty is a true rendering of this yearning for America. She pictures the Goddess of Liberty saying to the listening world:

> Give me your tired, your poor,
> Your huddled masses yearning to breathe free,
> The wretched refuse of your teeming shore,

> Send these, the homeless, the tempest-tosst, to me,
> I lift my lamp beside the golden door.

I stand up gladly to bear both personal and representative witness to the reality of this call. Every ancestral line in my family heard it—and so did yours! In our own family tradition people in Germany, Scotland, England, Ireland, and Sweden were weaned away from every precious tie to homeland and encouraged to set out for a new land with a new hope for a new world—a land, a hope, and a world in which this magic, mysterious word "Freedom" would "come alive and walk up and down in the hearts of men."

This holy fact of freedom has interpreted itself in various kinds of freedom which we believe deserve to be built into our common life and institutions. Freedom of worship, freedom of speech, freedom of press, freedom of assembly: these, our Founding Fathers held to be of paramount importance. All through the intervening century and a half men have proposed other freedoms as of comparable value: freedom from fear, freedom from want, freedom of information—and many others. I suspect the end of this list of candidates has not yet been reached. Nor can it be until freedom has permeated every nook and cranny of our common life.

Yet this will take a lot of doing before it finally gets done! For freedom is a dangerous thing in the sight of many people. They are frightened by the specter of change, deep, unpredictable change, which it carries with it. Their fear forces them into what amounts to a curtailment of freedom in order, they say, to preserve it. It is hard to recall a time in our history when we have had a worse attack of jitters on this matter of freedom than right now.

What would happen to a political leader in Washington today if he should say, "Whenever the people of this country 'grow weary of the existing government, they can exercise their constitutional right of amending it, or their revolutionary right to dismember or overthrow it.'" I am sure that many more than Senator McCarthy would sit up and take apoplectic notice! Yet this statement was made some years ago by a political leader from the State of Illinois who was seeking the Presidency of the United States. His name was Abraham Lincoln.

Believers in academic freedom are hard pressed on every side now. The president of Georgetown University—a Roman Catholic institution in Washington, D.C.—has called academic freedom "a fabulous formula," "the sacred fetish," "the soft under-belly of American education," and has asked for the kind of limitations on it that have characterized his church's schools since the Council of Trent in the sixteenth century.

Nor is he alone in this approach to the problem of academic freedom. The Board of Regents of the University of California recently released some faculty members who felt that a recently devised oath of loyalty was an infringement on their freedom. Serious as each of these examples is in its own right, their true seriousness lies in the fact that they are straws in a modern wind that is blowing dead against some of the deeper meanings of freedom.

Freedom of religion along with every other fundamental freedom prized in America must make its way against a head wind of misunderstanding, criticism, and hysteria that, at times, rises to gale proportions. Because I believe in the holy fact of freedom; because I believe in the way we have been trying to make it live in our common life; because I believe in freedom of religion as we have been trying to work it out in the history of this country—I propose that we lift it up for examination and try to determine what is happening to it today, and what our responsibility to it is or should be.

II

Sometimes I wonder how many of us realize what a novel experiment we have been attempting in this business of freedom of religion. Even today the large majority of mankind have never experienced anything like it. Not more than half a dozen among the sixty odd nations are with us in it—the rest being committed to some other ideal or goal. And when the idea was first broached a century and a half ago it must have sounded utterly fantastic. Look for a moment at the European background of what we are trying to do on freedom of religion.

Our effort to establish religious freedom grew out of the passionate desire of men to worship God according to the dictates of their own conscience. *Their own conscience,* mind you! Not the dictates of an absolute church or an absolute monarch or an absolute state, but the dictates of their own conscience. This perennial desire of the human spirit that no church could wholly satisfy or human power wholly suppress kept breaking out all over Europe with increasing frequency from the thirteenth century on in the form of brotherhood movements of one sort or another. The great state churches—both Roman Catholic and Protestant—tried to control them by threats and persecution or to stamp them out by crusades. But they continued to erupt.

Once such eruption occurred in a rural area of England in the seventeenth century. A small group of sincere people refused to conform to the religious laws of the country. They insisted upon setting up their own liturgy and life without reference to the state church. In fact, they were most critical of that church. Discriminatory laws, mob violence, and actual persecution finally convinced them that they had to give up either their homeland or their desire to worship God as they saw fit. Consequently, they made ready to move to Holland. After a long period of almost heartbreaking difficulty this was accomplished. But it was not as satisfactory as they had hoped it would be, and they began to investigate the possibility of crossing the Atlantic Ocean to the New Land and building a home where they could realize their desire for an unfettered worship of God. After another period of great anxiety and even greater difficulty the actual transfer of the small colony to America was accomplished, and they found themselves clinging precariously to the eastern edge of an unexplored and literally unknown world. The historical novel *Saints and Strangers* is a vivid account of all this—and of the subsequent steps in the history of the Plymouth Colony.

Soon other religious groups from Europe followed suit. The Puritans, the Quakers, and the Roman Catholics from England; the Huguenots from France; the Moravians from the Rhine Valley; the Presbyterians from Scotland and Ireland—to name but a few—headed westward. Then, as so often happens, human nature asserted itself here even as it had in Europe. While each group wanted to worship God as it saw fit, it also wanted everybody to worship God the same way! The European pattern of a preferred, or favored, or state-supported church was duly established in nearly every colony in America. And all other religious groups in the colony had to take "second-class accommodations." Quarrels were constant and bitter conflicts frequent. For nearly one hundred years it looked like the shameful European history of religious persecution and suppression was going to be reenacted in this new world.

Finally, and for a number of reasons—some religious, some political, some just plain "practical"—cooler heads gave events a new turn. They determined to make the experiment of freedom in religion. So they wrote into the basic law of the new nation a right of free exercise of religion. Every man was granted the right to worship God as he pleased. There would be no state church, no preferred church, no exalting of one church above another—all churches, whether large or small, poor or wealthy, would be on a plane of equality before the law. This was something new—and difficult—but the promise it carried of peaceful living among religious groups warranted both the risks of the novelty and the certainty of the difficulty.

III

Freedom of religion, as we understand it, is one of three possible ways whereby a state can deal with religious groups. To call them by name, they are tyranny, toleration, and freedom. Since all three are being tried today, since freedom is being tried by the smallest number of nations, and since powerful forces in this country want us to change from freedom to something else, we ought to look at them together for a moment. Then we may appreciate the novelty of the idea of religious freedom.

Tyranny is the policy whereby a state accepts one religion or church as the true one and seeks to stamp out all others. When this is carried out with resolution, as it was in Islam or has been in various countries in Europe and Latin America, terror runs riot. If any one fact is clear in human history, it is this: persecution may curb but cannot kill religious insight and faith.

Toleration is the practice whereby the state favors one church but permits others to exist. The favors bestowed on the one church are very concrete: financial support at least in part for schools and shrines; sometimes protection against encroachments by other religious groups (as in Spain today); ready entree to councils for formation of the state's major policies. And there are all degrees of toleration for other churches. In England, for example, it is so generous as to be almost indistinguishable from freedom. Whereas in Spain, it is so limited as to be indistinguishable from tyranny. But, whatever the degree of it, toleration is not freedom of religion as we are attempting it here.

Freedom is the practice whereby the state places all churches and religious groups on a plane of equality before the law. It will not grant to one favors it cannot grant to another. It will grant to one what it can grant to all. It will not grant one a kind of recognition and status that cannot be shared by all. Naturally enough, churches that have matured under the favors of either tyranny or toleration are restless when placed on a plane of equality with every other church or cult imaginable and are forced to secure the total support of their organizations through persuasion and voluntary contribution. Such churches have not accepted our tradition of freedom with good grace and have sought steadily to modify it.

Freedom of religion means the right of churches—all churches —to live with dignity and equality before the law. If I believe in it, I will seek for my church only those rights that can be shared with all other churches; I will not think that a church of ten million members is entitled to any more consideration before the law than a cult of one thousand members.

Freedom of religion means the right of churches—all churches —to grow by every means of persuasion at their disposal. The plea that Evangelical churches, that is, Protestant churches, should be curtailed in Spain or Mexico or Argentina because the population already belongs to the Roman Catholic Church makes about as much sense to a believer in freedom of religion as it would be to argue that the Roman Catholic Church should be kept by law out of the Southern States because most of the people there are at least nominally Protestant. Under the discipline of freedom—the right to live, the right to grow—a movement that is capable of winning a hearing and a following by persuasion is entitled to do so. A church that cannot maintain itself in the face of criticism and challenge belongs in the museum, not in the market place. And he who will not grant this does not believe in freedom of religion. He may be religious himself; he may believe in the policy of tyranny or toleration, but he does not believe in the policy of religious freedom which we have been trying to develop here in America for one hundred and fifty years.

IV

Precious as is this right of freedom of religion, it can be lost. Yes, we in the United States can lose it—that much is quite clear. We can lose it in any one of three ways, and, it seems to me, a significant number of our fellow citizens, if not fellow churchmen, are working at all three of them.

We can lose freedom of religion through actual neglect of the practice of religion. This, I think, is our greatest danger just now. Men will not long cherish as socially valuable something that is not personally important to them. And it is difficult to build up a convincing case for the proposition that we are a God-fearing people much less a Christian people. The known facts about our behavior and our relationships simply do not fall that way. Out of some one hundred and fifty million people, we have difficulty finding half—seventy-five million—who are vitally enough interested in the practice of religion to be listed in any kind of even nominal relationship with churches or synagogues. And, I assure you from long acquaintance with church statistics that seventy-five million is a most generous figure. Actually, it is probably two-thirds of that—some fifty million. I do not say that everyone else is either irreligious or unconcerned about the freedom of religion. But I do say that they cannot be counted on to be convinced or convincing advocates of freedom of religion because they simply do not sense the positive, creative force which religion either is or ought to be in human life and society.

Most of the citizens of this country who neglect the practices of religion want to live and do live in communities that have Christian churches. Not many of them would be drawn to a community that openly advertised itself in some such fashion as this: "No churches allowed. A good place to have a home: no bells or chimes to disturb your Sunday morning slumbers! Your children will not be exposed to the influence of church schools and youth organizations sponsored by churches! You can live like the pagans you are: uncriticized by the conscience and undisturbed by the insights of the great religious traditions of the modern world."

Advertising like that would kill any community in America. And yet, half of the adult citizens of this country, so far as their own personal practices are concerned, ought to feel at home in some such community. Whereas their forefathers were willing to take three months to cross three thousand miles of ocean in order to worship God as they pleased, their descendants will not get up two hours earlier on Sunday morning and go across the street to the church of their choice to worship God. They want a church all right, but they want someone else to belong to it, to run it, to support it, and to keep it a vital fact and factor in community life.

It is an open question how long people who do not know through their own experience the warmth, the strength, the courage, the sense of renewed life which come through the practice of religion will be vitally interested in the right of the free exercise of religion. Not long, I fear. The most we can hope for by way of support from them is the conclusion that freedom of religion should be regarded as one of the "secondary" freedoms of the country. He who has not found it to be a primary freedom in his own life cannot be expected to accept it as of primary importance in the life of this country.

A second way of losing freedom of religion is through the abuse, or the distortion, or the domestication of religion itself by its friends. Religion to fulfill its mission in life must truly be free. It must be in the world yet not of the world. Although it can seek to operate within any and every form of society, it cannot be identified with any known form of society. Great religion is trying to build the Kingdom of God, beginning wherever it is and with the materials at hand. While it is more at home in a democracy than in any other form of society, it cannot be identified with democracy. The late President Roosevelt once said, "Religion and Democracy stand or fall together." This is a stirring statement. So far as I can see it has only one defect—it isn't true. Christianity rose under the absolutism of Caesars, it matured under feudalism, and it has continued its growth and spread under many forms of modern society. To say that it stands or falls with any of them—and they have all claimed it!—is so much historical nonsense. Christianity will seek to enter into the life of any and all forms of society, as leaven in the lump, always seeking their transformation until His kingdom comes, and His will is done on earth as it is in heaven.

Now, against this background, it must be plain that a vital Christian faith and a vigorous Christian Church cannot be content with the status quo and forbidden to criticize and to seek its transformation. Whoever asks this of Christianity is trying to pervert her divine commission. Yet this very thing has been and is being asked by many friends of the faith. The World Council of Churches, for example, was roundly condemned because it was critical of the shortcomings of both communism and capitalism. The communist press called the Council a capitalistic-imperialistic venture. The capitalist press called it a "fellow traveler" in many of its utterances. Each was indignant because the Council had dared criticize its way of life. Each wanted the Church to be its ally—and wanted the alliance to bind the Church to obedience.

Within the last decade a determined effort has been and is being made to silence the leaders of the Methodist Church who are outspoken in their criticism of the evils which exist in and weaken our common life. Powerful—at least well-financed—lay groups have been formed to carry on this program of intimidation. In some instances such groups have asked Annual Conferences to pass supporting resolutions. I have read several such resolutions and confess that I am appalled by their meaning. The Caesars asked no more of the early Christians than some of these resolutions ask of our church. They ask us to forswear the right of fundamental criticism of our social order, to preach the Gospel within the limitations imposed by that social order—but not to challenge those limitations.

A church that will accept such an ultimatum, even when delivered by friends, is not worthy of the name Christian Church. We need not worry unduly about freedom for such a church it will not need freedom; it will not want freedom; it will soon lose all sense of freedom—it will surely die.

The third way we can lose freedom of religion is by surrendering the idea of freedom itself and retreating to either of the two alternatives to it: tyranny or toleration.

We are in the midst of a sustained attack on two ideas that have been closely related in our life and thoughts: separation of Church and State, and freedom of religion. Our Roman Catholic friends do not accept the traditional interpretation of either of these principles. The Roman Catholic Church wants collaboration between herself and the state, and she wants the preferred church status here as well as everywhere else. I am not now debating the merits of these claims. I am citing them in order to prove the point that powerful forces are at work seeking a radical modification of our idea of religious freedom. Maybe this is what the American people want. Perhaps they want an Italy, or Spain, or Mexico, where one church is regnant, protected by law, given special privileges by law, with schools supported by public funds, while other churches are permitted to eke out a precarious existence so long as they keep discreetly quiet about the preferred church. If so, if this is what we want, if this is to be final policy of this country, then the men and the women who came over on the *Mayflower* have been given the lie by their spiritually degenerate children.

For the overwhelming majority of us, to move in this direction is unthinkable. We simply cannot afford anything less or other than freedom of religion. The spirit, language, and policy of intimidation and coercion are out, so far as our country is concerned. The ways of persuasion are open to all; the ways of coercion are open to none. Churches that are in sympathy with the American dream of freedom should publicly renounce all recourse to coercion in any form as a curb on the activities of any other religious group. Difficult as it is to live with some of the noisy, insulting sects that roam the streets, it is downright dangerous to try to create a situation wherein they are not free to disturb us. Let us remind ourselves that the religious group that fashions a club of coercion for crushing other religious groups will find it used on their own heads sooner or later.

Frankly, I am not pessimistic about this happening in America. An alert, aroused citizenry, sensitive to the profound meaning of freedom of religion and keenly aware of the enormous difference between this and its alternatives, simply will not let it happen here.

V

So when we are asked—whether by our children or those reared in alien cultures—"What mean ye by these stones?" why this holiday? this celebration? we can say:

It means freedom—freedom under God.

It means the freedom to live a personal life blessed with privacy, dignity, usefulness, and security.

It means the freedom to build a society blessed with cooperation, compassion, and community.

It means the freedom to worship God according to the dictates of one's own conscience—and the responsibility so to do.

It means that this nation shall have not alone a new birth of freedom but a rebirth of confidence in the principle and the practice of freedom.

XII

Should the United States Have an Ambassador at the Vatican?[1]

SCRIPTURE LESSON: Galatians 5:1–15

I

JAMES BRYCE, later and better known as Lord Bryce, was one of the distinguished teachers and public figures in England at the turn of the century. He served as Britain's Ambassador to the United States from 1907-1912. He was a lifelong student of American affairs, particularly of our law and government. He published in 1888, and revised in 1912, his famous study of American life, *The American Commonwealth*. Believing it a good thing to see ourselves as "others see us" I find myself going over this work upon occasion. Each time I do it, I am impressed with the many changes—some good, some doubtful, some evil—that have come about in our life over the last forty years.

Bryce opens his chapter on "The Churches and the Clergy" (written in 1912) in this way:

In examining the National government and the State governments, we have never once had occasion to advert to any ecclesiastical body or question, because with such matters government has in the United States absolutely nothing to do. Of all the differences between the Old World and the New this is perhaps the most salient. Half the wars of Europe, half the internal troubles that have vexed European States, . . . have arisen from theological differences or from the rival claims of Church and State. This whole vast chapter of debate and strife has remained virtually unopened in the United States. There is no Established Church. All religious bodies are equal before the law, and unrecognized by the law, except as voluntary associations of private citizens.

[1] This sermon was preached October 28, 1951.

128

The Federal Constitution contains the following prohibitions:
Art. VI. No religious test shall ever be required as a qualification to any office or public trust under the United States.
Amendment I. Congress shall make no law respecting an establishment of religion or prohibiting the free exercise thereof.
No attempt has ever been made to alter or infringe upon these provisions.

In a later discussion of what he calls the "Pleasantness of American Life," Bryce says:

There are, moreover, other rancours besides those of social inequality whose absence from America brightens it to a European eye. There are no quarrels of churches and sects. . . . No Established Church looks down scornfully upon Dissenters from the height of its titles and endowments, and talks of them as hindrances in the way of its work. No Dissenters pursue an Established Church in a spirit of watchful jealousy, nor agitate for its overthrow. . . . Between Roman Catholics and the more educated Protestants there is little hostility, and sometimes even co-operation for a philanthropic purpose. . . . There is not a country in the world where Frederick the Great's principle, that everyone should be allowed to go to heaven his own way, is so fully applied. This sense of religious peace as well as religious freedom all around one is soothing to the weary European, and contributes not a little to sweeten the lives of ordinary people.

You must feel, as I do, "Oh what a falling off there has been" in this matter of harmony between and among religious groups since Bryce wrote these words forty years ago! This is the fourth time in the last twelve years that I have found myself a most reluctant participant in a battle over one or both of the two principles that Lord Bryce hailed as cornerstones of religious peace and harmony in this country, namely, freedom of religion, and the separation of Church and State. Knowing how difficult it is for a protagonist properly to evaluate his reasons and motives for conflict, I nonetheless feel as did the younger brother of two boys who were fighting underneath our apartment window many years ago. The mother, hearing the conflict, called to the older boy, "Tommy, what's the matter?" Tommy replied, "Make Johnny stop fighting!" Then Johnny's tearful voice came floating up, "I'm not fighting, Mother, I'm just fighting back!" When either of these principles—freedom of religion or separation of Church and State—are threatened by distortion or denial, then those of us who believe in them have no choice but to "fight back." Yet, I repeat, this has not always been true.

Until twelve years ago I was one of an increasing group of clergymen who dared to hope that the main outlines of the proper relation between religion and government were understood, appreciated, and respected by the religious groups and the political strategists of our country. We knew, of course, that there was enough active and latent religious prejudice in America to blow up any amount of achieved harmony. We had lived through the presidential campaign of 1928; we had lived through the last upsurge of the Ku Klux Klan and had fought it all along the line; we had felt the sting of the Klan's counterpart in the Roman Catholic faith, particularly in the vast and frequently vicious pamphleteering efforts of the Knights of Columbus, but we continued to cherish the hope that wise statesmanship on the part of Protestant and Catholic leaders would combine to keep such expressions of bigotry within narrowly restricted and relatively harmless limits.

I am still of the opinion that we were not then living in a fool's paradise as might now seem to have been the case. We were in the midst of fashioning concrete evidence that something new in the area of interfaith relations was struggling toward maturity in this country. The best example of it was the formation and active existence of the National Council of Christians and Jews which, working over a period of years, had set up thousands of round-table discussions in churches, schools, and community centers. Those of us who shared in these time after time were delighted with them and their portent for the future. American audiences, accustomed to outright or poorly disguised conflicts among religious leaders, rubbed their eyes in amazement. For they saw a Jew, a Catholic, and a Protestant sitting down at a common table and discussing points of agreement and disagreement among their respective religions, and doing it in a spirit of fraternity and understanding. Far and wide this method was called the "American Way" of dealing with religious differences. It was hailed as the democratic alternative to the age-old method of bitter strife and outright persecution. This method has done and is continuing to do an incalculable amount of good. It continues to impress many of us as the "American Way" of dealing with religious disputes. It is thoroughly realistic about the fact of religious differences between religious faiths. It makes no attempt to bridge these by superficial structures that cannot possibly carry the traffic of increasing interfaith relations in our common life. The round table is the place where we can learn to understand and respect the intellectual integrity and personal sincerity of those who hold religious convictions quite different from our own. It is, in other words, a step in the direction of learning to live in harmony with our differences. However, traveling that road toward increasing harmony has proved to be very difficult. But until twelve years ago it seemed likely that at least major conflicts in the field of interfaith relations might be avoided. That has not proved to be true.

For a dozen years storm signals have been flying along the coast line of Catholic and Protestant relations here in America. Every reliable indication points to an approaching storm of hurricane proportions over the next few months. Farseeing religionists, whatever their faith, tremble at that prospect. For there has never been a time when they stood in greater need of one another's sympathetic co-operation than now. It is a truism to say that the major international developments over the last fifteen years have been highly inimical to the interests of all forms of religion. Protestant and Catholic leaders know, or should know, this. They should realize that interfaith quarrels today will inevitably, perhaps irreparably, weaken religion in the titanic combat with the irreligious forces that now threaten us all. But our dire need for mutual understanding is not of itself sufficient to produce it. The grim fact seems to be that our protestation of need for one another's co-operation seems upon occasion to be little more than the perfunctory touch of gloves which always precedes the opening gong of a fight. I would not press this figure of speech so far as to say that I think a serious religious conflict is inevitable, but I do mean that if outright conflict is to be avoided, leaders in all religious groups must recognize the danger implicit in the mounting tension and take immediate steps to relieve it in conformity with the American conception of the proper relationship between religion and the state.

II

Lest you think we are merely fighting straw men, let me sketch briefly the nature of the four conflicts that have come up over the last twelve years.

The first was in 1939, and it revolved around the principle of the separation of Church and State. It was touched off by President Roosevelt's surprise appointment of Mr. Myron Taylor as his personal representative to the Vatican. Most of you will recall that furor. Cardinal Spellman proclaimed that "21,000,000 Catholics approved the appointment." He proceeded to insinuate that the only ones who opposed it were bigots (a favorite word of Cardinal Spellman's as he deals with anyone who criticizes a position which he supports). Protestants insisted that that appointment was an infringement on the principle of separation of Church and State because it singled out for preferential recognition the head of one of our churches. I do not know of a single non-Roman Catholic church in this country that did not protest the appointment of Mr. Taylor on this ground. The President denied that this was his intention, but his denial did not carry conviction to the aroused sentiment of Protestant churches. In fact, the criticism of the Protestants mounted to the point where the President finally and reluctantly wrote Dr. George Buttrick, President of the Federal Council of Churches, and assured him that nothing in the move could be construed as pointing toward a resumption of formal diplomatic relations with the Vatican.

In June, 1946, President Truman assured a representative group of Protestant ministers that the personal representative of the President to the Vatican was "a temporary measure made necessary by war" and that it would be terminated as soon as world conditions permitted.

The second conflict followed hard on the heels of the first one. I occurred in 1942 and involved the principle of freedom of religion. The actual occasion for it was the determined, public effort made by the American hierarchy of the Roman Catholic Church to have the Evangelical missionaries withdrawn from Latin America on two grounds: (1) Latin America was Catholic and therefore the missionary efforts of other groups could only cause trouble; (2) the good neighbor policy, so essential to the unity of the Western Hemisphere during the war, was being imperiled by the disturbing presence of non-Roman Catholic missionaries. Roman Catholic leaders in this country did more than openly assert these arguments; they kept up a drumfire of criticism in their church press and, finally, brought sufficient pressure to bear on the State Department to make it difficult for our churches to send missionaries to Latin America.

Once more the Protestant churches erupted and charged that this effort was entirely out of keeping with the principle of freedom of religion. The struggle was so acute and widespread that it was watched with interest and concern throughout the world. I heard echoes of it both in Brazil and Argentina as late as last summer. Fortunately, the State Department quickly gave up the effort to shut down on the free flow of missionaries to Latin America, and such difficulty as we encountered on this score came from the Latin American countries themselves. But that too passed, and we soon had complete freedom of movement.

The third conflict is far from over even though it began to get considerable public attention in 1940. I refer to the struggle of the Roman Catholic Church to get some measure of public support for her parochial school systems. Schoolbooks, transportation, teacher salary, health care, lunches—all these have been the subject of litigation not once but repeatedly in various sections of the United States. Determined efforts on the part of an overwhelmingly Caholic school board either to declare a parochial school a *de facto* public school or to put nuns on the teaching staff of public schools and at public school salaries have produced explosions in Ohio, North Dakota, Missouri, and New Mexico.

Every effort to get the Federal Congress to enact a bill providing for federal aid to education has been blocked by united Catholic opposition because the proposals did not place parochial schools on the same footing with public schools relative to Federal Aid. While the Catholic Church has not been powerful enough to pass a law to her own liking, she has been able to block those she did not like. Here again the issue at stake is not— as Cardinal Spellman in one of his many tearful public moods put it—whether a public school bus should stop on a rainy day and pick up a poor little Catholic boy and drop him off at the corner nearest his church's school—the issue is that of the principle of separation of Church and State. It is the continuing contention of the Roman Catholic Church that her schools—her schools, mind you—are entitled to at least partial support from public taxation. In opposition, Protestants say that a church's schools are her schools: to build, to man, to support. The moment you move beyond that the state undergirds the religious teaching program of a certain church—which is a distinct violation of the principle of the separation of Church and State.

This issue is still with us, with cases pending in several state courts now. The Roman Catholic Church is pushing her contention with all her might, and she is meeting an informed, aroused, and organized resistance all along the line.

The fourth conflict is the one that burst on us last week with President Truman's announcement that, subject to the approval of the Senate, he proposes to open full and formal diplomatic relations with the Vatican. There is little doubt that the Roman Catholic Church in America and throughout the world will welcome this proposal. There is no doubt whatever that Protestant Churches are opposing it with unanimity and fervor. Much as we dread the prospect, we find ourselves standing on the verge of the most serious struggle between Catholic and Protestant forces that this country has yet witnessed.

The contention advanced in a half-hearted fashion by some defenders of the President's proposal that it is purely a political matter dealing with the heads of two governments hardly deserves serious recognition. Strip the Vatican City, for one moment, of the one who is the accepted head of the Roman Catholic Church, and what do you have left? You have a country of 108.4 acres entirely dependent for its livelihood on charity from outside its borders and whose population of about a thousand souls lives under the absolute rule of one man. If the issue were whether or not we should have diplomatic relations with that kind of a political entity, I doubt whether it would ever have been raised. There are at least a hundred chieftains in Africa who better deserve diplomatic recognition on purely political grounds. But when you admit for one moment that the matter involves the recognition of the political power of the head of the Roman Catholic Church, as indeed it does, you have a head-on collision with the American principle of the separation of Church and State.

The further argument that we should have an embassy at the Vatican because 37 other countries do, overlooks three things: (1) there are 23 countries that do not have embassies there; (2) most of the 37 are countries in which the Roman Catholic Church is the State Church; (3) none of them has the American principle of the separation of Church and State. What countries do who do not have this principle is their own business and is not to be judged from our own perspective, but what we do should be in conformity with the fundamental principles of our common life.

We who are opposing this proposal believe that if the Roman Catholic Church would withdraw its overt or covert support, the proposal would die at once. Therefore, we have to consider why it is that the Roman Catholic Church will not only not withdraw its support but will undoubtedly fight for the adoption of the proposal to the very end. The root of the matter, I believe, is this: The Roman Catholic Church either does not understand or will not respect the principle of the separation of Church and State which has been fundamental to religious harmony in this country. We saw in the Taylor appointment the nose of the camel coming into the tent of the religious life of America and now with Mr. Truman's proposition we see the rest of the camel trying to get in.

The nub of the matter, I repeat, can be stated this way: non-Catholic groups in America are opposing Mr. Truman's proposal because, in their judgment, it is an irresponsible and profound violation of the historic principle of the separation of Church and State; the Roman Catholic Church is unmoved by this reason because it profoundly disbelieves in this principle. The Catholic leaders spoke for themselves on this point when the Taylor matter was up in 1939, and the principles involved in the two proposals are almost identical, differing only in the added degree of seriousness involved in Mr. Truman's proposal.

Cardinal Spellman then referred to the principle of separation of Church and State as "the shibboleth of separation of Church and State." A chorus of "amens" went up from a long list of Catholic writers and educators. One such referred to the principle of the separation of Church and State as "that bogey." Another scoffed at the opposition because Mr. Taylor's appointment "was held contrary to some imaginary American tradition." To these gentlemen, the American principle of the separation of Church and State may be a "shibboleth," "bogey" and "imaginary," but to all non-Catholic groups it is a fundamental religious as well as civic principle.

The issue between the Roman Catholic Church and non-Catholics on this matter is clear cut, and it constitutes the center of the approaching storm in Catholic-Protestant relations here in the United States. The Roman Catholic Church does not believe in the ultimate validity of the principle of the separation of Church and State. It believes in the *union* of Church and State. It has a recognized and official Catholic conception of the *union* of Church and State where the Church is the Catholic Church. This conception has been stated with admirable clarity in the Papal Encyclical entitled *Immortali Dei* of Pope Leo XIII, issued on November 1, 1885, and used as definitive by the Catholic Church and canon law from that day to this. This encyclical is interpreted clearly and honestly by Fathers Ryan and Millar in their book entitled *The State and the Church*, first published in 1924 under the imprimatur of the late Cardinal Hayes, and republished in 1940 under the title, *Catholic Principles of Politics*. We have no choice but to regard it as the official Catholic interpretation of the proper relationship between Church and State.

It [the book] explicitly states that as there exists only one true religion, Catholicism, the Catholic Church must establish itself as the State Church in the United States of America. This is in accordance with the fundamental doctrine of the Popes "that the State must not only have a care for religion, but must recognize the *true religion*" (Leo XIII). In short, Catholicism must be made to prevail and eventually eliminate all other religions. This has as its authority the encyclical written by Pope Leo XIII, called *Catholicity in the United States*, in which the American separation of Church and State is condemned.[2] Though Fathers Ryan and Millar are realistic enough to admit the necessity of beginning with America as it is, they are true to their Catholic faith as interpreted in the encyclical in wanting to move America in the direction of the position of the union of Church and State that is approved by the Catholic faith.

III

In sharp contrast to the Catholic position there is the historic American principle of the separation of Church and State both as it is stated in our Constitution and as it has been interpreted in the growing social experience of this people living under the Constitution.

Note that word "historic," for it suggests where to look for the origin and the meaning of the principle of separation of Church and State. You cannot understand the American emphasis on this principle apart from at least some of the history which has gone into the making of American life. Time permits us to do little more than note two reasons why our Constitutional Fathers chose to separate Church and State.

In the first place, they had vivid memories of religious oppression in Europe. The colonies were founded largely by men and women seeking refuge from religious persecutions of one kind or another in Europe. Even though commercial and political motives had their influence in the formation of large colonial companies, great bodies of immigrants in the early colonial period were willing to come because of religious oppression in their homeland. And for Protestants to blame the Catholics, or vice versa, in this matter, would be for the pot to call the kettle black.

[2] Alvro, Manhattan, *The Vatican in World Politics*, p. 302.

Pilgrims and Puritans came to Massachusetts and the rest of New England in order to escape the persecution of the Established Church of England. Later, when the Puritans under Cromwell acquired control of England, the old line Anglicans felt safer elsewhere. They settled in Virginia, Maryland, and the Carolinas. But Puritan and Anglican in England agreed in this: both persecuted the Quakers, forcing them to seek refuge in New Jersey and Pennsylvania. The Scotch-Irish Presbyterians, seeking to escape the recurrent religious wars between Catholics and Protestants, settled in the central colonies of America. Dutch, German, and French immigrants came in large numbers, some fleeing Catholic, others Protestant persecution.

Our Constitutional Fathers learned one lesson as they looked over this European background: *Grant any church political privileges and access to the public treasury and to police power, and that church will restrict the free functioning of dissenting religious groups.* This restriction is always resented and opposed, giving rise to civil conflict.

The second reason why the makers of our Constitution determined to separate Church and State was the trouble brought about by the continuation of the European pattern of an established church in early colonial life. Most colonies accepted the European system of a preferred or an established church and without exception found themselves plunged into the same kind of civil discord that had characterized the European scene. Finally Baptists, Quakers and Congregationalists took the lead in the agitation to separate Church and State. Rhode Island and Pennsylvania began by setting up colonial, and later state governments that would make no discrimination among the various religious groups. Franklin and Jefferson reflected the deliberate judgment of most thoughtful Americans in their explicit statement that there was no other way of providing a basis for harmony than that of separation of Church and State. So the Constitutional Fathers wrote into the Constitution the provision which called forth the admiration of Lord Bryce, the provision that no church should be established or favored by the law of this country.

IV

This stricture has worked no hardship on American churches. And by American churches I do not mean churches that are restricted to America but those churches that have either developed or matured in terms of their experience in this country.

Baptist, Congregational, Methodist, and American Lutheran are American churches in this sense, though they have their brethren all over the world. Churches like these have had to face from the start the necessity of supporting and expanding their programs by voluntary contributions and efforts and by free persuasion. They have been forced to build their schools and churches, and train their clergy on their own responsibility, paying the bills themselves from the first to the last cent. They had never known a time when they were *the one* church, but have always been *one among other* churches.

But the churches that had reached their full stature in terms of a European background had a hard time meeting the difficulties imposed on them by the principle of the separation of Church and State. Various churches were forced to surrender the favored-church status which they had enjoyed in Europe or in Colonial America. It was not easy for Lutheran, Protestant Episcopal, and Presbyterian Churches to do this, but they did it and now enjoy the complete confidence of other churches in this country. The Roman Catholic Church alone has refused to move in this direction.

The Roman Catholic Church never liked and never accepted the principle of separation of Church and State. She had nearly fifteen hundred years of favored relationships with the state written in her history, during which time she had enjoyed the favor of the mightiest state powers in Europe. Historically speaking, it is easy to see why this church was not and has never been able to accept the principle of separation of Church and State. The doctrine and polity of the Catholic Church matured in Europe and under historical circumstances where kings and rulers were willing to grant it the favored-church status. The changes forced on the Catholic Church by the American principle of separation of Church and State have been disturbingly practical.

As a State Church, it had enjoyed the security of an income paid by the state; here in America it was wholly dependent on voluntary contributions. As a State Church, it had been in a position to influence if not control the growth and structure of educational facilities; here in America it was free to construct its own school system, if it chose, but it had to foot the bill. As a State Church, it felt free to form political parties and use its vast resources to secure the adoption of various kinds of social and economic programs; here in America this activity would have been suicidal. *Perhaps the greatest change of all is summed up in the single word, "prestige."* As the State Church it was *the* church; here in America, under the principle of equality, it was *a* church with just as many but no more rights and privileges than the smallest religious sect in the country. Small wonder, then, that Catholic thinkers have never accepted the principle of separation of Church and State.

The Catholic criticism of this principle can and should be stated by their own writers. Father Ryan puts his initial objection in these words: "In governments which prefer absolute neutrality toward religion, the actual policy is one of hostility." Now this allegation is refuted, in the first place, by the simple fact that all religions have flourished in America as in no other place on the face of the earth. That, in itself, ought to be the sufficient answer to what happens when you separate Church and State. In simple, historical, numerical fact, Father Ryan's charge is untrue. *The only hostility latent in the principle of separation of Church and State is toward any church which claims to be, and acts as though it alone were, the only true church, and persists in regarding all others as imposters.* That hostility is not to be found in any intention of the Constitutional Fathers or of the Constitution. It is to be found in the reaction of men who claim that their faith is the only true faith. The same "hostility" would be felt and claimed by Methodists or any other church that should seek the favored-church relationship in America.

The strongest possible criticism of the American principle is the approved Catholic position as developed by Fathers Ryan and Millar in their book:

> The state should officially recognize the Catholic religion as the religion of the commonwealth; accordingly it should invite the blessing and ceremonial participation of the church for certain important public functions, as the opening of legislative sessions, the erection of public buildings, etc., and delegate its officials to attend certain of the more important festival celebrations of the church; it should recognize and sanction the laws of the church; and it should protect the rights of the church and the religious as well as the other rights of the church's members.

But what of other religions? Will they be tolerated? I quote again:

If these are carried on within the family, or in such an inconspicuous manner as to be an occasion neither of scandal nor of perversion to the faithful, they may properly be tolerated by the state. (Italics mine.)

Three things need to be pointed out about this position. In the first place, it has no precedent in American history. It is as thoroughly un-American in historical antecedent and moral content as any principle could possibly be. In the second place, it is precisely the position against which all non-Catholic Christian groups have protested from the very inception of the protestant movement. In the third place, and referring not alone to religious precedent but to observable, historical fact, this position has been the prolific mother of discord not only among religious groups but also between the Catholic Church and the State. Let Italy, Mexico, France, and Spain witness whether the relationship with the Catholic Church has been one of increasing or decreasing discord! Their records are plain. And so are the records of other countries, like England and Germany, in which other churches are the state church. The singling out of some one church for civic favors inevitably leads to conflict both with other religious groups and between the favored church and state. Therefore, when we remind our Catholic thinkers that we, in America, are proceeding on a principle which is peculiarly our own and one which has the impressive support of all non-Catholic religious groups in America, we are talking in terms of historical fact.

The position of non-Catholic religions in America can, I believe, be outlined in these propositions:

1. We believe in the principle of "a free church in a free state."
2. We believe that strict adherence to this principle constitutes one of organized religion's greatest contributions to the strengthening of the democratic principle of equality now under fire throughout the world.
3. We neither seek nor want special privilege from this or any other government. Our message and our churches must spread and grow by free persuasion, else they will, and should, perish.
4. We believe that the elastic character of democratic government and education enables us, better than any other known medium, to secure a hearing for the eternal values of religion.
5. We cannot, we dare not, and we will not stand idly by and see any forces, whether political or religious, tamper with

and modify the existing American principle of separation of Church and State.

V

To many of us it is simply inconceivable that responsible leaders in the Roman Catholic Church and the government of the United States will persist in an action which can end only in the most serious kind of discord in the life of America. It does scant credit to the honesty of our Catholic friends to try to place the blame on us for this discord. We stand where we have always stood and will continue to stand on the principle of the separation rather than the union of Church and State. We will continue to "fight back" every time any effort is made to modify that principle to the advantage of any group.

This is not the first time in our history when political strategists have tried to capitalize on the religious solidarity of the Roman Catholic Church and what they thought was the irremediable disunity of Protestant groups. We are not disunited on this matter—as every issue of the daily paper now shows. We say to political strategists: You cannot purchase, by granting special recognition and privileges to any religious group, the political support of that group without at the same time and on the same issue alienating the support of all other religious groups. Political strategists must face this question: Are you willing to assume responsibility for starting another forest fire of religious strife in this country? All such moves should be labeled by the line from King Lear, "That way madness lies!" Yet that is precisely the way in which Mr. Truman's proposal has clearly moved the sentiment in this country, and will continue to move it unless that proposal is either withdrawn or defeated.

I should like to remind our Roman Catholic friends (and I would like to say colleagues in the Christian Faith if they would let me!) that the struggle between the Roman Catholic Church and the Protestant churches can be dealt with on either of two levels and probably will find some kind of expression on both. The first one I like the least, not because I think we will lose the struggle, but because I am most fearful of what it will do to the unity and community of our life in America. This is the level of creating political blocks along religious lines and fighting it out on all issues just as they have done in half a dozen European countries. Know it for a fact, the existence and cultivation of "a Catholic vote" will call forth another block of "non-Catholic votes"; this, if human nature be not wholly changed, will soon become an "anti-Catholic vote." The final result will be something common to the political history of Europe but utterly alien to our own.

Our Catholic leaders should be realistic enough to know that this is actually happening now wherever "the Catholic vote" is in existence. They should face squarely the simple fact that the opposition is taking form swiftly, and that the result can scarcely be in doubt since there are at most no more than fifteen million Catholic voters as over against some fifty million non-Catholic voters. There is not the slightest doubt in this world that the Protestant churches intend to preserve the principle of the separation of Church and State even if we have to meet the Catholic vote with the Protestant vote in order to do it.

I confess to nothing but alarm at this prospect. The worst fight on earth is a religious one. Once we get into it the bigots and zealots on both sides will get out of hand almost at once and have a wretched field day at the expense of the best interests of every church and of our country as well.

The second level is that of trying to understand and co-operate with one another in the effort to build here in America something new—an example of peace on earth and good will among men. It should not be too difficult for Roman Catholic leaders to grasp the simple fact that the American tradition of separation of Church and State is utterly different from their conception of the union of Church and State. They should see that they as a church have profited at least as much as any other church under the discipline of freedom of religion and the separation of Church and State here in this country. They should face with complete candor the choice that is before them: Either abide by the traditional American conception and modify their church law and doctrine accordingly and publicly announce that this is what they are doing, or continue their steady attack on these traditional conceptions of our common life, knowing full well that they are plunging all of us into the sharpest kind of conflict—one from which we will not draw back.

There is dread rather than joy in my soul as I see the conflict shaping up before our very eyes. Yet we as Protestant churches have a very simple choice before us: Either we resist every effort to bend and finally break our conception of the proper relationship between Church and State, or we as churches accept a subordinate status to the Roman Catholic Church in the practice of our country.

Those of us who refuse to do the latter will make it abundantly plain to Mr. Truman and the Senate that we will never accept his proposal to compromise the principle of the separation of Church and State. We will make it plain to him that we expect him to withdraw the proposal and, if he fails to do that, we will both single this out as a major political issue and form ranks to fight it with every means at our disposal. And having won this fight, as win it we shall, we must keep right on struggling until the ancient American ideal and effort to establish freedom of religion through the separation of Church and State has been rescued from the confusion and contradiction which now threaten it, and we find our way once more to that high plateau of religious good will and harmony among all religious groups dwelling on a plane of equality and in the spirit of community that Lord Bryce thought one of our greatest characteristics.

Meantime, as we move into this struggle, I call upon us all to do so without hysteria, fanaticism, and hatred of fellow Christians or anyone else, but to do so with firmness yet moderation, with conviction couched in a spirit of good will, with a determination to serve the right as God gives us to see the right, yet with the realization that in His Kingdom there is a place for all.

XIII

Is Drinking a Religious Problem?

SCRIPTURE LESSON: Isaiah 5:11–16

I

THERE is only one reason why I have ever hesitated or hesitate now to deal with this theme of drinking: I am afraid that you who have wrestled or are now wrestling with this problem in a personal way may misunderstand my motive in so doing. I would not for the world want you to feel that I am covertly crying "for shame" at you or anyone else. Nor do I want you to think for one moment that I am either unsympathetic with or unwilling to assist in every way I can in the hard struggle you have had or are now having as you try to keep this problem under control in your own personal life. That, I hope, will be apparent from the very outset and through everything that I may say on this matter.

The problem that involves you involves all of us directly or indirectly, and that is why I have no choice, finally, but to deal with it carefully and directly. I propose to keep what I have to say on as high a level as possible of facts and clear interpretation.

It is hard to get a fair hearing in our country today on this matter of drinking alcoholic beverages. It is almost as hard to get a hearing today as it is to secure a clear witness against the use of alcohol from the Bible itself or from the practices of Christian churches. A study of the Bible will reveal that there is no one mind in the sacred Scripture on this matter.

One Biblical attitude encountered a number of times is akin to the Homeric notion that wine is the "nectar of the gods." Both Old and New Testaments seem to take the use of wine for granted. In view of the fact that one of the important factors in the economic life of the Hebrews was a cultivation of vineyards,

144

it is easy to understand this attitude. In fact, it is little short of a miracle that any other attitude ever did develop.

But another attitude did develop, and its emergence in the life of Israel must be regarded as an inescapable protest against a social evil that was endangering the life of the people. The strongest kind of protest was lifted by Isaiah when he was listing the evils that had brought his people under the judgments of God, and his nation to the brink of ruin. He reduced them to two: *injustice* and *drunkenness.* He charged that drunkenness had brought about a subversion of all values wherein black becomes white, good becomes evil, and people no longer can distinguish between them. Because of injustice and drunkenness Isaiah charges that his people are in turmoil and in disaster. God "looked for justice, but behold, bloodshed; for righteousness, but behold, a cry!" (R.S.V.).

So, without attempting to try to make the Bible say one thing where it plainly says two, it is important for us to realize that when it does oppose the use of drink it does so because of widespread damage and danger in the total life of a people.

The same sort of indecision is found in the witness of the churches. There is no point in my pretending that the churches are united on it. So far as I know, all churches are opposed to drunkenness, but not all are unambiguously opposed to the use of alcoholic beverages in any form. An increasing number of churches are beginning to bring the entire drink habit under judgment. The history of the Methodist Church on this point is instructive. Beginning without any sharply formulated opposition to it our position has now matured to the point where it seems wise, necessary, and Christian to oppose the use of alcoholic beverages. That is the clear and unequivocal position of our church today and one with which I gladly associate myself. If we should feel the need of any unusual kind of moral support in our own church this morning, I am sure we could get it from the spirit of Frances Willard, one of our most distinguished daughters, who, I am convinced, is trying to break out of that stained-glass window over there and shout her "Amens" to what I shall be saying.

II

There are several important reasons why it is hard to get a fair hearing today on the drinking of alcoholic beverages. One is the serious wounds inflicted in our common life during the battle over prohibition—wounds that are not yet healed. Those who lived through it will recall it as one of the bitterest battles in the life of America. It was a long one lasting from 1900 to 1933, and it is beginning to rage again with real intensity. The mere mention of alcohol as a problem in any form starts blood boiling on both sides of that battle line. Another reason for concern is the widespread fear about any further infringements on personal rights and freedoms. This, most of us will agree, is a legitimate fear these days. The advocates of the use of alcohol are ringing the changes on the claim that every move looking toward the regulation of its use constitutes, in some sense, a curtailment of personal freedom. Add to these two reasons a third, namely, the future of a multi-billion dollar liquor industry, and you can understand why it is difficult to get a hearing for this business of drinking.

Yet we must seek that kind of hearing because the problem is being thrust at us. We cannot let it alone and continue to live in this civilization of ours. There is no way we can evade or escape it.

There can be no blinking the well-documented fact that there is a rapid increase in the amount of drinking and actual drunkenness. The Yale School of Alcohol Studies leaves no doubt on this point. Alcoholics in America are increasing at the rate of more than 50,000 a year. And what they call problem drinkers (namely, those who need two or three bracers a day) are increasing at the rate of 200,000 a year. Not even the most fanatical defender of a man's right to drink anything he wants, any time he pleases, can ignore the simple fact that a million Americans have been killed in traffic accidents, and of this million, 200,000 met their end in accidents where liquor was directly involved.

And, if you are interested in watching the telecasts of sporting events, you will find yourself facing a literal barrage of very enticing liquor advertisements that certainly give your children the wrong impression of the relationship of drinking and sports. I happened to be watching the opening game of the White Sox. Of course, I looked at it through the jaundiced eyes of an old Cub fan, and as I looked at it, I could readily understand why White Sox fans might be driven to drink by what they saw! But even so, I could not rid myself of the feeling that here, taking full advantage of our native love of sports, was the commercialization of a habit which, as it fastens itself upon people, knows neither sportsmanship nor fair play nor respect for human personality in any way, shape, or form. Open any one of our major news magazines these days and you find "men of distinction" wearing roses (when they should be wearing lilies), giving the impression that success and efficiency in business and personal relations go hand in hand with the drinking habit. Drink the right thing at the right time—you are bound to be a man of distinction—apparently!

You may have read the letter of protest that was written by a family who had tuned in their television set recently to enjoy the antics of one of the great comedians of our time. The writer of the letter said, "We gathered together as a family expecting to have a pleasant evening of fun, and we discovered we had a drunk in our home." The writer proceeded to tell how discouraging it was to have the family go through that experience. Personally, I have never been able to laugh at the antics of one who has been drinking. It may betray a distorted sense of humor on my part, but I can no more laugh at that than I can at someone who is either under the influence of opium or addicted to some other form of dope or narcotic. I have nothing but complete sympathy for Shakespeare's ejaculation, "O God! that men should put an enemy in their mouths to steal away their brains; that we should, with joy, pleasance, revel, and applause transform ourselves into beasts."

Any way you want to look at it, drinking is not simply one problem; it is several different kinds of problems all rolled into one. That, I suppose, is one of the reasons why it is so difficult to deal directly with it and to get a fair hearing for it.

No one denies, for example, that drinking is a health, an economic, and a law-enforcement problem of gravest proportions. Yet it is denied by many that it is a moral and religious problem! What they mean, to put it simply, is this: It is their own business if, when, where, and how much they drink. They contend that it concerns them and no one else, whether God or man. This is precisely the point with which I wish to take issue, and to do so in terms of reasons drawn up and stated by Dr. Haven Emerson, who for many years has been one of the foremost medical scientists in the study of the meaning of alcohol in human life.

Among the fourteen basic facts which he gives about the meaning of alcohol, four have an especial bearing on the problem of whether it is a moral and a religious problem. (1) "Alcohol is a narcotic which, by depressing the higher centers removes inhibitions; (2) By releasing inhibitions, it makes for social ease and pleasure, and herein lies one of its great dangers; (3) It impairs reason, will, self-control, judgment, physical skill and endurance. (4) It is used primarily for its psychological effect as a means of escape from unpleasant reality." Yet some claim that the habit which produces these effects in human life lies beyond the concern of religion! The religious implications of reasons like these are written in letters so large that even he who runs may read. Look at them for a moment.

III

Drinking removes or releases inhibitions, the physicians tell us. What, precisely, does this mean? That depends, of course, on what an inhibition is and whether it is always bad. An inhibition is an internally imposed curb on action, the curb usually being the work of conscience or, sometimes, the emotion of fear or dread due to past experience. Many inhibitions resulting in shyness, cowardice, and other unsocial reactions are definitely evil in their effect on human personality and need to be managed if not removed. Other inhibitions are usually called "social controls" and grow out of our environment, training, and ideals. They constitute our standard of taste, judgment, and values. One brought up in a home presided over by soft-spoken parents "instinctively" flinches from the sound of parents screaming at their children. One who has been trained to respect the possessions of others must get over a tremendous internal hurdle before he can misappropriate funds. A man who has been trained in a thoroughly realistic way to honor the dignity and person of women approaches them with a distinct sense of what is proper and improper. One trained in a Christian home has a definite standard of values by which he judges the rightness and wrongness of proposed action. Such inhibitions are as good as those mentioned earlier are evil.

What does drinking do? It removes or releases inhibitions indiscriminately—good ones and bad ones alike. One and the same drink not only conquers shyness and promotes easy conversation; it numbs conscience and encourages easy morals. It results in an easement of all inhibitions, in the lowering of the threshold of conscience of all moral matters. It is futile for anyone to argue that this is not a profoundly religious concern. Religion seeks to create inhibitions in human life by encouraging positive loyalty to high ideals. But the ability to say "Yes" to these ideals means the ability to say "No" to their opposites. When any habit or practice aims at the dulling of both the wit and wisdom to say "No" as well as "Yes" in terms of noble ideals for personal and social living, that habit or practice is viciously immoral and irreligious. If it is not a religious problem, then there are no religious problems.

It was given to the New York Liquor Authority to sum up the relationship between drinking and social disease in one biting sentence: "The more alcohol the more syphilis." Dr. John W. Churchman, writing in the *Journal of Preventive Medicine and Public Health* on "Prevention of Venereal Diseases," points out that "alcohol is the best salesman and procurer known and is a constant and essential stock in trade for the promotion of prostitution." Testimony like this warrants the assertion that all is not well when the inhibitions by which we try to regulate human relationships are indiscriminately lowered if not removed by indulging in alcoholic beverages.

Drinking, we are assured by the doctors, *impairs reason, will, self-control, judgment, physical skill, and endurance.* What, we may inquire, remains of a man when you remove these qualities? An animal—nothing more. What, concretely, is done by the habit which impairs these human faculties?

To begin with, it unfits a person for work—careful, exacting, discriminating work—whether physical or mental. A few glasses of "non-intoxicating" (that is the legal phrase for it) beer under the belt of a subway engineer in New York City a few years ago—and the essential lightninglike reaction to signals was blurred, and one of the worst wrecks in the history of the New York subways resulted. It has been demonstrated by actual tests that a cocktail or two before driving a car make it necessary for the driver to have a few more feet—six by actual test with a glass of beer—in which to stop the machine. The man who takes that drink may say it is his own business, but if my child is in that six-foot death margin, it's not his own business! It's mine as well. The severity of the punishment which is meted out by law to the man who drives a car while under the influence of alcohol is an indication of our growing awareness of the seriousness of this phase of the problem. It is no accident that one of the first questions asked of an applicant for a position which requires exacting mental or physical abilities is "Do you drink?" I can only applaud the good judgment of the ruling of the president of one of the large firms in the city of Chicago that "addiction to drink is the equivalent of a resignation from any position in this firm."

It simply does not pay to employ a man who does drink if other men of anywhere near comparable skill are available.

If what the doctors tell us about the effects of drinking is true, it unfits a person for intelligent, sensitive companionship. Wit and humor, under its tutelage, become, as a rule, a collection of off-colored jokes and a deliberate profaning of sacred things. A person may mix more easily with a crowd after a few drinks, but that is far from saying that he mixes more creatively. He just mixes. He may talk more fluently at first, but soon what might have been a worth-while discussion becomes a succession of points of personal privilege which must be granted on penalty of a quarrel. I submit that when a person's reason and self-control are impaired, his capacity for companionship on the distinctively human level is seriously challenged. Again I must conclude that if this is not a religious problem, then let it be admitted that there are none such anywhere.

The doctors tell us that *drink is used primarily for its psychological effect as a means of escape from unpleasant reality.* Who will underestimate the seriousness of this indictment? Just how successfully the drink habit accomplishes this is recorded in an address made a few years ago by Dr. A. C. Ivy while he was Professor of Physiology and Pharmacology at Northwestern University School of Medicine. Speaking on the theme, "Why People Drink," he said: "Alcohol gives temporary relief from worry; abolishes mental tension; disguises difficulties; relieves a feeling of inferiority; makes a weak person feel strong; an ignorant person feel smart; a poor person feel rich; an oppressed person feel free; a bad person feel good; and makes one imagine himself a good driver who may be potentially a motor car murderer."

As a matter of fact, this effort to use drink to escape unpleasant reality is an old way. A jaded Oriental, Omar Khayyám, looked intently at life once and found it either evil or pointless. And when he made that awful discovery, he forthwith called for a jug of wine to assist him in blotting it out. But the catch in his method is obvious: It is successful only so long as someone stays sober enough to furnish him the wine that will prevent him from ever becoming sober enough to get another good look at the world. It is hardly considerate of Omar to require someone else to face bitter reality in order that he might not have to see it!

It is the contention of great religion that to evade unpleasant realities is the height of bad religion and actually amounts to ethical atheism. It is an axiom of ethical religion that one must struggle to free himself from hypocrisy in dealing with the facts of sin and evil. Dodging is no good anywhere in the long run. A problem evaded is a problem magnified. The Christian faith (for all the Church's many sins against it) is interested in truth, not in lies or in deception as it seeks to face the evils in human life. It therefore refuses to accept as an ally in its effort to free men from fear and deceit that which is a deliberate dodge around them. Religion moves through truth and confidence in truth rather than through the encouragement of a habit which begins by weakening and finally paralyzing all regard for truth, honor, integrity, and common decency.

IV

For all these reasons, the Christian Church as a social institution, committed to the achievement of the abundant life for all men, includes in her legitimate concern for all serious human problems the problem of drinking.

We have a right to be concerned about the sick—and drinking is related to mental, physical, and social disease. We have a right to be concerned about the poor—and drinking is intimately related to much of the poverty in the land. We have a right to be concerned about disillusionment—and disillusionment runs rife, and many seek courage by means of drink. We have a right to be concerned about the criminal—and drinking is related to the extent and type of crimes actually being committed today. We have a right to be concerned about broken homes—and drinking is a prolific cause of domestic unhappiness and catastrophe. We have a right to be concerned with any business which systematically educates our children for vice—and the liquor business does just that! Therefore, we say to those who might wish us to keep silent on matters like these: Drinking, seen through the eyes of what it does to men, is a religious problem of major magnitude; we therefore call upon our people, individually and collectively, to face it as a major personal and social problem.

We call upon Christian people to pay renewed attention to the dangerous practice of drinking—yes, even occasional drinking. We ought to see that there is a kind of ladder of degradation involved in what we sometimes brightly call "social drinking." The first step is occasional drinking, the second is habitual drinking, and the last is the inability to control one's self—or acute alcoholism. Naturally enough, not all occasional drinkers become habitual drinkers, nor do all habitual drinkers become drunkards.

But it is a matter of hard fact that all drunkards begin as occasional drinkers; then become habitual drinkers before finally losing control of their life. I am not saying that all occasional drinkers wind up as drunkards, but I am saying that all who become acute alcoholics begin as occasional drinkers. I am saying, furthermore, that we must be willing to face this fact in full seriousness if we are going to do anything constructive about it. I am persuaded that it is the duty of the Church to call to the attention of her people the moral and religious significance of this problem. To the extent that we are able to do this we may be able to make some kind of creative beginning.

If this is to mean anything at all in a realistic way, it must begin with a personal avowal that we will break with this whole business of drinking—and break clean. I have admired the way the president of one of our great universities did this when he stepped into the presidency. He said, "I do not propose to try to control the total life of this university, but I will make this personal statement that never in my own home nor in any function of this university for which I have any responsibility will liquor be served." I am not saying that it is not being served in various places in that university community, but I am saying that, so far as this man's personal influence and position are concerned, he has made his witness, and it is a strong one. For us to oppose drinking means that we will use our influence to discourage the habit among others. It means that we will help people instead of weaken them when they are trying to avoid this pernicious evil of social drinking. It means that we will strengthen them in their determination rather than weaken them by ridicule—as so frequently happens. It means that we will help with every means at our disposal those who are in the grip of the habit—and keep on helping until they win a complete victory.

I should like, in this connection, to pay my personal regards to the fine work being done by that organization called Alcoholics Anonymous. They are willing to go to help anyone who is in need and help as long as they can be of assistance. It is one of the finest examples of mutual aid I know anything about. I should like to believe that it is possible for me to turn to anyone in this congregation and ask you, too, to extend a helping hand to someone who needs your encouragement and help in this matter of the struggle to break the drink habit. Actually, of course, there can be no effective social witness against the evils of drink unless we both renounce it ourselves and are willing to stand by those who are having a battle with it and help them in every way that we can.

Collectively, there are a number of things we can do. We can see to it that there is a clear witness against it in our own homes. There is no reason for our children to be in doubt as to what we think and why we think as we do about this matter. The practice of our homes ought to be to confront our children with a clear witness against the evils of it—a witness that is incarnate in our own behavior. We ought to encourage our schools to broaden and intensify their already splendid educational program on the nature and meaning of alcohol and its use. It goes without saying that in our church school program there ought to be steady and effective units of education on matters like these.

When I look over a community like Evanston, I could wish that our businessmen particularly in our service clubs, composed as they are of business and professional people, would come more alive than they now are on this matter and do it with a clear-sighted intelligence and persistence that will cultivate and deepen respect for the provisions already in existence in this city for the regulation and the control of liquor traffic. The number of people who are willing to laugh out of the corner of their mouths at the effort on the part of our city to establish some kind of control is one of the more discouraging phases of trying to maintain present community regulations here in Evanston. When Jack Lait and Lee Mortimer were writing their self-advertised "cheeky, impudent, uncensored, shocking account of that fast, fabulous and fascinating city" of Chicago they were forced to dismiss Evanston with a few dreary phrases: "Evanston is the stately seat of Northwestern University and the cradle and the home of the Women's Christian Temperance Union. Prohibition was invented there. Evanston has always been arid, and its municipal government sternly means business." Therefore, they conclude, if you want to indulge in a "high good time," stay away from Evanston. If the citizens of this community actually "meant business" in terms of their own personal habits and in their own homes on this matter, it would be easier to believe that our municipal laws and government could mean business in community life. This manifestly is a matter of genuine concern to all who live here—not just to the police.

This is the proper time to record my own feeling that the control of the liquor problem is not primarily a matter of law. Law enters in—but the actual control and management of it does not begin there. The social control of drinking can better come *from within the organization or the community than from the outside through law enforcement.* It is easier and far better for a fraternity or a sorority, for example to control the problem by group morale from within than it is for the university to attempt to control it from the outside. The most and the best the university can do will not be enough—that we know. The same thing is true of the larger community in which we live. While laws are necessary for the regulation of the liquor traffic, it is important for us to realize that there is no way you can put a law on the law books that will take the place and do the work of personal resolution and will, that will do the job of an aroused social conscience within a group. Law cannot do what these alone can do.

Which is a way of saying that the religious approach to the problem posed by drinking requires of every individual and every group that it accept the seriousness of this issue, that we stop bypassing it and trying to make light of it, that we recognize it for the serious threat it is to personal and social morale in life; that, as churchmen, we must address ourselves to this threat to the personal and social welfare of ourselves and our people.

We shall be poor interpreters of the Christian life if we permit ourselves to be maneuvered into a position of silence by jeering cartoonists and other caricatures of our position. Christian men and women and Christian institutions have, in the life and teachings of our Lord, a standard of what we believe constitutes the abundant life. That standard means that we shall seek to bring the abilities of individuals and groups to their maximum and not cut them down or cripple them in any way, shape, or form. We know that although we are not good witnesses to our faith in this abundant life, we are nonetheless called upon to do so. There is no place in the Christian witness for the acute and progressive degradation of the human personality, for the cheapening of human relationships that are inseparably related to this whole business of drinking. For us to refuse to lift our voice against it for whatever reason, is to forswear the right to stand out boldly against any other social evil. We want to challenge it—in our own personal living, in our own homes, in our churches and schools, in our communities—challenge it because we believe that there is such a thing as the abundant life, and because we are opposed—unalterably opposed—to whatever cheapens or cripples or destroys the human personality.

XIV

Who Owns This Earth Anyway?[1]

SCRIPTURE LESSON: Matthew 25:14–30

I

IF YOU are a lover of stories about Abraham Lincoln as I am, you
have encountered the incident of the interrupted conversation he
was having with a friend in his own home. Two of his boys had
fallen afoul each other upstairs, as boys will do, and the quarrel
had become so loud that the guest finally asked, "What's the
matter with those boys?" Lincoln replied, "Only what's wrong
with the whole world. There are three chestnuts and two boys;
they're fighting over the odd chestnut."

In his penetrating way, Lincoln was describing much more than
the difficulty his two boys were having. He was calling attention
to one of the oldest and most difficult problems men must face,
the problem of the meaning of ownership, of possession of property. This, unfortunately, has not been an academic concern
through the ages. It has drenched the earth with bloodshed as far
back as our records go. Men have fought about every conceivable
kind of property—their land, cities, and nations, their temples,
homes, rights, and persons. Indian tribes in the early days of this
country used to fight over the salt springs in the South Central
States, and they fought just as savagely as modern nations now
fight over rubber plantations, tin mines, and oil fields. The only
difference is that this practice of collision over property is now
on a world scale and we have a far greater ability to harm one
another than we have ever had before.

A wise student of the twentieth century once remarked that the
basic problem of our day is the meaning of ownership, of property. The economists, political scientists, and jurists who are
specialists in this field know it to be true. They have filled li-

[1] This sermon was preached January 27, 1952.

155

braries with their answers to the problem. Not answer, but answers—pluralized and frequently highly contradictory answers —that is what we find in these libraries. And as I go through them and pull book after book off the shelf, spending some time with them, I get the depressing conviction that if we were to put clubs in the hands of the theories and sometimes the theorists, they would beat one another's brains out before our very eyes. I cannot say I blame them for taking themselves seriously in this matter. The whole world is watching them, scrutinizing everything they do and say and write, whether in books or in articles. What they say is studied not only line by line but in these days between the lines. The hardest spot to fill and the hottest spot to occupy in college and university faculties now is just anywhere in the field of economics or political theory. Let a man veer a little to the left and he is set upon as a radical, a socialist, and a communist. Let him veer a little to the right, and he is denounced as a fascist and a reactionary. Let him hold firmly to the center and he is spat upon by both sides as a Caspar Milquetoast sort of fellow who cannot make up his mind, who wants it both ways, who wants to have his cake and eat it. Thus the war rages in the libraries of the scholars as well as throughout the whole of life on this matter of ownership and property.

Religion is no spectator in this or any other area of human conflict. She is a participant. She participates because she belongs where people are troubled in mind, in spirit, or in human relationships. She has been a participant in struggles like these from the beginning of her historic career. I cannot claim that she has been welcomed by other combatants in such conflicts. She does not take their separate sides quite as readily or as freely as they think she should. They are human enough to want her support; also human enough not to relish her criticism. It seems to me that it is high time we had a fresh go at this business of the meaning of ownership and property, yet it is awfully difficult to do it. But the issue presses in upon us so sharply these days that we must make the effort. When we claim that religion does offer a fresh approach to the problem of ownership we are not calling it a new one. Rather, it is fresh in the exact sense that we have not been willing to take it seriously as yet. We have tried every other approach and they have led us to our present plight. Sensible people see this and are now asking whether or not there may be another angle on this business of ownership and property that may put it in a manageable perspective, lest we find ourselves opening the arteries of civilization in our conflicts over this matter. Religion has much to say, both directly and indirectly, about the proper approach to the meaning of ownership and property. In fact, I am inclined to urge the point that she has so much to say and that it is so vital that specialists in political science and economics and law will want to recast their answers if they should take seriously the religious approach to the subject.

Let this be said at once and never forgotten: *Religion's approach is born of human experience.* What it has to say is guaranteed to make all of us re-examine our thinking on this matter. And if we are not prepared to re-examine our thinking in the light of religious insight we are not prepared to have religion help in the resolution of these difficulties. Religion's contribution can be summed up in two tremendous statements taken from the Scriptures, one from the Old and the other from the New Testament: the first, the twenty-fourth Psalm; and the second, the parable of the talents.

II

The writer of the twenty-fourth Psalm unrolled a cosmic canvas before our very eyes when he said in no uncertain terms, "The earth is the Lord's and the fullness [or the fruit] thereof, the world, and they that dwell therein." God is the only real owner in this universe. The earth is His; it belongs to Him. We belong to Him. We are the sheep of His pastures, the people of His hand. The earth is the Lord's by right of creation, by right of maintenance through His law, by right of redemption through His chosen people and, later, through His son, who brings His holy will into historic reality. Thus reasons the Psalmist and later the Christian, who is wrestling with the proper approach to life itself.

It is against this background of the ownership of all the earth by God Himself that the prophets of ancient Israel approached the kings, princes, and priests of their day. What they said was simply this: Whatever power, whatever ability we have we hold in trust from God. Who can measure the difference this approach makes, if taken seriously? Nor was this enormous difference lost on the hearers of the prophets! For political leaders in that day— as in our own—liked to think that somehow or other they were laws unto themselves. Hitler, Mussolini, and Stalin did not invent the notion that the state or the social order is an absolute good in the universe. That is an ancient delusion, and the prophets of ancient Israel challenged it in the light of the claim that God owns all. For, if God owns all, then the prince must submit to God, and account for his stewardship to the God of the universe. If God owns all, then men of property must be prepared to submit to the God of the universe a full bill of particulars in terms of their dealings with all God has entrusted to them. Let a king forget for one moment that he is answerable to God, and he will play the tyrant every time. Let him realize that he is answerable to God for his power and the use he makes of it and he is likely to deal honorably, considerately, and in a spirit of freedom with his people.

Amos, for example, saw that a property holder without a due sense of God's ownership of life and possession would soon find himself in a situation where he would be willing to sell a poor man for a piece of silver. Amos saw that if a property holder is keenly aware of the fact that he is the steward of his property in the sight of God in whose sight all men are precious, he will never sell a poor man, or anyone else, for a piece of silver because life is infinitely more valuable than any other kind of property he could conceivably have. Isaiah, studying his day, saw that people were trying to run their lives and affairs as a nation without reference to the will of God, and he raised this ominous warning: "Seek ye the Lord while he may be found, call ye upon him while he is near." This old prophetic refrain was not particularly welcome then, nor has it been since. But it is an inevitable refrain if you believe that God owns the earth, and that all who live on this earth are stewards of the trust He gives them.

No one saw so deeply into or grasped so firmly the total meaning of the divine ownership of earth and life as did Jesus Christ in his parable of the talents. You recall how the owner of the property gave three servants various talents, one five, another two, and the third one. Telling them to take care of these to the best ability, he went on a far journey. While he was away, the man with five talents made five, the man with two made two, and the man with one buried it. When the owner returned, he rewarded the first two and condemned the third.

The parable is susceptible of many interpretations, only one of which concerns us just now. *The talents belonged to their owner all the time.* He had them on call whenever he chose. He had merely loaned them for use or misuse to the three stewards. Whether a man got five talents or two talents or one talent, he was answerable to the one who owned them all along. The question before the stewards was not, "Who owns these talents?" They knew the answer to that. The only question before them was, "To what use shall I put the talent which has been entrusted to me?"

Study life in the light of this parable for a moment and we come up with three conclusions that strike home to our property-conscious generation:

1. Everything we say we own, we actually share with others, that much is clear. We share our possessions with our fathers before us, our neighbors round about us, our children who are to come after us, and the God who reigns over us all.
2. We must live in terms of this multiple responsibility if we are to live wisely and well.
3. We are stewards before God of all that we have.

What a difference that parable makes throughout life if we take it seriously! Note some of them for a moment. We like to say this life is mine; I'm my own boss. As I heard one young man dreaming of some great gift he wanted the future to bring, he said, "I want the time to come when I can be my own boss." It is easy to appreciate something of what was going through his mind as he said that. But you wonder whether anywhere on this earth or anytime in this life or even in the life to come you are ever your own boss. The whole earth belongs to God. Life belongs to God. The use we make of our life as we live from day to day is a use that is paraded as on a stage before God Himself. Our bodies, our minds, our spirits, our relationships, everything we are pleased in a moment of absent-mindedness to call our own actually belongs to God. Take out of our own life what we share with others, and what is left would not be worth a plugged penny. Point to something that is literally your own: your own creation, your own to enjoy and to share with no one else. If you can find anything like that in life, it isn't even worth talking about, much less fighting over. God, the Creator of life, put it together in such fashion that we share it with others, that there is nothing worth while that isn't shared in some significant way with others, that there is no such thing as worth or meaning in life that does not grow out of a shared relationship with someone else. When we say we want to reach a time when we are our own boss we are looking for a time that will never come on this earth or in any kind of heaven ever foreseen by saint or seer.

III

The apostle Paul put his finger on the right word when he said we are "stewards of the mystery of life." Stewards of the mystery of this life that God has given us in this day in which we live, enriched by the relationships we have with all other people—there you have it. *We are stewards!* We can be bad stewards, or we can be good stewards of this life we have. We are all of us such poor stewards upon so many occasions that it does not behoove us to point a finger of blame at anyone else in particular, but you cannot read the biography of John Barrymore written by his friend, Gene Fowler, *Good Night, Sweet Prince,* without realizing that you are holding more than a book: *you are holding the chronicle of a wasted life.* Given five talents in the art of dramatic interpretation, here was a man who wasted his talents. Not just one talent buried, but five thrown away as only a prodigal steward could waste the life and ability that God gave him. The really big question we face is not whether we have five or two or one talent. The big question is whether we are good stewards of what has been given.

The stewardship of life means the stewardship of the limitations and handicaps which come the way of all in some form or other. It is far from easy to be *stewards of the handicaps* that do come our way. Whenever I think along this line I am reminded of William James, one of the greatest teachers ever to grace the halls of Harvard. Never robust, he had to guard his health with the greatest of care at all times. Yet William James occupied the chair of Professor of Philosophy at Harvard and went about his work with great gusto. In order to do this he kept in close touch with his doctor. The doctor kept a careful eye on the way he was using his energy. James said, "Tell me how to do it and I'll obey." The doctor began by saying, "Don't spend more than two hours a day at intensive reflection." After a few years, James complained of headaches and returned to the physician. The doctor said, "We must cut the work down to an hour a day now." Down, down it came until finally he was able to give only fifteen minutes a day to his work. That was all the energy he had, but he was a good steward of it. He played fair with the handicap from which he could not escape. Sometimes the complaints made by people who are delayed as much as ten minutes by a bus make one wonder if the universe is toppling because of their delay.

All too frequently we are not even good stewards of little inconveniences.

Many a time we have said or would like to say, "My time is my own." Not in a universe that is answerable to God, your time is not your own. Your time belongs to Him. Your days are in His hands and what you do, the way you invest your life must be invested as in His sight, as indeed it is. It is a sobering thing to realize with the poet, "I shall not pass this way again." Which is to say that there is something irrecoverable about every moment, every relationship, and every opportunity. Something irrecoverable in the sense that with the passage of time the doors open and close never to open again quite that way. True enough, other doors may open but the former ones are closed forever and locked by the key of time that only God can hold. Knowing all this, we continue to fritter away the days and the opportunities, humoring ourselves this way and that as though our time were our own. One of the hardest challenges of stewardship revolves around the wise use of time and opportunity. And there is no reason to think we can meet it in a satisfactory way unless we are guided daily by loyalty to a high standard of values in which first things have prior claim on our time and efforts.

How easy it is for us to say, "This is my business," or "This is my church." To people who talk this way, the Christian faith warns, "Nothing worth while is yours alone; you share it with others."

One of our weekly news magazines recently gave us a picture of that very stern young man, Mr. Henry Ford II. He looked competent and confident enough to carry the world on either one of his shoulders. And in an interview recorded in the magazine, it was quite clear that he regarded the company of which he is the head as "his" company, though not in the usual limited and personal meaning of "his." He could say, "This is my business," and point to the legal fact that he and his family hold the controlling interest in stock in the Ford Company. But the moment you start to investigate what that means, you ask yourself, "Could Mr. Ford by himself build one Ford car over the rest of his natural lifetime?" He would have to go to Venezuela to get the ore, and that would be quite a row in a canoe—after he made the canoe. He would need to go to Bolivia or over to the Far East to get tin—some of which they still use. He would need to dig the oil wells and refine the oil. He would need to design and make the dies and then mount and operate them. In short, he would have quite a job! You wonder whether he could make one Ford by himself throughout the rest of his natural lifetime, and in the spirit of generosity, you might give him two lifetimes. Whose business is the Ford Company? Everyone who has ever worked there! It is that vast network of all the people all over the earth who have shared somewhere or other in the creation and development of that gigantic enterprise that bears the name *Ford* and for which Mr. Henry Ford II bears responsibility. It is his in the sense that his is the tremendously crushing responsibility of stewardship for all who have been, all who now are, and all who will be involved in it one way or another over the years to come. They, too, are a part of the Ford Company; they are his responsibility. If a man wants to stand up and say, "This is my business," and mean all that, he has ceased to prate about ownership and he has begun to pray about stewardship. For that is the only significant meaning of ownership any more.

IV

We in the Christian tradition are called upon to be good stewards of this tradition. We who belong to this church have a right to look about us this morning and say, "This is my church." We have a right to rejoice in its beauty, in the storied line and color that give such eloquent expression to the deep meanings of our faith. It is a beautiful church. It was built over a long period of time. Even if we tried, we could not determine the number of people who have built a part of their life into it. The building of this church goes back through the ages to the beginning of human history—and many of man's deepest needs and aspirations have made these windows.

Yes, this is our church; most of us here this morning can claim little of the credit for it up to this point, but it is ours now. The whole tradition which built it is ours, too. The whole of the Jewish-Christian tradition that seeks expression in human life through this fellowship is ours. Every human hope that men built into it, every prayer that has been said here, every great insight that has ever been expressed here—they are all ours, and we are stewards before God of it all. Like the servants in the parable, we are either good or bad stewards. As good stewards we take this church with a sense of our infinite obligation to the men and the women who preceded us and the ones who share now with us in the discharge of this responsibility and pass it on to our children who will come after us enriched by what we do; or, as poor stewards, we treat the church as an optional opportunity which we can pick up or lay down, which we can invest or bury, which we can nurture or dissipate at will. All too many of us think we can play fast and loose with our responsibility for the church. Instead of thanking God for the richness of our religious tradition and for the existence of this lovely sanctuary in which we may worship and work and train our children to love God, all too many of us assume or appear to assume that somehow or other the church just got built and maintained, and that, somehow, it will continue. At least we hope so—even though we propose to have very little to do with meeting the problems which the church faces today.

When I consider that there are six hundred million people in this world today who bear the name *Christian* and realize that this world is on the brink of hell itself, I am driven to the conclusion that we have had a lot of poor stewards in this Christian tradition. We have received insights from the Bible which should have transformed life for all men as they did for a handful of disciples two thousand years ago. We have fought against the full meaning of those insights from the very beginning of our own Christian experience. We have wanted them close enough to gain comfort from them and find strength in them when we have needed comfort and strength, but we would not let them into the innermost part of our life as a new life and a new way for us. Close, but not too close; near, but not too near; powerful, but not too powerful—that is the way we have wanted it.

We know now that it won't work that way. Time and history have caught up with us. We are either going to be good stewards of the luminous light of the will of God that bursts into our midst in Jesus Christ, or we are going to be bad stewards, and we and our children after us will pay the price of our bad stewardship. We must answer to God and indeed, we are answering to Him all along for the talents He has given us: For the life, for the opportunities, for our relationships with other people, for our religious tradition.

V

We are free to invest our talent or bury it; that is true. But we are not free to escape a judgment on what we do. And for the simple fact that all life and all action finally belongs to God. All opportunities belong to Him and are treasured by Him. That makes of life what religion has said all along it was—it is sacramental. In it there is nothing common or unclean. Life is sacred, and the living of it ought to be regarded as a sacred trust. The possessions we have are opportunities for service. Success is defined in terms of the stewardship we render others, not in terms of the service they render us. Henry Ward Beecher was right when he said, "This world is God's workshop for making men." And as you wonder what kind of man He is making of your life, you come to the sobering realization that He is not doing half with it that He could if you would co-operate with Him! What couldn't God do with the world if six hundred million Christians acted like good stewards of His!

Yet life is a stewardship in freedom where God cannot force Himself upon us. It is a matter of choice, but God stands before us as both the inevitable Companion and the inescapable Conclusion that must be faced. He is not simply standing at the end of our life; He is standing at the terminal of each moment and each opportunity and each relationship. And as a result of how we spend and use these, our life is either richer or poorer and mankind is the richer or poorer for our having lived. The most devastating moment in life is when we realize that we have been poor stewards of it. When that realization burst upon Satan in Milton's *Paradise Lost*, he cried, "Myself am hell." But when we feel that we have earnestly tried to be good stewards as we understand this responsibility, there comes the peace of mind, a confidence in ourselves and others which can only be expressed in the words of the Master, "Thou hast been faithful over a little." Whether it is five talents or two talents or one talent that we have, it is still only a little when considered against God's total richness! It is not the amount we have entrusted to us that counts in God's economy; it is how we take care of it. Good stewardship is the glory of life. Christian stewardship is the crowning glory of the Christian life. He that is faithful in a little looks forward not to that which is less and that which finally ends, but looks forward to that which grows and becomes more and more until finally the greatest of all is given—fellowship with the Living God.

XV

The Christian Faith and Economic Problems[1]

SCRIPTURE LESSON: Jeremiah 7:1–7; 31:31–34

I

UNDERLYING the different denominational and sectarian formulations of the Christian faith here represented is an essential unity in the conviction that in Jesus Christ we have our clearest revelation of the will of God for the life of man. Underlying the many specific problems which will engage our time and attention, and tax our wits, if not our charity, is the permanently important problem of the relevance of the Christian faith which we profess to the social problems which we confront. However much we may disagree on the nature and meaning of an "applied Christianity"—and one of the most stimulating and rewarding aspects of a conference like this is just that variety of opinion and insight—we are one in the conviction that the Christian faith is not only relevant to social problems but, further, that it is our clear responsibility to explore and describe as best we can the way in which this relationship can be declared most fruitfully.

That this task is going to be difficult goes without saying. That it involves us immediately and on to the end in some of the most complex problems of our day is obvious. As we gird ourselves for the journey we may find some comfort in a conversation Daniel Boone had with a fellow townsman when the great scout had returned from a six-months' trip in the wilderness. The

[1] Given at the opening worship service of the National Study Conference on the Church and Economic Life in Detroit, Michigan, February 16-19, 1950. This conference was convened by the Federal Council of the Churches of Christ in America.

165

townsman asked, "Daniel, did you ever get lost?" "No," said Daniel, "I never got lost, but I was puzzled once for three days." I strongly suspect that we too are going to be puzzled for about three days! Yet I am sure none of us is unduly alarmed at that prospect. We share Bishop Francis J. McConnell's sturdy conviction, once expressed to some young men going into the ministry, "If you want to drown, don't do it in a mud puddle. Get out where the water is deep!" One look at our Conference agenda reminds me of nothing so much as the deep blue waters of the broad Pacific—yet sail them we must, and drown in them we may!

Let us, then, recall to the forefront of our consciousness as we enter upon this task the convictions which underlie our differences, making us truly one:

We are here to celebrate our common faith in Jesus Christ as one in whose life and teachings we find our clearest revelation of the will of God for the life of man.

We are here to commit ourselves to the task of trying to find our way in God's will as revealed in Jesus Christ.

We are here to articulate our Christian faith and commitment in terms of a realistic concern for the concrete problems that must be faced in one of the most disturbed areas of our world—Modern Industrialism. We are dedicated to the task of trying to bring about the redemption of our life by the proclamation and, as best we know how, the implementation of the Christian gospel of salvation.

II

A major conference devoted to the study of the relationships between the Church and industry is a relatively recent development. And new developments ought to be willing to present their intellectual passports to any who may be doubtful or critical of the project. This, in a sentence, is what I should like to try to do in this service. And do it by finding and stating our purpose in terms of the deepest questions, uttered or unexpressed, of friend and critic alike. I can only hope that the necessity for brevity will help explain and perhaps mitigate not only the speed with which we move from one point to another, but also the seemingly dogmatic, if not truculent, spirit in some of the utterances.

As nearly as I can determine, the doubts and criticisms to

which we are subject revolve around one or more of these questions: (1) On whose authority do you meet? (2) By what right does the Church concern herself with the problems of industrialism? (3) To what end do you seek to move our common thought and life in these matters? All of these are honest questions and deserve an honest attempt at answer—one which we should make gladly.

III

We might content ourselves by saying: on the authority of the Federal Council of Churches, or of our respective churches—yet I am certain a deeper answer is both possible and necessary. It is suggested by something that happened when Gandhi visited England in the late twenties. Some of the papers in England called attention to the fact that he held no official position in the Indian government and asked, "On whose authority does he come?" Gandhi never missed that kind of opportunity and replied, "I come clothed with authority—the authority of the needs of my people."

We are asked, "On whose authority do you meet?" And we make answer:

We come here clothed with authority—*the authority of the living God*, the Creator, Sustainer, and Redeemer of the world in whom we live and move and have our being, and who seeks today as of old the welfare of His children. The God who spoke to Moses saying, "Come now, therefore, and I will send thee unto Pharoah, that thou mayest bring forth my people the children of Israel out of Egypt"; the God who spoke to Israel through Amos saying, "Let judgment run down as waters and righteousness as a mighty stream"; the God who spoke to Judah through Isaiah asking, "What mean ye that ye beat my people to pieces, and grind the faces of the poor?" The God of the probing ethical conscience of ancient Israel is seeking to speak to the troubled heart and life of mankind today through people neither better nor wiser than we are—and we meet here clothed in his authority.

We are here not by permission of men but by commission of God—the God whom we meet in transcendent glory in the New Testament; who seeks the welfare of all of His children even as a shepherd searches for one lost sheep or a father for one lost son; whose nature is love and "who so loved the world that he gave his only begotten Son, that whosoever believeth in him should not perish, but have everlasting life"; who commissioned His followers to go to the ends of the earth making disciples of all men.

We come here clothed with *the authority of the evolving ethical conscience of the Christian tradition* through nearly two thousand years of history. Without claiming for one moment that all has been well with the Church through the centuries, the plain fact remains that she has rendered an incalculable contribution to human welfare and well-being both in the living of life here and in the anticipation of the life to come. Schools, hospitals, asylums, orphanages, and churches—these are some of the creatures of the maturing ethical conscience of the Christian faith. Practice after practice—slavery, infanticide, racism, nationalism, and war—have been brought before the bar of Christian judgment and pronounced evil. Whenever, wherever, and for whatever reason the health of the bodies, minds, and spirits of men is endangered either by injustice, misunderstanding, or fratricidal conflict—there we have not only a clear duty but also an unassailable mandate both to be present and to be present as ministers of the living God.

IV

We are asked, "By what right does the Church concern herself with the problems of industrialism?" And we answer in the most uncompromising manner: By right of the plain fact that the whole range of life belongs to God. Nothing human is alien to Him, nor can it be to us. Gone is the day when churchmen would permit themselves to be either shoved unceremoniously or bowed politely out of any area where human values, human relationships, and human lives are at stake. The Church is involved all along the line in every major problem of industry, since the Church is composed of the men and women in the management, labor, and consumer groups. Whatever affects them—any of them—affects the Church, and the Church has the right and the duty to take serious cognizance of the situation. Whoever argues otherwise would say, in effect, that a hole in the hull of a sinking ship is the concern of the captain and the crew but not of the passengers!

A further, and more affirmative, answer to the question is this, "The Church concerns herself with the problems of industrialism because she is needed there. She has a contribution to make apart from which the problems of modern industry cannot be solved."

In a volume of his *Study of History* published before 1939, Professor Arnold Toynbee says that "industrialism" and "democracy" are the two distinctive characteristics of modern civilization. Both are in grave trouble just now, and it is an open question whether either can survive. As a matter of fact, Dr. Toynbee argues that the basic conflict in the modern world is between industrialism on the one hand and democracy on the other.

The case as he develops it proceeds something like this: The needs of modern industry created huge pools of workers in cities. In its early days, industry was the personal property of one man or of a few men at most. It was essentially feudal in its pattern of power and responsibility. Owners were laws unto themselves in policies of purchase and sale of goods, as well as in the hours, conditions, and wages of labor. Understandably, the ferment of democracy which over two centuries had overthrown the doctrine of the divine right of kings and the absolute monarchies of Europe, placing the right of franchise in the hands of citizens, produced movements for greater freedom, dignity, and security among workingmen. It is difficult to see how the leaven of democracy could have been prevented from working in the field of industry. The logic of democracy is inexorable: each man is the bearer of infinite worth because he is the child of God; each man is entitled to a voice in the determination of the laws under which he lives and the selection of the government which is to administer the laws; each man is entitled to a voice in the determination of the policies, the life, and the structure of the industry on which he is dependent for his livelihood. Until and unless we can find some way of compartmentalizing ideas, thus restraining the meaning of democracy to the area of citizenship, it will keep right on challenging any and every allocation of power beyond the reach of the persons affected by the use of that power.

In these latter days, both industrialism and democracy have been and are being challenged by various forms of fascism and communism which, if successful, will alter them beyond recognition. So the problems we face in the field we must study at this conference are all tangled up with history, politics, international events, and policies. Emerging from the many problems in detail are certain problems in principle—and these are now under discussion and dispute. They might be phrased this way: (1) the democratizing of power; (2) social stability through social change; and (3) personal and group freedom in community. To one who challenges our right to consider problems like these arising as they do in the field of industry, we say that the Christian faith is prepared to make a contribution to the solution of these problems apart from which they cannot be solved. And that contribution lies in both the end to be sought and the reason why we seek it.

V

In answer to the query, "To what end do you seek to move our common thought and life in these matters?" we must say, at the risk of triteness, "Toward the Kingdom of God." That is the goal, the end, the ultimate purpose of the Christian Church because it is the ultimate aim of the will of God as found in Jesus Christ. That is the banner under which the Christian Church enters this and every other area of human conflict. Justice, security, peace, and community—the importance of these nearer goals should not be minimized. Yet the most certain way for the Christian faith to minimize them is to wrench them out of the context from which they derive their final validation, i.e., the concept of the Kingdom of God. We do not dishonor them by putting the Kingdom of God first; rather we thereby supply the frame of reference in terms of which they find the widest possible scope of meaning. Separate them from the idea of the Kingdom of God and they become prudential instruments for the removal of conflict without any affirmative convictions about the nature of the life that will result. The question "Why seek justice?" could be answered, "To remove conflict and injustice." But a persistent skeptic will want to know, "Why remove conflict and injustice?" Without a further affirmative notion as to what life ought to be like, there is no real answer to that. With the idea of the Kingdom of God in mind, a final answer can be given.

While we are not able to produce a set of blueprints for realizing the Kingdom of God in human life, we may make certain general statements about its nature that will indicate its relevance to our life and history.

First, it is God's Kingdom, the condition in which His will is owned and obeyed. Nor are we wholly in the dark as to what His will is. Certain beliefs about the nature of God have finally won their way to general acceptance in the Christian tradition. The idea that God is love is probably the most fundamental one and, with it as background, we find it easy to understand a very realistic conclusion which William Temple found in it: "The Kingdom of God is the sovereignty of love, and the subordination of power to love is the principle of that Kingdom." To believe in love as the true order of reality, to feel its power toward oneness is to live in the Kingdom of God even now. The Sermon on the Mount is no tract for Utopia; it is a series of simple declarative statements about the meaning of full citizenship in the Kingdom of God.

A second statement about the Kingdom of God is this: it reminds us that all our plans, policies, institutions, and creations must finally square with the fact of God—or perish. History is not morally neutral. The Kingdom of God is both within us and within history as guide and judge. The Kingdom of God is not a "far-off" day toward which the whole creation moves"; it is a reality—in part actual, in part potential—in human life and history. Hence, the Christian faith insists that the question, "Does this proposal or practice or institution square with the meaning of the Kingdom of God?" is not only the one ultimately important question, but it is also the most immediately relevant one as well.

It adds up to this: the Christian faith insists that what we do we ought to do for God's sake and for the sake of His Kingdom. The Christian faith is not primarily concerned with the preservation of democracy, of the American way of life, of free enterprise, of capitalism—even *laissez-faire* capitalism—of unionism, of the white race, of the Protestant, or of the Catholic Church. It is or ought to be characterized by humble devotion to the petition: "Thy Kingdom come, thy will be done on earth as it is in heaven." And if in the actualization of that will, even cherished national or cultural or social conventions and practices need to be altered if not abandoned, so be it—let His will be done.

Study the notion of the Kingdom of God for a moment and you see two great centers of confidence emerging from it: God can be depended upon, and man, under God, can be depended upon. We are not trying to build bricks without straw when we try to build the Kingdom of God with and of men neither better nor wiser than we are. There is an essential core of dependability and reliability about man, the child of God, and upon this we can and must rely. Indeed, no new answer is possible to the problems we face if we act on any other assumption. On any other assumption—democracy is a mockery; community is a fool's paradise; and a world of justice, peace, and security is a myth.

Believing as we do in God, in the activity of God in life and history, and in man, under God, we are able to say without hesitation that the end we seek is the fuller discovery and more perfect realization of the Kingdom of God in our common life and history. We approach the problems of industry, or racial relations, or denominational relations, or international relations with this end and only this end in view. It and it alone can be given our supreme loyalty. I repeat: We are not here *primarily* to make modern industrialism or capitalism or socialism or labor unionism work—we are here primarily to bring this entire troubled area in the life of mankind before the judgment bar of the Kingdom of God. To the extent that we are able honestly and humbly to do this we will have made a supreme effort to separate the better from the worse in each and to preserve the better. But, let it be known, the judgments "better and worse" derive from the nature and reality of the Kingdom of God and not from any other standard or reality.

To the extent that we are able to let the logic of the Christian faith control us, we shall neither be surprised nor appalled at the certainty that deep-lying changes in our social order must be consciously and persistently sought in order that the Kingdom of God may come. We shall confront the confusion of our times confident that it can be brought to a stable order if we are able to discover the meaning of the Kingdom of God in its disorder.

VI

When Jesus came teaching and preaching and living the convictions that (1) God is the supreme fact in life and the world; (2) all men are His children; (3) life is a divine trust and all living is a dealing with God, He unfurled a banner of salvation that has quickened the pulse and exalted the lives of men ever since. For these convictions are not so much ideas to be weighed as paths to be followed. If we follow them to their end, we shall find ourselves in possession of a far different view of life and history than we now have, and, what is immeasurably more difficult, under the compulsion to be instruments of the redemptive will of God as He seeks to transform the world from what it is to what it ought to be.

No one knew better than Jesus that these convictions pre-figured the complete transformation of life and history. To take them seriously is to become a new creature in Christ. Difficult as it is to live with them, we are finding life without them liter-ally impossible. We are learning the hard way that unless life is treated as a divine trust the human situation rapidly becomes intolerable. Treat other persons, or races, or nations as means to your end, as instruments in purposes that serve your own wel-fare, and you, to the extent that you are successful, have made revolution inevitable. Yet the illusions nourished by power, wealth, and position continue to darken our perception of this fact. Military power is such an impressive fact that in the day of confusion or uncertainty men turn to it as a kind of guarantor of security. We read the judgment of a military analyst: "We are the masters of our fate." We hear the judgment of a news com-mentator on world affairs: "History is what men make it. If we do not choose to get out and make it what we want, at whatever cost, it is going to be made for us by other men who are willing to work at it."

Such counsels are more than futile, they are fatal. To say that history is what we make it is to utter a most dangerous half-truth; the full version of which is this: History is what God per-mits us to make it. It is the scene of our dealings with God and His with us. It is true that we are free to try to build any kind of social order we choose; but the validity of our plan and the permanence of our building are determined by a Power entirely beyond our control. James Anthony Froude, after a lifetime spent in the study of history, bears this impressive witness: "One lesson and only one, history may be said to repeat with distinct-ness; that the world is built somehow on moral foundations; that in the long run it is well with the good; in the long run it is ill with the wicked."

Almost from the beginning of his ministry, Jesus sensed the costliness of such convictions. The transformation of life and history plainly implicit in them could not be accomplished by verbal proclamation of them; they had to "come alive," to be-come incarnate in the lives of men and in history before they could become the way of salvation. He made it clear that one could know the vocabulary of religion, could say, "Lord, Lord," yet not know or be known by its transforming power. Looking back upon the faith of Jesus as he went among his fellows and on the fate they meted out to him, Paul counseled his hearers to remember, "Ye are bought with a price." The Cross became the symbol not alone of the fate of Jesus but of the price which any man who follows him must be prepared to pay. Whether the gospel of salvation spreads slow or fast, every inch of advance is "bought with a price"—that is the unqualified testimony of nineteen hundred years of Christian history.

Confronted by our frailty and fallibility, it is small wonder that we, like Jeremiah, shrink from the task of proclaiming by lip and in life a gospel which clearly intends to bring life and history under the redemptive judgment and activity of the God of the universe, as revealed in Jesus Christ. Yet that is the clear meaning of marching under the banner of the Cross.

Ever since I first read it, I have been recommending C. S. Lewis' *Screwtape Letters* to my colleagues in the church. It is a collection of letters from Screwtape—an under-secretary in Hades —to one of his agents on earth, who is seeking his advice as to proper procedure in the effort to guarantee that a certain man will reach Hell safely. The earthly agent writes in great anxiety when his client joins a church, and asks, "Now what do we do?" Screwtape replies, in effect, "The situation is not as bad as you think; but you will need to proceed with great caution. Go with him whenever he goes to church, never leave his side, and always keep him aware of the little things; the squeak in the ushers' shoes, a misfit hat, some hypocrite or other. Keep him aware of the little things; don't let him see the church, with her banners flying—for that is the sight at which all Hell trembles."

We are here to make all Hell tremble!

XVI

The Moral Requirements of Public Leadership[1]

SCRIPTURE LESSON: Philippians 2:1–13

I

WHEN Paul counseled the Philippians "to work out your own salvation with fear and trembling," he, consciously enough, was stating the perennial task of religion and, all unconsciously, the watchword of democracy. John Philpot Curran was to give this watchword a memorable phrasing in his famous warning to Eighteenth century England: "Eternal vigilance is the price of liberty." Paul was talking about the salvation of the soul; Curran was talking about the salvation of a democratic state. Yet both perceived clearly the simple fact that the great ends of life are not won without persistent and responsible thought and work all along the line.

Difficult as it is for us to come to this conclusion, the plain truth seems to be that there is no place for panaceas—or magic cure-alls—either in religion or in government. Let a panacea get loose in the field of religion and a cult is born—to flourish vigorously for a while, then die. The roadway of religious history is dotted with the debris of tens of thousands of abortive efforts to work out some "quickie" solution to the profound and persistent problems of human life. Let a panacea get loose in the field of government and a tyranny, whether benevolent or malignant, is born—to flourish vigorously and tragically, for a while, then die. Students of political history are familiar with the great totalitarian states that have emerged in one form or another from the beginning of the human story. They flourish—or appear to

[1] This sermon was preached July 6, 1952.

175

flourish—in our own time with a new and terrible intensity. Although the most arresting samples of these political panaceas have taken root in other soil than our own, we are living in a fool's paradise if we think our soil is unfitted to their nourishment. If you saw it, you will never forget the motion picture *All the King's Men.* Nor can you forget that it actually happened here in America, at least in principle. There is something almost pathetic about the persistent belief and faith that men have, that there must be some short-cut, some easier way to the solution of human problems than that of long-range, patient, persistent effort.

Time and again brute facts grab our daydreams and short-cuts by the collar and remind us that we, too, must work out our own salvation in personal and social life with fear and trembling; that it is as true for us today as it was for eighteenth century England that "eternal vigilance is the price of liberty." Since the Christian faith is concerned with the whole range of human life there is a natural and unforced relationship between the Christian Church and the whole range of human problems that we face today. She approaches the problems of democracy with a concern born of her love for God and man, and her conviction that we are called upon to build as best we can the Kingdom of God in our common life. While the Church must seek to live in terms of the social and political patterns in which her lot is cast, she cannot be content with any of them. She must be studying at all times —and on peril of losing her sense of mission if she does not do it—the deep and abiding problems of the people to whom she ministers. That is one of the deepest reasons why the Christian Church in this country is concerned with the problem of democratic leadership. As Arthur Holt has so well put it, *"The modern church is working at the task of being influential in a social order which it does not desire to manipulate, but for which it feels a moral responsibility."*

It is in this spirit that the Christian Church approaches the problem of the moral requirements of public leadership. It is clear that there can be no long-range hope for a democracy unless we understand the peculiar meaning of both citizenship and leadership in a democracy. While it would be out of place for the Church to try to suggest the political machinery by which democracy should function, she is well within her role when she talks about the moral responsibilities that rest upon both citizen and leader alike if this form of government is to reach anything like its fulfillment in our common life. That is why it is of great importance, particularly in an election period, for the Christian Church to try to be influential in securing what she believes to be wise choices both of men and of policies. To do less would be tacitly to admit that we do not feel a moral responsibility for a realistic facing of the critical problems of the day in which we live. To the end, then, of discharging what seems to me to be the clear moral responsibility of our religious faith, I propose that we shall pay strict attention to the qualities of leadership which can make the most significant contribution to our common life and hope.

Right off, let it be stated and underscored that no leader can do all of the work for us who are citizens in a democracy. Also, no one leader can make or break a democracy as firmly rooted as ours in America. It will take a whole series of ruinous choices for us to undo the work of our forefathers, and no one with faith in democracy believes that most of the people will be fooled all of the time into letting their rights slip away.

But having said this the simple fact remains that leaders are very important in a democracy. Not only do they actually initiate many policies, but they symbolize the ideas and ideals of the citizenry of the country. In time of great crisis, like war and depression, we vote them enormous power and must trust them to use it wisely and return it to us intact when the crisis is over. It is therefore a matter of great importance when a democracy or a democratic organization chooses a leader. A healthy democracy and a democracy determined to maintain its health will measure any man who presents himself as a potential leader in public life against certain moral requirements. Though other institutions may be reluctant to press these requirements, it is the clear duty of the Church to do so. These requirements are not optional except as democracy itself is optional; they are determined by the very nature of democracy itself. They apply to all elections, all political parties, and to all men seeking public office. Four such requirements deserve our careful attention.

II

The leader we need is one whose word is his bond. Democracy is fundamentally a matter of faith in the collective wisdom of men over a long period of time. It could not be otherwise and live. It must make allowance for short-term mistakes due to ignorance and passion. Democracy is the one form of government which can admit mistakes and not destroy itself thereby. If one generation of Americans was unjust to the Indian, as they were, a later generation will recognize this and strive to make amends, as we are now doing. But always there is a fundamental faith in the long-time judgment and justice of the average citizen of this country. As Archibald MacLeish once put it: "Democracy is *belief in people*; not just some people, but *in all people*."

The basic institutions of a democracy lean heavily on this faith; they could not exist in their present form without it. Our schools, courts, banks, and our particular form of government by means of elected representatives simply assume this faith in the common citizen. Representative government requires that we finally entrust to our leaders the right to make decisions for us and in our name. Obviously they must appear before us and appeal for this precious right. In early American days they made their appeal at town meetings where it was a fairly simple matter for neighbors and friends to check their words and promises against their known character in community life and affairs. But their manner of appeal is and must be quite different now. Party platforms are drawn up; campaigns are waged; candidates speak at mass meetings and over radio and television; problems are discussed and solutions advanced for public consideration. All these are essential ways of encouraging the common citizen to have faith in the leadership of some man and some party *because he believes what they say, because he has faith in them and their public word*, and, therefore, gives to them one of his most precious rights— the right to speak in his name.

Under these conditions either a man's word is his bond or the whole machinery of democracy is disrupted. If a man says one thing, and does another, how far can you trust him in any sort of dealings? As citizens we have not only the right but actually the serious obligation to ask of any man who offers himself for public office whether his word is his bond, whether he can be trusted, whether he makes promises intending to keep them or intending simply to snare votes with them. If he has a long record in public life, we have the right to study that record with eagle eye and say publicly what we see.

To me, the most disturbing aspect in the life of American democracy today is the completely skeptical attitude of so many citizens toward the public utterances of political parties and candidates for the most important office in this country—the presidency. It is no new thing for us to be critical of men who

seek office; that is as old as democracy, and it is a thoroughly
healthy attitude. But that is not what I am referring to. I am
referring to the widespread decline of public confidence in the
spoken word of public officials. I am referring to the fact that
"Washington" is a synonym of mismanagement and the President
is unhesitatingly referred to by a rival, and many of his critical
friends, as "the cleverest politician and the worst President we
have ever had." The moral implications of such an attitude reach
far beyond the excuse of political expediency and strike a fatal
blow at the very nature of democracy itself. Democracy cannot
and will not long survive the collapse of public confidence in the
dignity of public office and in the integrity of its elected leadership.

As citizens we must indeed work out our own salvation with
fear and trembling in this matter. Nothing is more important for
the future of America than an immediate and determined effort
to restore confidence in the spoken word of public officials. Com-
pared to this task, the so-called issues in any campaign pale into
insignificance. We can survive, at great cost perhaps, mistakes
made on specific issues, but we cannot expect democracy to survive the growing conviction that the word of the elected leaders,
even of the President of these United States, cannot be trusted.

A second requirement of the leader we need is this: *he must
be one who unites us rather than divides us in our thinking and
planning for the future.*

Take a cross-section of the life of this country today, or any
other time for that matter—and you find it harassed by great
problems pressing for solution. You find embattled pressure
groups on both sides of the problem, and you find sincere people
among them despite what their opponents say! Just now our
ominous problems are, roughly, (1) the conflict between labor and
management for the control of industrial policy, (2) the race
question with its ugly implications, (3) the determination of
many underprivileged people to secure equality of opportunity
for themselves and their children while arrayed in almost unbroken front against them are the holders of privilege in the
status quo, and finally, (4) the matter of our relations with other
nations.

It goes without saying that there is no immediate solution for
such problems as these. No one man and no one party and no
one election is going to solve them. Strictly speaking, we are
constantly looking for the proper solution all of the time. One

hundred and fifty million Americans are thinking and experimenting with various ways of solving them, and, sooner or later, we believe, we shall be successful. Two things can help us in our quest for the right answer. The first is the earnest desire for the right, the fair, the just answer. Without this we shall merely be looking for ways of favoring ourselves. The second is a growing confidence in the integrity of those who are on the other side of the line in any given problem. It is at this point that one of the great qualities of leadership in a democracy is indispensable.

The leader we need will have the ability to stimulate the growth of mutual confidence across lines of division within a democracy. He must be able to do this not necessarily by political expedience and the art of compromise, though these have their place and are not to be scorned. But he will do it most definitely by bringing to the fore the more co-operative leaders in the embattled groups. If this is not done, the fighters, the unconditional-surrender type of men will surge to the front, setting the stage for riots and other forms of civil war.

It cannot be stated too strongly that he who seeks to lead by playing one group against another in our common life is engaged in nothing less than a betrayal of democracy. Call it good politics if you will, but it's rotten religion and I very much doubt whether it is good politics in the long run. This is no plea for soft-pedaling the gravity of the problems which are agitating us today—for that is a futile and finally foolish procedure. But it is to insist that every encouragement must be given to the conciliatory leaders within opposing interests; it is to insist that the United States government use its good offices as conciliator rather than exploiter of differences in our common life. It may be good politics to seek to "divide and rule" but it is discredited and dangerous strategy in a country which desires to remain a democracy.

This much is clear: We cannot afford to move into the ominous future with a lessening of confidence in one another! To move into a future of discord with increasing dissension in our common life will be sheer tragedy for everyone. To the end then of strengthening our common life we are duty bound to seek as public leaders the men best fitted to increase our mutual confidence, especially in areas of greatest tension.

A third requirement of the leader we need is this: *he must be one who accepts and exalts the disciplines of democracy.* Democracy, for all our glib talk about it, is the government of the people, by the people, and for the people. Students of our particular form of democracy say that it is a system of checks and balances set up by the Constitution for the express purpose of keeping power divided among the three branches of government—the executive, the legislative, and the judicial. The writers of the Constitution did not make this division in an idle and thoughtless moment. They well understood the tendency of power to become more and more centralized, resulting finally in some form of tyranny. They sought to ward off this threat by arranging our three centers of power in a kind of triangular relationship in which each is dependent upon yet identifiably different from the other.

You do not need to be any better student of geometry than I am to realize that when you remove one point of a triangle the triangle itself disappears. And when you remove in letter or in spirit one point in our system of checks and balances the entire system collapses into—God alone knows what, but it will not be our form of democracy. It is, therefore, a highly questionable precedent when the President casts slurs at the Supreme Court, the Congress casts slurs at the President, and the Supreme Court at least by implication questions the sanity of Congress. Yet we have seen all these tendencies in operation in a more or less aggravated form in the last decade. There is room for criticism and unrest and a continual study of the adequacy of the system of checks and balances. Yet he who advocates a change must have a clear picture of what it is he seeks by the change.

One of the most difficult disciplines of democratic leadership is the giving and taking of criticism. The right and the responsibility of criticism is fundamental to democracy. *No man, no office, no policy, no institution can set itself up as beyond and above criticism.* I know—not all criticism is fair and responsible. But we have less to fear from hotheaded, rash, hasty, and unfair criticism than from the effort to curtail it. A democracy without the right of public dissent and criticism is a contradiction in terms. And a leadership which seeks to evade or stifle public criticism is a poor leadership for a democratic society. It's about time we got over the habit of equating serious criticism with concealed treason. Let someone criticize our foreign policy and he is sure to be told, "Stalin couldn't have done better!" Let the churches oppose U. M. T. and we are solemnly assured that we are "giving aid and comfort to the enemy." A democracy without the right of public criticism is not a democracy and a democracy that does not jealously guard the right of criticism and the free expression of criticism will not long remain a democracy. It will not be overthrown by attacks from without; it will fall by betrayal from within.

It ought to be axiomatic that a democratic leader is one who accepts and exalts the disciplines of democracy in that he will be a good citizen himself. Which is to say that he will seek to abide by the law of the land and not evade its clear intent by some devious means. If a law is outmoded—and this may well be —or if it obstructs the general welfare—and this may well be— the President, for example, has a perfect right to seek its removal from the statute books of the country, but so long as it remains there he should respect it. One of the frequent charges against the late President Roosevelt came from this area. As Mr. Arthur Krock of *The New York Times* once wrote: "The president has an uncanny ability to make end runs around existing laws!" In the last coal strike, and again in the present steel crisis, the President of the United States has not invoked the Taft-Hartley Act which was created especially to deal with such situations because he does not like it.

I ask you, what kind of a country would we have if each citizen specialized in making end runs around the laws of the land, if we obeyed just the laws we liked? To ask the question is to answer it in a single word: anarchy. The whole purpose of law is defeated if it is left up to the judgment and caprice of the individual. It is, therefore, a most dangerous precedent for a democracy which finally depends upon respect for law to have as leaders those who by their attitude and action, whether consciously or not, teach a disrespect for this elemental responsibility for citizenship in a democracy. If long persisted in, we shall find government by law superseded by government of men—which means the end of constitutional democracy as we have known it in America, and a creation of the kind of government dramatically portrayed in *All the King's Men*.

A fourth requirement of our leader is this: *he must be one who keeps us facing our deepest problems in domestic and foreign affairs*. This calls for statesmanship of the highest order. It calls for utmost fidelity not only to the problems themselves but also to the nature of democracy, lest in the very act of seeking to save it we betray it. Democracy is not, as someone has suggested, a government of the people, by the few, and for the rich; it is of, by, and for the people. Democracy requires, therefore, that every citizen must be kept aware of the problems, both internal and foreign, which this nation faces. Democracy does not ask of any man or any party that it pretend to know the answer to all such problems, but it does ask our elected leaders both to face these problems realistically and to keep them before the citizens. The right answers to such problems come from the bottom up not from the top down. I do not mean thereby to depreciate the role of public leadership in a democracy. Our grave problems must be studied by experts in our councils of state. They must be given the undivided attention of all of our elected and representative leaders. Creative leadership in a democracy is a co-operative matter, involving the free use of all persons to whom we the people delegate authority and upon whom we exercise the periodic right of recall through elections. We have something considerably less than democratic leadership when any of our elected leaders take the bit of decision in their teeth and plunge ahead with a whole series of either veiled or wholly secret commitments pausing only to tell us what they have done, not asking us to consider what they propose to do! And the whole matter becomes a farce when they appear before us and try to convey the impression that they are merely doing our will! They have been doing their will in our name! And their will can become our will only when we the people know definitely what they have been doing and have a chance to consider it carefully. Government by an individual or government by committee without reference to the will of the people prior to a commitment given in the name of the people is government, all right, but it is not government by the people.

It is one of the tasks of leadership in a democracy like this to guide us into a consideration of our common problems. This is the common task of the President and the Congress of the United States. They must help us understand the fuller nature of the problems we are confronting in domestic and international affairs. We expect them to suggest creative answers to such problems and submit them to us for consideration and approval or disapproval. Naturally this is a slow and tedious process, and it is understandable that we should seek to speed it up in various ways. But he who wants or seeks a short cut around it is wanting and seeking a short cut around an essential meaning of democracy.

One of the hardest tasks of democratic leadership is that of giving citizens an over-all view of national problems. Provincialism and sectionalism are among our besetting sins. It is natural enough, I suppose, to think that the pinch on us is the most painful pinch in the country, and therefore most deserving of immediate attention and relief. At least that is the way we act! Visit the agricultural areas and the woes of the farmer are poured into your ear. Visit the industrial areas and you hear the woes of labor and management alike. Visit anywhere in our Southland and white and colored alike have much to complain about—and they complain! You come away from the survey of our country's woes about ready to conclude that democracy is one big headache!

Of course it is the business of government to help alleviate such pains. But it is also the business of government both to get the total picture itself and to keep that picture before the people in a serious and sympathetic way. In fact, Senator Paul Douglas recently gave it as his considered opinion that "the gravest danger we face today is economic and political disintegration into competitive groups, each placing its own interest above national interest. The times demand on all sides a new degree of public-mindedness, a greater sense of responsibility for the general interest, a self-discipline that marks the wise use of freedom." He further said, "If I were limited to only one conclusion based upon my term in office of the Senate, I would make it this: We must guard against breaking our population into self-conscious, selfish segments commonly known as pressure groups."[2]

To this end, we as citizens should try to send the fairest men we can find to our elective offices. A man who presents himself for our vote under the plea that he will be primarily concerned with our own interests ought to be suspect forthwith. Our elected officials are, as it were, our eyes for seeing the whole picture, not just our part of it which we know well enough. A carefully informed citizenry is much less likely to be split up into warring groups if the government does a good job of keeping us informed about the whole range of the problems in the nation and in the world. In peace, no less than in war, most of us are willing to bear our share of hardship if we are fairly sure that everyone else is doing likewise. The creation of this consciousness of oneness is one of the essential functions of government in a democracy. This, I know, is in violent contrast to the idea that good government is merely a matter of taking care of whoever shouts the loudest and controls the most votes.

[2] *Collier's Magazine*, February 11, 1950.

III

Can we find men like this for leadership in a democracy: men whose word is their bond, men who unite us rather than divide us, men who exalt and exemplify the disciplines of democracy, men who keep us facing our deepest problems in domestic and foreign affairs? Can we find men for leadership of whom it can be said that they can face oppositions without animosity, criticism without rancor, flattery without conceit, and defeat without despair? This is our most pressing problem just now, and we must be prepared to work it out with fear and trembling, not simply in the elections in the immediate future, but especially in our own conduct as citizens in a democracy. These moral requirements of leadership in a democracy are not optional unless the Hebrew-Christian conception of the moral nature of the world is wholly wrong. But if this conception of the structure of the world is right, these moral requirements arc not simply requirements for the election of any one man—they are the requirements of survival for democracy. The only person who can afford to take these requirements lightly is the atheist. The rest of us will exercise the privilege and the responsibility of citizenship in a democracy, whether as citizens or leaders, by taking them as the watchword of our thinking and living. "Eternal vigilance is the price of liberty" in a democracy. The problems we face are tremendous, but so are our resources if we lose not faith in God and man.

XVII

The Christian Faith
Challenges Communism[1]

1. The Conflict Between Philosophies
of Life

SCRIPTURE LESSON: Psalm 43:1–11

I

THE main purpose of this series of sermons is clearly stated in
the title, "The Christian Faith Challenges Communism." I want
to compare and contrast the Christian faith and communism on
certain fundamental matters. I shall not be studying in any direct
fashion the present conflict between the United States and Soviet
Russia, though that, of course, is implicated all along the line.
Neither shall I be comparing the economies of capitalism and
communism, though that too is indirectly involved in this under-
taking. Matters like these are of great importance, and we are
fortunate to have an abundance of books treat them in a system-
atic fashion.

I shall be taking full advantage of the splendid study of Christianity and communism made by the faculty and friends of Garrett Biblical Institute two years ago. Many of you know of this
study, and I commend it to the rest of you. It is available at Garrett for the modest sum of one nickel. It is the best brief summary
of the many points of tension and conflict between Christianity
and communism now available. I shall be centering attention on
some, not all, of its conclusions, and endeavoring to enlarge upon
and interpret their importance for our day.

[1] This sermon was preached October 21, 1951.

186

If I might express one hope, it would be that there might be two results from this effort: one, direct; the other, indirect. The direct one would be to separate the conflict between Christianity and communism from its present involvement, if not actual blurring, in social, economic, and political tensions, and see it for what it is—*a conflict in basic philosophies of life.* Having seen this, we then face the necessity of choosing between them, personally, and, as a Christian Church, we have the right and the responsibility of asking all men to choose between them.

The indirect result hoped for will be to put to rest, once and for all, the notion that a Christian can be a communist or a communist a Christian. This simply is not possible. If one claims to be both he is either an unorthodox Christian or an unorthodox communist. How one can deny God and still claim to be a Christian defies understanding. How one can affirm belief in God and claim to be a communist is equally baffling. Between Christianity and communism there is a great gulf fixed, and I propose to investigate why this is so and why it must remain so until one or the other disappears from the affairs of men. In this battle, no compromise is possible and no plea of prudence or discretion will be admitted. It is a fight to the end—not between peoples or nations nor with guns or bombs—but between systems of ideas or philosophies of life.

The importance of a philosophy of life was given an unforgettable statement by Gilbert Keith Chesterton some fifty years ago: "There are some people—and I am one of them—who think that the most practical and important thing about a man is . . . his view of the universe. We think that for a landlady considering a lodger, it is important to know his income, but still more important to know his philosophy. We think that for a general about to fight an enemy, it is important to know the enemy's numbers, but still more important to know the enemy's philosophy."[2]

We have been treated to some pretty grim evidence in substantiation of this extreme emphasis upon the importance of a philosophy of life. Mr. Alistair Cooke, American correspondent to the *Manchester Guardian*, attended the Hiss trials and wrote his impressions in the book entitled *Generation on Trial*. Mr. Cooke contends that Mr. Hiss, Mr. Chambers, Mr. Fuchs, and a host of others fell into communism because it offered them a dynamic, hopeful philosophy of life—one in which they could

[2] *Heretics*, pp. 15-16.

live and work in an effective and useful way. That they were disillusioned is a truth tragic enough for them and even more so
for those they betrayed, but, just now, I want to emphasize the
fact that their and our generation is on trial simply because we
have refused to give the Christian philosophy of life anything
like the same consideration we have been willing to bestow upon
other philosophies of life oriented to economic and national concerns. We have "heiled" our Hitlers but proudly refused to bow
down before our God as though the act of obedience were unworthy of us. We have embraced the philosophy of humanism in
all its forms because it rings the changes on the word "man," and
we love to hear ourselves paged in the corridors of the cosmos,
but we have turned away from the Christian philosophy of life
because it is centered in the reality of God.

Most of us are prepared to agree with Chesterton that the
most important thing about a person or a movement is its philosophy of life, its view of the universe, its conception of the meaning of human life and works. Since the deepest cleavage between the Christian faith and communism occurs precisely in
this area, we begin there.

II

The communist philosophy of life is built upon the ancient
foundations of materialism. I say "ancient" advisedly because
some form of materialism, on the one hand, and some form of
idealism, on the other, have candidated for the control of our
view of life from the heyday of Greek culture. Socrates, Plato,
and Aristotle numbered among their persistent opponents some
of the great materialists of ancient Greece. Three hundred years
later, the Christian faith took form under the still strong star of
materialism. We usually associate the name of Democritus with
Greek materialism, and probably fairly so. He believed that
everything in the universe could be explained in terms of what
he called "atoms and the void." He argued that these atoms
were the only real things in the universe. He believed that he
could explain such tremendous values as truth, beauty, goodness,
and love in terms of atoms and their interrelations. He disagreed
with those who argued that mind or thought could not be reduced to atoms in motion. He decreed that "matter in its form
and motion is regarded as that which alone is truly real." He
concluded that "the entire mental or spiritual life" is derived

from matter.[3] Democritus and his disciples used this principle of the finality of matter as the foundation on which to build a philosophy of life.

In contrast with materialism, idealism argues that the true foundation for thought and life is the finality of a mental or spiritual principle. Not matter but mind or spirit or purpose has the last word in the universe. Believing this, Plato and his great colleagues insisted that ideas and ideals, minds and wills, purposes and goals cannot be explained in terms of atoms. These discerning Greeks stated in no uncertain terms that it is far easier to reduce matter to mind than mind to matter. We call them idealists because, for them and for all who oppose materialism, the final truth or fact in the universe must be stated in some nonmaterial terms like mind or will or spirit.

The mind of Western civilization has oscillated between materialism and idealism as views of life for nearly two thousand five hundred years. During the Middle Ages and up to almost the end of the seventeenth century, idealism seemed to be winning a clean victory in the contest. Then came the advent of science with its remarkable development in discovery and theory, and materialism made a strong comeback. And until about 1900 the issue was in doubt. The great periods for materialism are the early Greek period, "the 18th century in France and Germany, and in Germany in the 19th century. . . . In England materialism has been endemic, so to speak, from (the 17th century) to the present time, and English materialism is more important than that of any other country."[4]

As a matter of fact, Karl Marx was born and educated in Germany at the beginning of the nineteenth century and he spent the latter part of his life in England, dying in 1883. He grew up with the credo of materialism ringing in his ears: There is no God but matter and science is its prophet. Although he himself was the son of a rabbi who had turned to Protestant Christianity, Marx seems to have spent his entire life during and after student days among people who accepted materialism as the true philosophy, holding that everything in the universe can be explained in terms of mass in motion. They believed, further, that "the business of the scientist is to explain everything by the

[3] Quotations from W. Wendelband, *History of Philosophy* (Macmillan, New York, 1907), p. 111.
[4] *Encyclopedia Britannica*, "Materialism."

physical causes which are comparatively well understood and to exclude the interference of spiritual causes."[5]

It was not long after Marx's death that science and philosophy began to move away from materialism toward idealism. We may now safely say that "largely through the influence [of major developments in science and philosophy over the last fifty years] contemporary science is tending away from materialism and mechanism toward the recognition of other nonmechanical factors in the phenomena, even the physical phenomena of nature."[6] Thus the pendulum swings back toward a new appreciation of some form of idealism. We have a profound study of the *Idealistic Reaction against Science* by Aliotta, an Italian thinker. Sir Arthur Eddington, famed British scientist, describes *The Nature of the Physical World* and concludes in the vein of idealism. Sir James Jeans, another English scientist, writes of the relationship between science and philosophy and concludes that the science of today has so far forsaken the position of the science of half a century ago that one must now admit the reality of an element of purpose, design, and will in the universe not in order to be religious but in order to be scientific.

While we have cause to rejoice in this trend we need to keep a steady eye on the single fact that when the basic ideas of communism were being fashioned by Marx and Engels, materialism was the reigning philosophy in the minds of most scientists, philosophers, and educators all over Europe and, to a large extent, here in the United States as well. Every philosophy of government or science or education formulated during this period was either openly or covertly materialistic in nature or leaning. Materialism might be called the very atmosphere in which men lived, moved and had their intellectual being.

So when Marx and Engels were fashioning a philosophy for revolution they placed it squarely upon what, to them, was the firm foundation of a materialistic view of life and history. This became an essential part of the philosophy of communism, and continues to be just that to this day. It is the official philosophy of the Communist Party, and no man can hope to be in good standing in government, education, science, art, or military life in communist countries unless he accepts the tenets of materialism and the conclusions drawn from it by its revered interpreters: Marx, Engels, Lenin, and Stalin. One of the open secrets of the

[5] *Ibid.*
[6] *Ibid.*

power of the Communist Party in Russia has been its insistence
upon conformity to the party line and its ability to enforce its
insistence. The judgments of the Marx-Lenin-Stalin triumvirate
are the party line, and they are materialist to the core. Science
may now repudiate the conclusions which Marx took for granted
when he embraced materialism, but the party line on materialism
cannot change. Biology, genetics, as well as sociology and philosophy must wheel and march with the precision of Rockettes to
the score written by the Party. All of which underscores the
seriousness with which we must deal with the meaning of materialism if we would deal adequately with communism.

III

The biography of communism might be put in three brief
sentences:

1. It began as a system of ideas or a philosophy.
2. It became the center of faith, action, and organization, seeking social reform by violence.
3. It is now the ideological heart or brain or both of one of
the most dangerous revolutionary movements in history.

Upon the foundations of materialism Marx and his disciples
built an imposing superstructure of answers to every question
known to man. They disposed of religion with a single blow.
Religion, they decreed, is a stupid, unscientific, idealistic superstition; it is the opiate of the people, and the Church is the tool
of the moneyed class in their oppression of the workers. Here
again they were but copying the judgments of many if not most
of the intellectual leaders of their day who were busy explaining
religion away for one reason or another.

One thing we must never forget about Marx and his disciples:
they were revolutionaries before they were philosophers, and
they demanded of any system of thought or idea that *it justify
revolution*. Because classical materialism seemed a little too
static to suit their purpose, they called themselves "scientific
materialists" and sped it up. They insisted that there is a peculiar
movement in the very nature of matter which, on the human,
social level, is the conflict between and among persons and
classes. For them, the principle which explains class struggle and
makes it both good and necessary to foment it in the affairs of
men is an essential part of matter itself.

This is the real foundation of communism's famous dialectical theory. Even as the atoms are in collision and conflict, yet seek stable combinations, so do men and groups. History is the record of the collisions and conflicts of group with group, conflict beginning in and among small groups and moving to large ones, finally, in our time becoming world-wide in scope. Early communist thinkers and writers contended that the moneyed, or capitalist, or owner class is locked in a struggle with the workers for the control of the tools of production; they argued that this struggle could end only when the workers overthrew their oppressors and worked out their own salvation. Once they have done this, the conflict in human history may well come to an end in the communist version of the Kingdom of God or matter!

This, then, is the theoretical justification of the unending, costly, and tragic class warfare preached and practiced by communism. But what about the Communist Party? Where does it fit into the conflict? It leads the workers in the fight. It is their general staff, so to speak. It furnishes the informed, alert leaders in the battle with the capitalists. As a leader, it must really lead and see that its discipline is observed. It demands strict conformity from Party members, on penalty of expulsion if not liquidation, and it requires loyalty from those whom it seeks to lead. The Party must seize and control the instruments of power and control and direct the state until the workers of the world have been able to work out a socialist paradise on a world scale. Then, the Party will be needed no longer and the political apparatus of the Party—the state—will wither away, leaving peace and justice to reign for aye in the affairs of men.

It was the conviction of Marx, and even more so of Lenin, that the right answer to every human problem could be found within this system of ideas. And you must give them credit for this: They took their philosophy of life seriously enough to make it the center of action. It became the center of faith, action, and a social organization seeking social reform by means of ruthless violence. Some early communists were "gradualists" rather than revolutionaries, but they were soon declared unorthodox and expelled from the Party. Only those who were committed to completely violent revolution at the opportune time were permitted to stay in the organization. Discipline became the watchword of the Party, and death the penalty for disobedience. Jan Valtin's book, *Out of the Night,* is a terrifying picture of the Party at work in the lives of its own members.

Yet it will not serve us in our struggle against communism to depict it as the last refuge of social malcontents. Men like Marx, Lenin, and Stalin became communists from conviction, and they suffered for their choice many a long year before it won the power they had sought all along. You cannot work your way through their writings without sensing on every page their *esprit de corps*, the reality of a great purpose and the conviction that they were the chosen instruments of history. Communism, for the elect Party members, has been and is a form of religion, and it will never be properly evaluated if this fact is ignored.

Marx and Engels lived when the industrial revolution was remaking the entire life of the Western world, and doing it by means of one great social convulsion after another. They lived through the French Revolution; they saw England brought to the brink of one; they saw the gathering storm of deep unrest in Germany, Russia, and all over the world. They more than saw it; they anticipated it with eagerness, looking forward to the day when they or their disciples would touch the match to the existing forms of society and burn them to the ground. Lenin even named his newspaper *Iskra*, the Spark.

When the philosophy of communism took form and root in this kind of world, it inevitably flowered into revolution. It fought every known form of government, every form of church, all newspapers, and every convention that tended toward stability in a social order. It felt that every form of society had to be subjected to drastic change when the revolution came. And it insisted that the revolution had to come and that men had to accept it when it did come.

There is a sad truth in the story that was prevalent in New York City during the depression. The communist orator in Central Park was encouraging his hungry hearers to be loyal communists because, very soon, the revolution would come. And when it did, what a change-about there would be! He said, "Now you eat bread and water while the swells on Park Avenue eat strawberries and cream. Come the revolution, they will eat bread and water while you eat strawberries and cream." Someone objected, "But, Comrade, I don't like strawberries and cream." The speaker eyed him a moment, "Come the revolution, you eat strawberries and cream."

The broad outline of the story of the way in which a small band of determined, disciplined revolutionaries, headed by Lenin, moved into a Russia engaged both in a war with Germany and in civil war, and convulsed by widespread strikes and civil violence everywhere, is either known or should be known to all of us. John Reed, writing of it, called it *The Ten Days that Shook the World*. That is an understatement, if anything, we must say as we look back to 1917 now. And the end of that beginning is not yet—of this we may be sure.

IV

How does the Christian faith challenge communism in these basic matters on which all else depends? The first thing to say, I am sure, is this: We find no new foe in communism. It is as old as the materialism in the world of the New Testament. It may have new techniques of propaganda and new possibilities of social control today, but it has no new insights into human life and history. We have met them all before, and we face them without the least fear again.

The Christian faith challenges the materialistic foundation of communism and does so not only in the name of philosophical idealism but even more deeply in the name of a vital belief and faith in the reality of God. To the communist who says the world is basically mass in motion we say the world is basically God in action. The arguments for the reality of mind, spirit, will, purpose, and order are the armory from which the Christian draws or should draw his weapons for this fight. Contemporary science has cut the very foundations out from under the materialism of communism, and we both ought to know that and say it without ceasing. If the epithets "blind, stupid, and superstitious" are to be used at all, then they apply, not to the Christian who believes in God, but to the communist who continues to chant that "there is no God." He cannot appeal to science or philosophy or history now for the support of his position, while the Christian faith can and does appeal to all three for the interpretation and vindication of its faith in God.

What do we make of the fact of conflict in history? Well—it's there, and not even a Pollyana can deny or justify it. The Christian faith looks on the pages of history, stained as they are with tragedy, and argues that there was nothing inevitable or inexorable about it. We do not say that there is no tragedy in history; we do say two things about it: (1) it is of our own making, by and large; (2) God is in history trying to redeem it—He has shown us the way in the life and teachings of Jesus Christ. Lenin could call history "one bloody lump"—as indeed it is—but the Christian faith cannot let the matter rest there. History is the scene of moral law. History is the record of God's dealings with men, or rather of man's determination to live as though there were no God, only to discover from the pit of tragedy that there is One after all.

We agree with the communists that man is at least in measure responsible for the trend in the historical events of our day. Neither we nor they are fatalists in this matter. But we challenge their conclusion that we can give history any turn we choose. We say we are answerable to the God of righteousness no matter how powerful we may think we are.

Both communism and Christianity believe in morality, in conduct according to prescribed rules. But there is this significant difference: morality for the Christian is not to be found in obedience to the Party, but only in obedience to the will of God. The communist has no need for conscience; the very word is anathema to him. And well it might be—it is fraught with danger to his whole philosophy. Once recognize that man is the bearer or creature of conscience, and therefore answerable to the intimations of conscience, and you have laid the ax to the roots of communism.

V

I cannot conceive of two more utterly dissimilar philosophies of life than communism and Christianity. Even where they seem to be alike, they do but parallel each other for a while—and that is a quite different matter.

Both are out to transform the world—but what a difference there is between the ends sought and the means used by each!

Both believe that people like us must share in the transformation, but communism holds that men are answerable to themselves and history, while the Christian holds we are answerable to God in and beyond history.

Both demand all that a man has, but communism refuses to grant freedom of exercise to the mind, spirit, and conscience of men, while the Christian faith must make its primary appeal to these.

There can be no compromise between these philosophies of life; the Christian faith has seen and said this for two thousand years now, and we shall keep right on saying it. When President Truman issues his lament about his difficulty getting religious groups to stop their bickering and help him fight communism, when the American Legion pretends to be a modern Paul Revere riding from one hilarious convention to another warning us that the communists are coming, the Christian faith makes reply, "We have been fighting communism, root and branch, for two thousand years now, and such urgings from these Johnny-come-latelies are quite unnecessary." It seems never to occur to President Truman that it is possible for Christians to be united in our fight against communism without being united behind him!

We hear a lot about fellow travelers these days—so much so, in fact, that the term has lost most of its precision. I should like to go on record as saying that I think it is both a good word and that it describes a number of types very accurately.

A fellow traveler is one who either denies or seeks to restrict the meaning of spiritual and moral considerations in life.

The psychologist or sociologist or scientist or philosopher who tries to reduce the manifold richness of life to a few simple measurable facts about it is a fellow traveler of materialism in all its forms.

The historian who tries to account for the facts of history on the basis of the economic determination of history is a fellow traveler of materialism, even though he may disown its expression in communism.

The economist or businessman who tries to separate financial profits from spiritual and moral considerations about the public and the worker is a fellow traveler because, with the materialists of all ages, he denies that man is the child of God, the bearer of infinite worth, and deserving of a concern born of love.

The man who argues that the end justifies the means, who believes that peace can come only through violent means, who seeks to deny the power of love, is a fellow traveler because he ranges himself against every idealistic and spiritual argument of the ages.

The man or people who believe that history is what we make it, and that we can make it what we will if we are powerful enough, is a fellow traveler with every form of materialism known to man.

The Christian faith eyes all such men and says with an ancient Jewish teacher: "I fear God, and after that I fear the man who fears him not." I am not afraid of the communist philosophy incarnate in life if we can meet it with the Christian philosophy incarnate in life.

XVIII

The Christian Faith
Challenges Communism[1]

2. The Clash Between Practices

SCRIPTURE LESSON: *Philemon*

I

THE Christian challenge to communism grows out of the simple fact that they are radically different philosophies of life. So different that the matter can be summarized in some such way as this: A Christian cannot be a communist; a communist cannot be a Christian; if one claims to be both he is either an unorthodox Christian or an unorthodox communist, or he is muddleheaded about either or both communism and Christianity, or he is a deliberate deceiver. There has never been and there can never be any compromise between their basic philosophies. We need to remind ourselves of this conflict in philosophies of life before surveying the clash between the two in actual practice.

The foundation on which communism builds its entire view of life is the nineteenth century version of the ancient philosophy of materialism. From the day in early Greece when Democritus and his disciples proclaimed that all life could be reduced to atoms in a void to the heyday of scientific materialism in the eighteenth and nineteenth centuries when the disciples of Newton (but not Newton himself) proclaimed that all life could be reduced to mass in motion—throughout this long period of over two thousand years materialism was an active or latent force in the thought of Western man.

[1] This sermon was preached November 4, 1951.

197

Whenever materialism got the upper hand the emphasis upon the reality of life, spirit, mind and will withered away and matter reigned supreme. Science, the high priest of matter, was the oracle of all knowledge and truth. The artist and the seer were smiled on benignly, at best, as strayed ghosts of an earlier age of superstition, or, at worst, were roughly denounced and discarded as useless, if not dangerous, baggage. Atheism—the denial that a spiritual power or principle is ultimate in the universe— flourished in these periods, not as the creation of malicious minds, but as the inescapable corollary of materialism.

The Christian faith, born as she was under the star of the materialistic philosophy of many Greek thinkers, has fought materialism from the beginning of her historic career. She has always chosen as her champion in this conflict some one of several forms of idealism. For idealism denies that matter is ultimate; it insists upon the ultimacy of mind, or will or spirit. The great idealistic systems of thought, for all their differences, perhaps inadequacies in this detail or that, have been solidly united in the contention that the universe is the scene of the active operation of a cosmic mind, or will, or spirit. The philosophical systems of Plato, Plotinus, and the rest have provided Christian thinkers like Origen and Augustine with tremendous alternatives to materialism which they seized with eager minds and spirits.

The firm opposition of the Christian faith to materialism is so deeply ingrained in every branch of the Christian Church today that a priest in the Russian Orthodox Church, writing in 1948 and counseling the need of the church's maintaining some kind of peace with the government, nonetheless said, "Naturally, we reject materialism." There is no reason to doubt this simple statement: it fits in with the unbroken position of the Christian faith relative to materialism for over two thousand years.

II

Communism was set over against the Christian faith from the very outset. The early and now classical communist thinkers —Marx, Engels, and Lenin—were materialists to the core. They called themselves "scientific materialists" and referred to their system as "dialectical materialism."

Their theory of history exudes materialism. In fact, it is usually called "historical materialism" or the "materialist's interpretation of history." They held that since "men must be able to live in order to make history . . . the economic factor is fundamental for all social institutions and particularly for their historical development. . . .[2] They scoffed at the medieval Christian conception of the world as a "vale for soul-making" and argued that it was the scene of an unending struggle for existence. The Darwinian notion of "the survival of the fittest" played into their hands, and they have clung to it as their gospel ever since—even though science has long since discarded it as a useful hypothesis. The world, they proclaim, can only be interpreted in terms of conflict, and the history of man is the history of conflict for the production and control of the necessities of life.

The communist theory of class conflict is a natural corollary of this kind of thinking. Various groups get control of the necessities of life, and hold on until they are overthrown by other groups. Feudal lords owned the land and ruled the lives of all until the capitalists came along and broke their control by developing the power of an industrial society. That was the end of feudalism and the beginning of the reign of capitalism. But, now, capitalism is being challenged by the workers, the proletariat, who are determined to wrest control of the means of production from the owners. This, of course, is the proletarian revolution of our times, and, if it is to be successful, it must have the political leadership of a group of trained revolutionaries. The Communist Party came into being in order to furnish this leadership. Lenin made it clear "that if you wanted to make a revolution you must have something to make it with, and that this could only be a centralized and disciplined party."[3]

Communism's theory of government presupposes both a philosophy of materialism and the emphasis upon class conflict as the clue to history. Government, for communism, did not begin as ours did in a New England town meeting; it began in the determination of a band of revolutionaries to seize and control all essential powers of a people's life. Accepting the obvious fact that they were in for the severest kind of fighting, the Communist Party regarded themselves as the general staff of an army. They kept party power in the hands of a few—Lenin dominating it from 1903-1923, Stalin from 1923 to our time. Though they might speak of "the masses" in unctuous tones, they never trusted any large number of people with actual power. Certainly, com-

[2] R. N. Carew Hunt, *The Theory and Practice of Communism* (Geoffrey Bles, London, 1950), p. 43.

[3] *Ibid.*, p. 147.

munism has never made even a pretense of being a government of the people, by the people, and for the people. Even its most ardent supporter would not claim that! The most he could claim is that it is a government of the people, by the Party, and for the welfare of the people, as understood by the Party.

To the Christian faith all this theorizing of communism is both an attempt to revive the corpse of materialism and a reversion to the jungle. The Christian faith believes in God. It holds that there is an eternal spiritual power at the heart of the universe. It constructs beliefs in man, society, and the future on this firm foundation. The Christian faith holds that the God of the universe is not only real but also is best described by the word "Love"—which is to say that there is a power in the universe— trying to create a genuine oneness, or unity or community among men. The Christian faith believes that the power—the power of God—is working in individual lives as well as in groups and in history, moving all life toward the divinely ordained end of the Kingdom of God. The Christian faith holds that all men are souls in the sight of God, are His children, are stewards before Him of their life. The Christian faith holds that no institution —Church or State—has a right to step between a man and God. This is a sacred relationship in and through which Father and Son commune with each other, in and through which the word of God comes to the spirit and conscience of man, in and through which man discovers himself, his neighbor and his God at a deeper level of meaning, in and through which man makes or renews his commitment to find the way of his life in the will of God.

III

Wide as is the chasm of disagreement between communism and the Christian faith on all these matters, they are in agreement on one point only: *Both seek to change the world.* Marx once wrote, "All philosophies have sought to explain the world; our business is to change it." Change it they have tried to do by action or reaction wherever they could! And the end is not yet as we well know to their efforts to change the world. The Christian faith has held as one of its deepest convictions that the God of the universe was creating a new heaven and a new earth in the life and teachings of Jesus Christ. Vachel Lindsay struck a permanent note in his quatrain entitled "Foreign Missions in Battle Array":

> This is our faith tremendous,—
> Our wild hope, who shall scorn,—
> That in the name of Jesus
> The world shall be reborn![4]

Nor can this hope be charged off as the sort of wishful thinking to which visionaries and fanatics are usually addicted. Charles Norris Cockrane opens his unparalleled study of the relationship between *Christianity* and *Classical Culture* with this observation: "The theme of this work is the revolution in thought and action which took place during the first four centuries of the Christian era."

Both communism and Christianity, then, are calls to action— but an unbridgeable chasm continues to yawn between the ends they seek and the means they use.

It is risky business, I know, to attempt to reduce the goals of widespread complex social movements to a single word because an injustice is bound to be done somewhere along the line. But I do believe it is possible to suggest a cleavage between the ends sought and the means used by communism and the Christian faith in two words. *Communism seeks solidarity; the Christian faith seeks community.*

The principles advocated by communism look toward the day when "the masses," "the toilers," "the workers," or "the people" have undisputed control of the production and distribution of the goods of life. All opposition will have been liquidated en route, and the rising generations of men will have been educated to live in what communist writers are fond of calling either a socialized order or a true democracy of the people.

But the road to that end is a hard and twisting one at best, and the journey over it will be long and difficult. A successful journey requires three things: (1) the utmost vigilance of the Communist Party; (2) absolute discipline within the Party; and (3) the complete confidence of people in the Party and their leadership. These factors are the stuff of the communist notion of solidarity, and they furnish the clue to the inevitability of those practices of communism that are so abhorrent to us.

Even as I begin the detailing of such practices I want to make it clear that I am not unmindful nor, I hope, do I underestimate the many contributions for good which have been wrought in the life of the Russian people since 1917. A miracle of industrial

---

[4] Used by permission of The Macmillan Company.

transformation has come to pass—that we know. There seems little reason to doubt that the ordinary Russian is no worse off and may be better off now than he ever was under the Czars. But, having said this, I cannot help wondering whether they, like young Benjamin Franklin, have not paid too much for their whistle.

Apply the notion of solidarity to government, and you wind up with some kind of dictatorship every time. In Russia, and under the guidance of the economic and political theories of Marx and Engels, the thrust toward solidarity produced the Soviet regime. You do not get far in the utterances and deeds of this regime to discover its messianic complex. It "believes itself to be always right, all other regimes to be always wrong. The Soviet leaders alone know where mankind is going, they alone are for the victory of truth, justice, humanity. This belief in their own infallibility and righteousness is combined with an extraordinary flexibility—for the aim will be accomplished only after conditions have matured, after the right moment has arrived."[5] Hence the monotonous claim that "the party is always right, that it cannot tolerate any opposition, and that it must control the whole of life."[6]

There must be no public division of opinion within the Communist Party. It must present an unbroken front to enemies and friends alike and at all times. The official *History of the Communist Party of the Soviet Union* does not mince words on this matter: "The history of the Party further teaches us that unless the Party . . . wages an uncompromising struggle against the opportunists within its own ranks, unless it smashes the capitulators in its own midst, it cannot perform its role of organizer and leader of a new proletarian revolution, nor its role as the builder of a new, socialist society."[7]

This, then, is the real background of the periodic purges that have swept through the Communist Party since 1917. And as you study the records of those purges, it becomes increasingly clear that, even within the Party, there is no real security for anyone except the Dictator himself, and for him only so long as he successfully controls the reins of power.

I am certain that we who have been reared in our radically dif-

[5] Waldemar Gurian, editor, *The Soviet Union,* (Notre Dame Press, 1951), p. 5.
[6] *Ibid.,* p. 7.
[7] P. 359.

ferent traditions have wholly misunderstood the thorough discipline that has gone into the make-up of the Communist Party. When victims of the purges spoke up in court, confessing their crimes against the Party and admitting the justice of the punishment about to be meted out to them, we rubbed our eyes in astonishment. "Crimes, what crimes?" we asked. "All they did was to criticize Party leadership and refuse to carry out instructions that seemed to them mistakes." That, to us, may upon occasion seem to be ill-advised, but never a crime. What we did not see was the simple fact that it was and is a crime for a Communist Party member to criticize or refuse to carry out the orders of Party leaders. It is more than a crime in the sight of the leaders; it is a crime in the sight of every good Party member as well, Hence, when the criminal was brought face to face with the true nature of his defection, he could only confess: "The Party hath given, the Party hath taken away, blessed be the name of the Party." So long as the Communist Party is in being and has the power to do so it will purge its membership in the interests of purity and absolute obedience.

Purges within and terrorism without—these two go together in the practices of a government which believes itself to be infallible. Forced labor, slave labor—not everywhere and all of the time to be sure, but everywhere it is needed, and as long as it is needed; the vast and vicious apparatus of terrorism in a police state; the stark ruthlessness and violence that stalk the land, throwing over it a blanket of fear—the sheer callousness of it all is appalling to an outsider. Bertrand Russell tells of a conversation he had with Lenin shortly after the communists got control of power in Russia. Lenin was describing in high good humor how they had set the laborers on the small farms over against the owners; how they had encouraged the laborers to hang the owners. "Why," he said, "go down any road, and you would see some of those fellows hanging from trees or poles. Haw! Haw! Haw!" Russell records that he turned away sickened by this incredible callousness. Winston Churchill reports on his conversation with Stalin about the liquidation of the small farmers. Stalin said that it had been an awful struggle because some ten millions of small farmers were forcibly deported, killed, or otherwise liquidated. After Stalin said this, Churchill reports that "there was a considerable pause," during which he tried to visualize the immeasurable human agony wrapped up in those phrases. When Lady Astor visited Stalin after one great purge she asked him,

"How long are you going to go on killing people?" Somewhat shaken by the directness of the question, Stalin nonetheless answered according to the book, "As long as it is necessary."

Accept the notion of solidarity as the goal of society, and you get a totalitarian government bent on creating a monolithic society—a society in which there are no divisions of any kind. You get a government which will not submit itself to the criticisms of a free press, a free church, or a free school. Lenin candidly said that he saw no reason why a government that was doing what it thought best for the people should permit criticism of its personnel or policies by a hostile press or party or institution. Liberty, he said, is so precious it must be rationed. And ration it he did! (Would to God he were the only man in our time who wanted to ration it.) He believed that the Party determined the morality, the art, the science, and all other activities of men. Hence we hear communist leaders proclaim that "there is no morality outside of politics." We hear their cultural experts say, "Drama, painting, song—all these are all means of propaganda and agitation carried on through artistic images and for this reason more accessible to the masses and deep in their penetration. Hence, it is clear how important it is for art to be a party, a Bolshevist art."[8]

The cry of "Art for Marx' sake" is paralleled by the cries of "Philosophy for Marx' sake" and "Science for Marx' sake." We have no record of any teacher of philosophy in the Soviet Union who is not a materialist and a disciple of Karl Marx. We have recently read in amazement of the way Marxism holds the balances between rival theories in genetics, psychology, and literature. This subordination of all creative pursuits to the end of political action aimed at solidarity hurts all of them, but some more than others.

Take literature as an example. A recent study of *Soviet Russian Literature* by Professor Gleb Struve of the University of Chicago is a record of "the progressive impoverishment of the creative artist under such conditions." A student of Russian literature insists that "the process of exterminating literature in the Soviet Union reached its peak when the Zhdanov in 1946 established the heresy of free, individual art." He banned the many literary groups for which Russia used to be famous and gathered all politically acceptable writers into a Union of Soviet Writers who

[8] Edgar Snow, *The Pattern of Soviet Power* (Random House, New York, 1945), p. 199.

immediately announced that "writers must be 'engineers of human minds,' that is, they must combine 'truthfulness and historical concreteness of artistic depiction . . . with the task of ideological remoulding and re-education of the toiling people in the spirit of socialism.' " The result of this action of subordinating art to politics is summarized in these telling words, "After this, few new works or authors of any enduring interest appeared. Humanity, personality, emotion and variety vanished in favor of dictated attitudes, characters and structure. . . ."[9]

This same determination to create a monolithic society has more than gripped all existing educational institutions; it has created others by the score. Newspapers, radio, the theater, and all public assemblies are absolutely controlled in the interests of solidarity. Books, magazines, and periodicals of every kind are printed prolifically and circulated widely—so long as they conform to the Party line. It may be observed truly and objectively that the Soviet Union is one great school and that the Communist Party is its teacher as well as disciplinarian.

Much as communist orators prate about the welfare of the masses, the simple and the grim fact remains that communism is incapable of creating anything but mass men. It strips the individual of his soul, spirit, conscience, and reason. Instead of a responsible person in his own right he becomes little more than a mechanical unit in a closed society, a society where someone else knows all the answers, someone else faces all of the problems, someone else initiates all action. Instead of permitting him to live, move, think, and associate freely with all men everywhere, it proposes to chart his life and relationships for him. All of this will be done for him and to him for his own welfare, to be sure, but it will be done for and to him by someone else. That much is clear.

Socrates, in Plato's *Republic,* is confronting Agathon with alternate kinds of societies, and he describes a dictatorship in which the government does everything for people, asking in exchange their liberties. Socrates asks Agathon what he thinks of that. Agathon answers that Socrates has described not a state but a sty! I turn away from the communist ideal of solidarity and the practices by which they seek to achieve it with Agathon's word ringing in my mind.

[9] Quotations from *The Nation,* October 20, 1951, pp. 332-33.

IV

Even as *Solidarity* is the great word for Communism, *Community* is the great word for the Christian faith. Whereas communism relies on coercion all along the line, the Christian faith is trying to build a society characterized by the free, unforced co-operation of all members. Whereas communism exalts *obedience*, the Christian faith stresses *consent*, based upon understanding and personal commitment. Whereas communism is in effect a closed society, the Christian faith is intent on creating an open society—open to all men and open toward the Creator of all men, even God himself. Whereas communism rests moral responsibility for decision and action in the ruling group, the Christian faith, insisting that all men are responsible before God for what they do, is trying to create a society in which all men actually share in the thought, decision, and actions of that society.

You cannot teach a man that he is a responsible creative child of God and then expect him to be a stupid, slavish, blindly obedient creature of the status quo! Teach him that he is a child of God, and you both acknowledge his reason and you free him to think, to criticize, to affirm or deny, to experiment, to discover, to reject, and to plan for the future. Teach him that he is a child of God, and you both acknowledge his creative spirit, and free him to express himself through the arts. Teach him that he and all others are children of God, and you acknowledge the most important thing about men, and you free them to explore ways and means of living as new men in a new world.

I would not even for one moment give the impression that it is an easy or comfortable venture to try to build what might be called a Christian society. As a matter of fact, it can be done by nothing less than complete commitment of all that we have and are to the will of God as we see it in Jesus Christ—a commitment that will not stop short of the cross itself, if need be. I wish it were harder than it is to document this fact of the difficulty we must face as we bear witness to the Christian faith in this world in which we live.

The Christian faith tries to draw a fine line between the individual and group, holding them in that delicate relationship of being together yet separate. We seek a society in which each person will feel himself to be and will be treated as a child of God and will himself treat others accordingly. When a society tries to dominate and extinguish the individual, the Christian faith objects. And when an individual seeks to dominate society, the Christian faith objects. Interested as it is in community—the ideal community called the Kingdom of God—trying as it does to prepare men to be fit citizens of a truly Christian community, the Christian faith is equally severe in its criticism of a socialism that subordinates the person to the group and of an individualism that subordinates society to the individual. It objects strenuously to a society like communism which cancels out the individuality, the personality, the rationality, and the moral responsibility of the person. And it objects no less strenuously to the individual who would ignore the human family and treat other persons as Robinson Crusoe treated the goats and the birds on his island home. When a social order asks an individual to forget that he is a man, it asks too much. When it permits a person to forget his membership in the human family, it permits too much.

I need not dwell on the point that in these difficult days the position of the Christian faith pleases neither the collectivists on the one hand nor the individualists on the other. Both want to subordinate the Christian faith to their own way of thinking. Both want the Christian Church and Christian ministers to follow along like priests clad in white robes behind the ark of their own peculiar social covenant, uttering solemn "Amens"! I can understand the impulse which causes them to ask the Church to do this; I cannot understand the deliberate betrayal of the Christian faith on the part of a Christian church that will do it.

When communism sins against the Christian understanding of Man and God, the Church must object by word and in life. When capitalism sins against the Christian understanding of Man and God, the Church must object by word and in life. When she objects to the sins of communism, does that make her a tool of capitalism, as communists claim? I think not! When she protests the sins of capitalism, does that make her a tool of communism, a fellow traveler, or a member of the pink fringe? I think not! What then does it make of her? At least this—a determined committed disciple and preacher of the Christian gospel as the way, the truth, and the life! Communists and capitalists who would silence the Christian Church as she seeks to perform this duty are like Mrs. O'Grady and the Colonel's lady—sisters under the skin!

Both communism and Christianity are efforts to change the world. Both accept the inevitability of change throughout the entire range of life. Both issues call to commitment to their own way of life: communism calling men to commit themselves to a zigzag mechanical purpose under the guidance of Karl Marx and the Communist Party; Christianity calling men to commit themselves to the will of God as seen in the life and teachings of Jesus Christ and to the fellowship of the Christian Church.

The Christian faith renounces hatred and conflict and exalts love and brotherhood as means to the end of a Christian society. It believes that the love of God can and will work through sensitive spirits and willing servants with a power sufficient to remake the world. It lays upon men like us and churches like this the responsibility of being a truly Christian society ourselves and of leading our social order and our day toward a Christian world. And it believes that the world must, can, and will be remade by the power of the love of God working through people like us. It bids us lift in our own day the triumphant cry of old:

> This is our faith tremendous,
> Our wild hope, who shall scorn,—
> That in the name of Jesus
> The world shall be reborn.

XIX

The Christian Faith Challenges Communism[1]

3. The Churches and Soviet Russia Today

SCRIPTURE LESSON: Revelations 2:1–11

I

THE greatest struggle in our times is not between armies, navies, airplanes and atom bombs; it is the spiritual struggle between the Christian faith and communism, with the prize being the minds, souls, and lives of men. This struggle began with the ancient dispute between philosophies of life: idealism on the one hand and materialism on the other. But it forced its way out of the halls of philosophic controversy and can now be found in every phase of personal and public life. Each philosophy has ceased being merely a pattern of words and has become incarnate in practices and institutions, through which the struggle is being waged. That is why the final movement in even an outline of the Christian challenge to communism is and must be a consideration of the relationship between the Christian churches inside and outside Russia and the government of that great and powerful country. There are so many misconceptions, if not actual misrepresentations, rife as to this relationship, that it is too much to hope to be able to do more than make a beginning at clearing them up in this single effort. But, I am convinced, if we stay close to the facts, we can get a long way in a little while on the road to a better understanding of the present relationship between the churches and Soviet Russia.

[1] This sermon was preached November 11, 1951.

The studied hostility of the Soviet regime to any and all churches is no accident of history. It roots in the official attitude of communism toward religion. Lenin describes, and, to his own satisfaction, disposes of religion with this analysis of the origin and value of religion:

The impotence of the exploited classes in struggle with the exploiters inevitably gives birth to faith in a better life beyond the grave, just as the impotence of primitive people in struggle with nature gives birth to gods, devils, miracles, etc. . . . To him who all his life works and suffers need, religion teaches humility and patience in earthly life, comforting him with the hope of heavenly reward. And to those who live by the toil of others, religion teaches philanthropy in earthly life, offering them very cheap justification for all their exploiting existence, and selling at low price tickets to heavenly bliss. Religion is opium for the people. Religion is a sort of spiritual moonshine . . . in which the slaves of capital drown their human figure, their demands for even any sort of worthy human life.[2]

It makes no difference to contemporary communists that not a single competent scholar in the origin and history of religion will accept Lenin's analysis; they keep right on repeating it as though it were the last word in the matter. When Stalin was addressing some members of the First American Trade Union Delegation to Russia in 1927, he made quite clear what the attitude of the Soviet government toward religion was and he spelled out what the government proposed to do about it:

We conduct propaganda and shall conduct propaganda against religious prejudices. . . . The Party cannot be neutral with regard to religion, and it conducts anti-religious propaganda against any and all religious prejudices because it stands for science, while religious prejudices go against science, since every religion is something contrary to science. . . . Have we oppressed the reactionary clergy? Yes, we have oppressed them. The trouble is only that they are not yet fully liquidated.[3]

Against this background, and as an essential part of it, it is not hard to accept the simple fact that the record of the Soviet government from 1917 to 1939 was one of constant and recurrently severe efforts literally to beat the life out of the churches and to discredit religion in every way and by every means at its disposal.

[2] Quoted, Paul B. Anderson, *People, Church, and State in Modern Russia* (Macmillan, New York, 1944), p. 58.
[3] *Ibid.*, pp. 101-2.

Since the Russian Orthodox Church is known as the Church of all Russians and has been the dominant Church in Russia for many centuries, it has borne the brunt of the attacks of the Soviet government. Charging that the Church was a tool of the Czarist regime and the hotbed of reaction against all liberal movements, Lenin and his militant disciples moved on her at once. There was some truth to their charge that the Church was closely allied with the government. Not as much as they claim, to be sure, but more than we like to think.

The Czars had favored the Church and, in return, the Church leaders had been partial to the Czars. The Reformation movement in Europe missed the Russian Church altogether, and the sluggish current of her vast life flowed almost to a standstill with the passing of the centuries. Her schools were too few and too poor to do a good job of public education. Her priests, with a few brilliant exceptions, were content to administer the rites of the Church and paid little or no attention to civil policies. They took the census and kept the vital statistics of births, marriages, and deaths for the government. In return, the government helped support most of the church schools and great cathedrals. It was of this Church that Tolstoi, himself a devout Christian, wrote, "The Church . . . has fulfilled its mission and is now useless."[4]

The early communists, determined to root out every possible source of reaction, singled out the Church as an enemy and treated her accordingly. As a matter of fact, the Soviet attack on the Church moved out along four lines.

First, there was the disestablishment of the Church, the cutting off of such income as she had formerly received from the state; the removal of priests from civil office and duties; the removal of marriage from the churches to civil offices; the stern prohibition of monks and priests from seeking support for monasteries, convents, and training schools for the priesthood.

Second, the government embarked on the largest and most ambitious educational program in history, aimed to orient the Russian people to the leadership of the Communist Party and to enlist their loyalty to the policies of the Soviet government. One of the fundamental emphases of this gigantic educational effort was to undermine respect for religion in the minds of the rising generation. This they sought to do by contrasting science and religion. It was never a friendly investigation of relative merits—which is always in order; it was and continues

[4] *My Religion.*

to this day to be the intellectually indefensible comparison of the worst in religion with the best in science. In this contrast, science is the white knight of knowledge, freedom, and power, while religion is the evil dragon of superstition, oppression, and weakness. The philosophy of materialism is exalted and every form and impulse of idealism is derided all along the way.

Third, the Soviet government launched a vast propaganda campaign against religion and the churches. To spearhead this immediate and outright assault, it created the League for Militant Atheism. Large sums of money were available for all kinds of publications, programs, parades, and traveling lecturers. The Soviet government made it plain that only an avowed believer in materialism and atheism could hope either for membership in the Party or for any kind of preferment in civil, cultural, or economic life. The most conspicuous way for anyone to demonstrate orthodoxy in this regard was to be an active member of the League for Militant Atheism. Consequently, the most able and aggressive young communists found their way into it. Artists, scientists, educators, as well as military and civil officials were careful to have their names inscribed on the membership records of the League. Naturally, this fact was bruited abroad, and the rising generation was confronted on all sides by this witness to the vital relationship between atheism and progress in the New Russia. There was strategy as well as malice in the fact that after many church buildings had been confiscated by the government they were turned over to the League and transformed into museums for the defamation of religion.

Fourth, the Soviet government sought to break the power of the Russian Orthodox Church by encouraging and nurturing a serious division within her ranks. Following Napoleon's advice, "divide and conquer," the government backed what was called "the Living Church" movement and sought to bring its leaders into positions of responsibility in the Church. These favored churchmen were, in almost every case, sincere priests who had been trying to bring about various reforms in the Church before the Soviet government came into power, and they were as much opposed to materialism as any of the more orthodox churchmen. The government nursed this split in the ranks of the Church, hoping thereby to break the power of the Church from within. For a few years, the effort looked as though it might succeed. It was at this same time and undoubtedly as a part of the same strategy that all other churches were encouraged by the government. The Baptists made the best use of this period of dispensation and grew with amazing rapidity. The Roman Catholic Church alone was discouraged as the tool of a foreign power.

As I read the records of that long period of bitter strife between the Russian Orthodox Church and the Soviet government, I get the distinct impression that the government confidently expected the Church to shatter before the savage onslaught of the many-sided attack. Never before in the annals of Christian history had a large Church been called upon to face so vicious and concentrated an attack upon principles, policies, institutions, and personnel. The persecutions engineered by Nero and other Roman emperors pale into insignificance beside the one that fell on the Russian Church.

The Russian Church was staggered, bewildered, and temporarily blinded by the wholly unexpected nature and intensity of the attack. Her leaders, like many others the world around, had either been paying little attention to or sadly underestimating the power of the writings and plans of Marx, Lenin, and their disciples. It seems never to have occurred to Church leaders that a serious effort would actually be made to kill their beloved Church. When the blow fell with unparalleled severity on all parts of the Church at once, they were stupefied—for a moment, but only for a moment. Then, they reacted swiftly and in line with the great tradition of the Christian Church.

First, and most important, the Church leaders called upon their people to reaffirm and hold fast to their faith in God, Christ, and the Church. Even though the government might close the buildings, sell their revered icons, and publicly defame religion, the people were urged to believe in God and in the Church as ever-present eternal realities. Priests went about such duties as they were permitted to perform, keeping alive the fellowship of faith.

The second step taken by the Church was to challenge the philosophy of materialism with bell, book, and candle—and with some of the keenest reasoning ever to be brought to bear upon a pagan philosophy by Christian thinkers. I do not know of a single indictment of the philosophy of communism made outside Russia, whether in papal encyclical, or the editorial columns of our newspapers, or by students of Russia, that deserves to rank with a document drawn up by a group of exiled bishops of the Russian Church. The document is known as the "Slovetsk Document" and it was drawn up for presentation to the Soviet government.

Accepting the right of the Soviet government or any other civil government to administer the civil life of Russia, the bishops pointed out the real source of friction between the Church and the government. As I read only a few sentences from this document, keep in mind the actual historical situation which provoked it.

Those who have signed the present statement are fully aware of the difficulty of establishing mutual friendly relations between the Church and the State under present actual conditions. They cannot be silent regarding this. It would not be true, it would be beneath the dignity of the Church, and besides it would be quite useless and unconvincing to assert that there were no points of discord between the Orthodox Church and the State authority of the Soviet Republic. . . . The discord lies in the irreconcilability of the religious teaching of the Church with the materialism and the official philosophy of the Communistic Party and of the government of the Soviet Republic directed by that Party.

Then the bishops detail the ways in which this conflict affects the lives of all persons in Russia, after which they reach this conclusion:

The Church wants religion to flourish. Communism wants it to perish. With such deep differences in fundamental principles separating Church and State, it becomes impossible that an inner nearness or reconciliation could exist between them. . . . For the very soul of the Church, the circumstance of its existence and the reason for its being, is just that which is categorically denied by Communism. . . . By no compromise or concession, by no partial changes in its teaching, by no explanation of it in a communistic spirit can the Church attain such a reconciliation. . . . The Orthodox Church will never stand on this unworthy path. It will never deny either the whole or part of that teaching which has come down to it from all that has been holy in the past centuries, in order to accommodate ever-shifting popular opinions. . . .[5]

This ringing denunciation seems to have registered in the Soviet government at least to the extent that it showed a new will to work with leaders of its own choosing in the Orthodox Church. It cast off the Living Church movement—which was stillborn anyway—and recognized the right of the Orthodox Church to be registered and administered under the leadership of Metropolitan Sergius. But if the government expected softer words from him than from the exiled bishops they must have been

[5] Anderson, op. cit., pp. 90-92.

shocked at the bluntness with which he made his position clear
from the very outset:

> But let us be sincere to the end. We cannot be silent about the con-
> tradiction which exists between us Orthodox and the Communist
> Bolsheviks, who govern our Union. They set as their purpose struggle
> with God and His power in the hearts of the people. We on our part
> see the whole sense and the whole aim of our existence in confession
> of faith in God and strengthening of the faith in the hearts of the
> people. They recognize only the materialistic interpretation of history,
> and we believe in the providence of God.[6]

Thus a severe battle was joined in the life of the Russian people
and their reaction to it is of utmost importance. If the Soviet
government was amazed to discover that the Church neither
folded up nor made a dishonorable peace with communism, it
must have been doubly amazed and chagrined at the reaction of
the Russian people to the attack upon the Church. After a promis-
ing and well-publicized start, the League for Militant Atheism
was virtually ignored by the Russian people. It became a professional Party organ, patronized by Party members and climbers
within the Party. There was open resentment at the manner in
which it ridiculed the Church and the religious beliefs and
practices of the people. Its membership declined steadily and its
influence clearly was very small—so small that the government
closed it down in the early days of the war and it has not been
reopened. The Soviet government started out to extirpate the
Church, but it was forced to settle by the separation of State and
Church. It did not repent of its materialism, you may be sure.
That philosophy continues to this day to underlie its educational
policies. But it did recognize the simple fact that it had been
badly beaten in the battle to discredit religion in the eyes of the
Russian people.

When the Constitution was adopted in 1936, it took a step that
Lenin feared they might have to take in case the Church was too
solidly entrenched, but a step that was an admission of defeat on
the part of the militant antireligious forces in the Communist
Party and the Soviet government. Article 124 of the Soviet Constitution reads: "In order to ensure to citizens freedom of conscience, the church in the U.S.S.R. is separated from the state,
and the school from the church. Freedom of religious worship

[6] *Ibid.*, p. 95.

and freedom of antireligious propaganda is recognized for all citizens."

The government moderated its open attack on the Church all along the line after 1939. Why, no one knows for sure, but the best guess given by a Russian churchman himself is that the government smelled war with Germany in the distance and was trying to heal the deep wounds made in Russian life by the struggle with the Church. When the war came the Russian Orthodox Church, true to her tradition of loyalty to Mother Russia, stood by the government. In surprised relief, the government while "holding firm to its atheistic conviction . . . discontinued the publication of anti-religious journals, closed the anti-religious museums and greatly alleviated the taxation of religious groups. . . . In the summer of 1942, a book appeared in Moscow entitled the *Truth about Religion in Russia*. It was beautifully printed and copiously illustrated and contained contributions of the highest dignitaries of the Russian Orthodox Church, as well as of a number of priests and laymen. There is reason to believe that the book was printed on the now-idle presses of the League of Militant Atheists!"[7]

Following the war, the Soviet government has continued the policy of easing up on the Church. It has permitted her to reopen her monasteries, schools, and churches. It is encouraging her to draw the scattered branches of the Orthodox Church, principally in the Near East and the Balkans, into a closer unity. The political motive in all this is obvious, but the actual meaning for the Church should not be overlooked. It can now be said that "step by step in the course of less than a decade, the Russian Orthodox Church, instead of being an object of relentless persecution has become an officially recognized body."[8]

A few statistics tell the story:

	1917	1941	1950
Churches open	46,457	4,225	29,000
Priests	50,960	5,665	33,000
Bishops	130	28	80

Add to these statistics the simple human facts that the great services of the Church are widely attended, that there is a significant number of young people in the congregation, and you have the Church's answer to the effort of communism to crush her.

[7] Gurian, p. 155.
[8] *Ibid.*, p. 157.

One of the most reliable students of the Russian Church draws up what he calls the balance sheet in some such fashion as this:

On the credit side we have these facts:
1. The Russian Orthodox Church is in an enormously stronger position relative to the Soviet government than she has ever been.
2. All other churches, excepting the Roman Catholic Church, have expanded their work and membership, the Baptists numbering between three and four million members.
3. The hostility of the Russian Orthodox Church to the Roman Catholic Church is of long standing and is a two-way affair. It existed all over eastern Europe before Communism took over the Russian government, and the government has capitalized on that fact. The Soviet government regards the Roman Catholic Church as an international political power and, as such, a real fifth column in the civil and political life of Russia. The idea being advanced by the Vatican today that the sole reason the Soviet government opposes the Roman Catholic Church is because she believes in God is historical nonsense.

On the debit side of the ledger certain depressing and dangerous facts must be noted:
1. The official and outspoken loyalty of the Soviet government to materialism and its continuing declaration that religion is superstition constitute an evil atmosphere in which the churches must live and work.
2. Although there is separation of Church and State and some measure of religious freedom for most groups, it is a severely limited freedom—and the government sets the limits. "A theologian could not publish a book or pamphlet attacking materialism. A group of parents could not organize a school in which their children would receive education in the spirit of religion. . . ."[9] The most that can be said for this situation is that our work has as much freedom in Russia as it now has in Italy or Spain where the influence of the Roman Catholic Church is all-powerful.

Of course the ledger is far from closed. Entries—good and bad —are being made on it every day. No one can foresee the outcome for the churches in Russia, but the issue is deeply, fully, and finally joined here.

[9] *Ibid.*, p. 193.

II

Time permits only the briefest kind of look at the relationship between the churches outside Russia and the Soviet government. The Churches outside Russia exhibit a variety of attitudes and policies toward the Soviet regime, but they share with the churches in Russia the complete and unqualified rejection of the materialism that underlies and determines communist thought and policy. I do not know of a single exception to that sweeping generalization. Here and there individual churchmen like the Dean of Canterbury, Harry Ward, and Jerome Davis have been apologists—and sometimes uncritical apologists—for Soviet policy, and they give the impression that there is much we can learn from that policy, but none of them makes any pretense of swallowing the materialistic philosophy which underlies communism. Arnold Toynbee once called communism a "Christian heresy." This, I must confess, is not the first time I have been mystified by judgments of this, our greatest historian. I find myself at a complete loss to understand exactly what he could mean by this because heresy is a deviation from, not a denial of, a norm. Materialism is an outright denial of the fundamental principle of the Christian philosophy and life. Hence the community of spirit which you find among Christian churches relative to communism.

But this unity soon breaks down and for good reason as we move from Roman Catholic to Protestant churches.

The Roman Catholic Church has never amounted to much in Russia for the very same reason that the Orthodox Church has not meant much in Europe: The Roman Catholic and Orthodox Churches are state churches and have used the powers of the state to keep each other out of their own territories. The Roman Catholic Church had some work in Russia prior to and after the Communist Revolution, but not for long. The Soviet government takes at face value the claim of the Roman Catholic Church to be a temporal power and regards it as an international political organization, and, as such, suspect in the civil life of Russia. Almost from the outset, the government made it literally impossible for the Roman Catholic Church to carry on work in Russia. Efforts to work out some kind of rapprochement after the recent war were made, but without success. The suppression of the Roman Catholic Church in territories conquered during and after the war, particularly in Poland, brought about an open conflict between the Vatican and the Kremlin. There is no question but that the Russian Orthodox Church has tried to move in on the Roman Catholic Church in these territories—just as the Roman Catholic Church followed Hitler's legions into the Balkans and tried to take over the Orthodox churches there.

I find it difficult to accept the current judgment that the Roman Catholic Church is the leader in the crusade against atheistic materialism or even against communism, for that matter. All churches inside and outside of Russia are against these and have been against them from the beginning. And the brunt of the battle has not fallen, nor does it now fall on the Roman Catholic Church; it falls on the Russian Orthodox Church.

The World Council of Churches has tried to avoid a direct collision with the Soviet government largely because it has been seeking a creative relationship with the Russian Orthodox Church. The Anglican and Russian Churches have had several commissions meet on plans for future co-operation. The Russian Church has not sent official delegates to the World Council Assembly because the assembly did not look toward the consideration of problems of the dogmatic reunion of Christendom. Other Orthodox churches in Greece and the United States were at the assembly representing the Orthodox tradition there.

The World Council has condemned the materialistic basis of communism without hesitation or equivocation. It has not tried to indict the whole Russian nation, and it has been careful not to include the Russian Orthodox Church in its denunciation. Fairness to fact as well as deep sympathy with the long and continuing struggle of the Russian Church with the tenets of communism demand this position.

Various utterances of the leaders of the Russian Orthodox Church over the last five years have been disturbingly like the releases of the Kremlin, but no more so than some of the pronouncements of the Anglican Church seem to originate in 10 Downing Street, and some of ours in the State Department. It is entirely possible that relations between the Russian Orthodox Church and the World Council of Churches will deteriorate steadily because each one is being oriented, willynilly, to one or the other of the two great centers of power in the modern world. If that happens, both will be guilty, and both will be weakened for the great task of preaching the Christian gospel to our times.

III

So far as I am concerned at this stage of the situation, certain great compulsions stand out:

1. We must and should gladly honor the Russian Church for the great fight she has waged and is waging to keep the Christian witness alive in Russia under circumstances of unparalleled severity. We must honor her leaders and people for their persistence and patience under persecution, their courage in defining their Christian faith in opposition to the philosophy of their government, the swift way in which they set about recovering their leadership after the abatement of persecution, their sense of duty to their people, their nation, and their God, which has led them into difficult and ofttimes embarrassing and ambiguous positions that easily can be misunderstood and misinterpreted as betrayal of the faith.

2. We must refuse to be led as a Church into a holy war against Russia. We must not make the mistake of identifying the Russian people and the Russian Church with the Russian government and the communist philosophy of life. It is not only utterly unfair but wholly dangerous to fall into this frame of mind. While we may and do sympathize with the Pope's concern to keep the Roman Catholic churches free from the domination of the Soviet government, we have a duty and a right to point out two things: (1) his concern for freedom of religion does not extend to our work in Italy and Spain; (2) the Russian Church rejects the philosophy of atheistic materialism as flatly as does the Roman Catholic Church and all other churches. There is no reason to have a holy war on this account, now or ever!

3. We must brace our brethren of whatever ecclesiastical connection anywhere in the world for the struggle against the challenge of the philosophy and practices and institutions of communism. Through the World Council of Churches we must articulate the Christian faith with clarity and in a spirit of sincere Christian fellowship to and through all Christian churches. To this end and in this spirit we should refrain from passing easy judgments on the ones who must bear their witness surrounded by the active and powerful hostility if not outright persecution of alien philosophies of life. We must never succumb to the hysterical temptation to indict a whole

people like the Russians, the Chinese, or the Indians—even as we hope they will not indict us as a people—because the policies of their governments seem to be dangerous to the ideals we hold dear as Christians. We must realize that there are many ways of witnessing against unchristian practices and philosophies other than outright conflict. We must realize that our brethren in Christ have repeatedly given evidence of their loyalty to Him and can be counted upon to continue to do so.

4. We must brace ourselves individually and collectively for the long-range challenge to and conflict with the philosophy and practices of materialism wherever found, whether in Soviet Russia, China, England, or the United States. Our belief in God must be so clear; our faith in Him so firm; our sense of His presence so real and personal; our awareness of His leadership so powerful that we too can confront our generation with the ancient affirmation: We believe in God the Father Almighty, maker of heaven and earth and in Jesus Christ His only Son our Lord. As a Church we shall want to have so pure and fine a covenant with the God of all men that we shall never by word or deed or prayer seem to exclude anyone from the Christian fellowship. May our faith in God and in the power of Christian fellowship and prayer be strong enough to keep all men in our hearts and minds and plans as we pray to God for His kingdom to come and His will be done on earth as it is in heaven.

Set in Linotype Baskerville
Format by Edwin H. Kaplin
Manufactured by The Haddon Craftsmen, Inc.
Published by HARPER & BROTHERS, *New York*